ROUTLEDGE LIBRARY EDITIONS:
COLD WAR SECURITY STUDIES

Volume 36

THE PATTERN OF WORLD CONFLICT

THE PATTERN OF WORLD CONFLICT

G.L. ARNOLD

Routledge
Taylor & Francis Group

LONDON AND NEW YORK

First published in 1955 by George Allen & Unwin Ltd

This edition first published in 2021
by Routledge
2 Park Square, Milton Park, Abingdon, Oxon OX14 4RN

and by Routledge
52 Vanderbilt Avenue, New York, NY 10017

Routledge is an imprint of the Taylor & Francis Group, an informa business

© 1955 G.L. Arnold

British Library Cataloguing in Publication Data
A catalogue record for this book is available from the British Library

ISBN: 978-0-367-56630-2 (Set)
ISBN: 978-1-00-312438-2 (Set) (ebk)
ISBN: 978-0-367-62070-7 (Volume 36) (hbk)
ISBN: 978-1-00-310780-4 (Volume 36) (ebk)

Publisher's Note
The publisher has gone to great lengths to ensure the quality of this reprint but
points out that some imperfections in the original copies may be apparent.

Disclaimer
The publisher has made every effort to trace copyright holders and would welcome
correspondence from those they have been unable to trace.

The
PATTERN
of WORLD
CONFLICT

by G. L. ARNOLD

GEORGE ALLEN & UNWIN LTD.
LONDON   1955

DESIGNED BY WILLIAM R. MEINHARDT
PRINTED IN THE UNITED STATES OF AMERICA
BY THE HADDON CRAFTSMEN, SCRANTON, PA.

CONTENTS

PREFACE   **1**

CHAPTER I: THE AFTERMATH OF WAR AND THE END OF THE NEO-LIBERAL UTOPIA   **3**

    1: *Lost Horizons*
    2: *Utopia Revisited*
    3: *Problems of Coexistence*

CHAPTER II: ATLANTIC WORLD AND EURASIAN BLOC   **27**

    1: *The Decline of Europe*
    2: *The Imperialist Pattern*
    3: *The New Power Balance*

CHAPTER III: DEFENSE OF THE WEST   **50**

    1: *The Cold War*
    2: *Toward Atlantic Union*

CHAPTER IV: THE ECONOMICS OF A TRANSITION PERIOD   **70**

    1: *The Dollar Gap*
    2: *The New Division of Labor*
    3: *Economics of Democracy*

CHAPTER V: THE PLAN ERA   112

    1: *The Permanent Revolution*
    2: *Rates of Growth*
    3: *The Cost of Stalinism*
    4: *Soviet Europe*
    5: *The Perils of Retardation*
    6: *The Market and the Plan*
    7: *The Poverty of Nations*

CHAPTER VI: THE PATTERN OF
                 CONFLICT   172

    1: *East Against West*
    2: *Nationalism and Revolution*
    3: *The Role of the Peasants*
    4: *The Communist Synthesis*
    5: *The Western Dilemma*

CONCLUSION   228

BIBLIOGRAPHY   237

INDEX   241

PREFACE

ANY ADDITION to the growing volume of literature on current affairs stands in need of some justification. If the topics discussed include such familiar ones as East-West relations, the cold war, and the prospect of "peaceful coexistence," the author is under a special obligation to show cause why he should add to the already large number of general and specialized studies devoted to these subjects. His best defense will be to assert the possibility of a new approach. In the present case this implicit claim has two buttresses: first, the standpoint here chosen is "Atlantic" sans phrase; that is to say, the Atlantic Community appears in the following argument not as something to be created, but as the overriding reality whose concerns already determine the lesser problems of its constituents, whether the latter are called America or Europe. Secondly, the methodical approach is neither liberal nor socialist in the usual sense; instead, it operates with concepts derived from the experience of planning and state intervention. These have been shown to be relevant to democratic and totalitarian practice alike; it remains to be seen whether democratic politics can in time produce agreement on the degree of public planning necessary to preserve the social health of the non-Communist world.

This study, then, attempts a synthesis of views common to liberal and socialist, American and European, supporters of planning. The hazardous nature of such an enterprise will

1

be evident to most readers. In addition, an effort has been made to combine the analysis of political trends in recent years with a brief consideration of long-term processes released by the collapse of the nineteenth-century system of world trade. The complexity of the resulting picture must serve as an excuse, however inadequate, for the medley of factual analysis and theoretical interpretation presented in the following pages. It has been necessary to attempt a shotgun marriage of concepts usually kept apart. Political science unfortunately has not yet reached the point of being able to discriminate clearly between its own domain and those of history, economics, or sociology. Perhaps such a demarcation will be assisted by further study of the political upheaval in which we are all caught up. Meanwhile the totalitarians are teaching us a lesson in how not to go about the business of synthesizing our concepts.

The first chapter of this book has appeared in *Partisan Review;* other extracts had previously been published in *Commentary* and *The Twentieth Century.* I wish to thank the Royal Institute of International Affairs for permission to reproduce part of a paper originally published under their auspices. I should also like to record my obligation to the staff at Chatham House for their unfailing help and courtesy. This is equally the place to thank the friends who have encouraged me during the writing, principally Mrs. Jane Degras. For advice on some important points I am indebted to Mr. Mark Abrams, to Miss Jean Bird, to Dr. Werner Klatt, and to Mr. Richard Lowenthal.

London, June, 1955

CHAPTER I

THE AFTERMATH OF WAR AND THE END OF THE NEOLIBERAL UTOPIA

1: *Lost Horizons*

FEW OF THOSE who have followed with attention the course of events since the Second World War ended in 1945 can fail to have been struck by the extraordinary discrepancy between the hopes fashionable at the time and the actual development we have witnessed. There is today an obvious temptation to conclude that the disillusionment which so swiftly followed the adoption of the United Nations Charter was no more than the recoil to be expected when utopian plans were brought into contact with reality. But what is so remarkable is the extent to which experienced statesmen, diplomatists, and other public figures shared in the movement that first led to San Francisco and then away from it to the Atlantic Pact, Korea, and the tacit acceptance of atomic and air power ("retaliatory power," in the current idiom) as the only real guarantees of peace—or, rather, of the absence of total war: for to this modest aim have the bright promises of 1945 shrunk in the intervening ten years.

3

It was doubtless an omen that while the façade of world government was being erected at San Francisco, the real business of settling the fate of Europe was accomplished at Potsdam, and that the principles proclaimed in one locality had no evident bearing upon the decisions taken or condoned in the other. Thus the uprooting of some ten million Germans, to facilitate the westward advance of Poland's frontiers, and the subjection of all eastern Europe to Soviet control, clearly were not actions that could be justified by any interpretation, however elastic, of the liberal philosophy underlying the Charter. And it is arguable that the same might be said of the decision, also taken at this time, to employ the first two atomic bombs for the purpose of forcing an already defeated Japan on the point of surrender to capitulate exclusively to the United States—a motivation which cannot be considered immoral, but which does not leave a great deal of scope for moral argument save on the assumption that Asians are somehow "more equal than" Europeans or Americans. But these lapses from grace could still be regarded as familiar instances of the tension between general aims and particular methods. What weighs more heavily in the scales, now that the 1945 settlement has disclosed its consequences, is that the aims themselves appear to have had only a very limited relation to the facts.

The casual manner in which the Potsdam decisions canceled ten centuries of European history (incidentally sanctioning mass expulsions, spoliations, and killings exceeded in scale only by Hitler Germany's own accomplishments) was already a sign that control had slipped from those who in former times had seen to it that European wars were conducted for limited objectives and brought to an end with the minimum of disturbance to Europe's general equilibrium. At the Potsdam Conference Great Britain appeared

for the last time as one of the Big Three, on an equal footing with the United States and the Soviet Union. At most
succeeding international conferences Britain was accompanied by France, and it gradually became clear that, save
on those rare occasions when she could rally the whole
Commonwealth, her status was that of a western European
country allied to the United States, rather than a "third"
center of power lying outside the American and Russian
orbits. But at Potsdam the wartime Big Three still met on
equal terms, and the British government once more
attempted, though without success, to perform that moderat-
ing role which Wellington and Castlereagh had exercised
at the close of the Napoleonic epoch, and which corresponded as much to Britain's tradition as it did to Europe's
interest. That so little real weight was placed behind this
effort must be debited to Churchill's obsession with the
Anglo-American partnership and to the mediocrity of his
Labor colleagues-and-successors, who, by their behavior
on this crucial occasion, gave advance notice of the fundamental helplessness they were to display during six years
in office.

The real authors of the settlement were, of course, the
United States and the Soviet Union, and their motives were
all too clear. On the Russian side, the wartime fusion of
chauvinist and revolutionary sentiment into the new imperialist amalgam led to a policy of conquest that pushed the
frontiers of the Soviet Empire as far west as they would go,
uprooting or steam-rolling everything that stood in the way.
On the American side, Roosevelt's policy—never acknowl-
edged in so many words, but implicit in all his actions—
of reaching an understanding with the U. S. S. R. at the price
of the permanent partition of central Europe was at first
continued after his death, and indeed came to its full flower-

ing at a time when its presuppositions were already beginning to crumble. Thus the British attempt to moderate the
destructive urge of the victors and preserve something of
the old European framework encountered resolute resistance
from the Russians, and at best obtained only very lame support from the Americans, who were just beginning to wonder
whether the wrecking of Germany and the transfer of
eastern Europe to Soviet control were really in everyone's
best interest. In the circumstances, Britain's halfhearted
resistance was foredoomed to failure, the more so since the
Polish bastion had already been surrendered at Teheran and
Yalta. But the fact that the newly elected Labor government, whose leaders replaced Churchill and Eden in the
middle of the conference, confirmed the decisions already
taken, instead of instantly dissociating itself from so gross
a travesty of wartime promises and declarations, lent
additional significance to these transactions by giving them
a kind of moral sanction. After Potsdam it was difficult
to maintain that any sizable body of opinion in the
Western world was prepared to act on principles radically
different from those professed and practiced by the Kremlin.
Liberalism and socialism had both been compromised, along
with their totalitarian ally and enemy-to-be. This display of
moral indifference was not widely commented upon at the
time; its effects only showed at a later date, when the outbreak of the cold war led to renewed emphasis upon the
general principles so widely proclaimed by the Western
democracies during the earlier, and militarily unfruitful,
part of the war.

The old balance of power having thus been destroyed,
it was clearly urgent to establish a new one, for only the
more naïve votaries of perpetual peace could imagine that
the San Francisco Charter by itself would make an end of

conventional diplomacy. Here the Western powers were at first favored by their short-lived monopoly of the new atomic weapon, a circumstance which caused some suspicion that the obliteration of Hiroshima and Nagasaki, hard on the heels of the vital decisions taken at Potsdam, was intended at least as much to impress the Soviet government as to hasten the Japanese surrender. However that may be, the expectations placed upon continued Western—or rather American—monopoly of the new weapon are now known to have been unrealistic even at a time when they seemed in accordance with the known facts. Thus if a belief that the Soviet Union was unable to produce atomic arms, or at least would take a decade over it, formed part of the mental background of Western policy-making, that misjudgment must be listed among the other notable intellectual errors of the period.

In actual fact it is doubtful whether those in authority were quite so naïve as they appeared to be some years later, when they allowed it to be inferred that but for Soviet espionage the secret of the bomb might have been preserved indefinitely. Like much else that came to be said and written, this suggestion belongs to the folklore of the cold war. Already in June, 1945, a Committee on Social and Political Implications, appointed by the Metallurgical Laboratory in Chicago and presided over by Professor James Franck, had presented a report to the U. S. Secretary of War which stressed the impossibility of the United States' retaining the monopoly.[1] (The signatories incidentally opposed the use of the atomic bomb against an already defeated Japan, a recommendation that was promptly ignored.) When in March, 1946, the U. S. State Department issued the so-called Acheson-Lilienthal Report advis-

[1] *Bulletin of Atomic Scientists*, Chicago, May, 1946.

ing on methods of atomic control, the warning was repeated, this time with all the authority of a committee including such figures as Vannevar Bush, James B. Conant, and Major General Leslie R. Groves, to say nothing of J. Robert Oppenheimer, who was partly responsible for writing the Report.[2] Thus, there was plenty of advance notice from those best qualified to know that within a few years an atomic arms race would be on, unless international ownership and/or control of atomic energy could be arranged. The problem consequently—except for those who seriously believed that the Soviet government would submit to outside control of atomic installations—was how to assemble the elements of a new world-wide political system before Russia had caught up in the race. This, of course, could not be stated, but it was implicit in Churchill's Fulton address (March 5, 1946) and in the actions of the Western powers.

Not for a moment did the existence of the United Nations make any difference to the crucial issue of reconstructing a new balance of power. At most it can be said to have confused the public about the situation, especially since Roosevelt's insistence on the inclusion of China among the Big Five had resulted in one of the five permanent seats on the Security Council being occupied by a Chinese government that was rapidly losing all authority at home. Only with the signing of the North Atlantic Treaty in April, 1949, was there a partial return to reality—*i.e.*, a partial admission that the real aims of Western statesmanship could not be pursued by enlisting the cumbersome machinery of the

[2] *A Report on the International Control of Atomic Energy.* The Board of Consultants responsible for its writing consisted of Mr. David Lilienthal, Mr. Chester I. Barnard, Dr. J. Robert Oppenheimer, Dr. Charles Allen Thomas and Mr. Harry A. Winne. The report was transmitted to the Secretary of State, Mr. James F. Byrnes, by a Committee consisting of Mr. Dean Acheson, Dr. Vannevar Bush, Dr. James B. Conant, Major-General Groves and Mr. John J. Meloy.

Charter. Although the reported explosion of the Soviet Union's first atomic bomb in the fall of that year was a coincidence, the conjunction of both events served to emphasize the transition from the euphoria of the immediate postwar period to the acceptance of a divided world, which thereafter became a commonplace.

On the Soviet side less time was lost in making their public understand that a new arms race was on. It has always been a cardinal point of Leninist thinking that every peace is a preparation for the next war—a Clausewitzian axiom whose ultimate sanction lies in Hegel's *Logic,* along with a good deal of actual experience—and that the closeness of war can be measured by the amount and intensity of pacifist talk in currency among governments and populations. Since atomic energy had now become the crucial factor, it followed that both sides would try to maneuver to win public support for their proposals regarding international control, and that neither would risk an open conflict until reasonably sure of having gained the upper hand in the propaganda war. To say that the Soviet government did not at any time intend to accept the American proposals for atomic control first put forward in 1946, or even to discuss them seriously, is an understatement. It never regarded them as anything but a bid for public support in the general drive to obtain control of the new sources of power, and as a maneuver intended to place America's rival in an unfavorable light. Any other assumption was excluded from the start, not merely by the habitual cynicism of the political practitioner, but by the intellectual framework within which the Soviet government has operated since its inception. It was hardly to be expected that these assumptions would be sacrificed to the rhetoric of American spokesmen, especially if there was ground for believing that the Soviet Union would shortly draw level in the arms race. That this has now occurred, or almost occurred, while the West is as far as ever from having restored the balance destroyed in 1945, is the largest and most disagreeable fact on the contemporary scene. It was, however, by no means unforeseeable ten years ago.

There is, of course, a sense in which every international system can be said to balance. Thus the present relationship between the NATO powers and the Russo-Chinese bloc is roughly one of balance, if by this is meant that neither group is significantly stronger than the other and that each would do well to refrain from putting matters to the test. But this is not what the Western governments had in mind during those wartime conferences on which so much startling light has been cast by the recently published Yalta Conference Papers and some earlier unofficial disclosures. There is, indeed, ample evidence that the Grand Alliance was never as solid as it looked on the surface, and that the cold war really began as soon as the Axis had obviously been defeated. But the quantum of wishful thinking that went into the Teheran, Yalta and Potsdam agreements was much larger than the American and British public had a right to expect from their leaders. No real effort was made to preserve either the independence of Poland (for which Britain and France had nominally gone to war in 1939) or the existence of a viable Germany. In the main this outcome reflected the emergence of two non-European colossi with world-wide interests quite different from those of the traditional European powers. It has proved a misfortune that Britain, even under Churchill, was unable to resist this trend, but in the long run the tendency for America and Russia to treat European interests as bargaining counters was bound to assert itself. That it did so under wartime conditions of censorship and official propaganda calculated to flatter the naïveté of the "common man" and his readiness to take a one-dimensional view of the world doubtless facilitated the operation but did not alter its essential character.

2: *Utopia Revisited*

THE NEOLIBERAL UTOPIA, of which the United Nations Charter was the most exact—*i.e.*, the emptiest—expression, had for a complement the belief that the time had come to restore the classic framework of international trade. It was, indeed, recognized that the golden age of liberalism could not be restored all at once and that the whole operation would depend on the initiative of the United States. With these qualifications, the neoliberal school around Keynes saw no reason to despair of ultimate success. The Master had, indeed, apostatized from economic orthodoxy, and his wartime proposals for a managed international currency represented a compromise between the older liberal and the younger socialist schools of thought at Oxford and Cambridge. But similar processes had occurred in the United States, and it seemed a plausible assumption that an American Administration committed to the basic principles of the New Deal would find sufficient common ground with Britain and western Europe to make a workable partnership possible. It is now a commonplace that this hope—never very firmly grounded—had already come to nothing by 1946.[3] Its disappearance has recently

[3] Cf. Roy Harrod, *John Maynard Keynes*, Macmillan, 1951, especially Chapter XV. Mr. Harrod was himself among the optimists at the time, and for some years continued to assert that there was, for Britain, no true dollar shortage. Since the advent of a Conservative government, which has found the shortage just as real as did its predecessor, he has signified a change of mind. It is all the more noteworthy that in his most recent discussion of this topic (*The Dollar*, Macmillan, 1953; especially Chapter IV)

been capped by the discovery that even the more modest expectations of the school—*e.g.*, the hope that the United States would substantially alter its tariff policy—are unlikely to be fulfilled in the measurable future. For practical purposes this means that Britain cannot expect to trade on a much enlarged scale with the dollar area. But the long-range implications do not affect Britain alone. They point inexorably to a widening gap between North America and the rest of the Atlantic world—a gap in productivity, in living standards, in the ability to withstand temporary recessions, and ultimately in the willingness to pursue common aims. The muttered European protest over American restrictions on trade with the Eastern bloc is merely a symptom of this divorce. Underlying it is the belief that the world is in essentials drifting back to the situation that existed before the Axis threat forced America and Europe to co-operate—the main difference being that in the interval America has become far more powerful, both absolutely and in relation to its partners. This is the background of the resentful neutralism of which so much is heard in Europe today.

The 1919-39 period was characterized by a sustained effort on the part of Western statesmanship to get back to 1914. The outcome was the great depression, Hitler's rise, the Second World War, and the spread of Soviet power to central Europe. Since 1945 we have witnessed a comparable attempt to restore at least the conditions prevalent in 1939. This tendency found an early expression in the Bretton Woods agreement, which placed the burden of restoring an international balance of payments not upon the

---

he pays eloquent tribute to the man who did more than anyone else to disillusion Keynes: Mr. Harry White. And indeed Mr. Harrod is not alone in holding that White, whatever his failings may have been and whatever imprudent actions he may have committed, was first and foremost an American patriot—and at times a rather intransigent one at that.

creditor but upon the debtor nations (principally Great Britain). As a sop to them it provided for an international monetary fund of $3 billion to close a dollar gap which between 1946 and 1949 alone amounted to no less than $20 billion. A further demonstration of the same state of mind was provided by the terms of the 1945-46 U. S. loan to Britain, which showed that a determined attempt was to be made to revive the economic system of the late nineteenth century—a system that depended for its functioning on the easy availability of sterling.

It is true that these exercises in neoliberal utopianism were followed by the Marshall Plan, hastily extemporized in 1947 to halt the disintegration set in train by the inevitable breakdown of Britain's attempt to make sterling freely convertible: an experiment undertaken by the British government, without the slightest chance of success, in response to American pressure to help build "One World." But the Marshall Plan, although a brilliant success as a rescue operation, did not effect any major structural changes. The west European coal-steel merger, planned by M. Monnet and blessed by M. Schuman, remained an isolated accomplishment. Above all, no sustained effort was undertaken to integrate the west European economies and merge them with the sterling bloc, so as to establish an international economic system outside the dollar area and independent of constant dollar support. On the contrary, tendencies in this direction were frowned upon, and it is only fairly recently that realism has gained the upper hand on both sides of the Atlantic.[4] Thus while the Soviet government drew the

---

[4] Cf. *The Economist*, January 30, 1954: "But if there is no excuse for a policy of Two Worlds, it is equally unrealistic to cling to the belief that the One World of postwar dreams—the One World without quotas, excessive tariffs, discriminations, or exchange controls—can be attained within measurable time."

logical conclusion from the collapse of the pre-1914 division of labor and the consequent disintegration of the single all-embracing world market, Western policy for some critical years pursued the phantom of a near-global free-trade system. It has taken repeated currency crises in western Europe, and the perpetuation of the "dollar gap," to convince the policy-makers that even the "free world" is, economically speaking, composed of two different halves which intersect but cannot be merged. As a corollary of this discovery it is now beginning to be appreciated that *planned* capital investment in the so-called backward countries is required, not as a philanthropic operation, but to establish an "international" division of labor outside the dollar area. This is a considerable step forward from the liberal solutions popular in 1945. The road would no doubt have been traveled more rapidly if utopianism had not had so powerful a hold upon Western statesmen and "practical" men of affairs.

In looking back on the period it is not without interest to note that the United Nations Charter, the Bretton Woods agreement on removing economic barriers, and the initial proposals for controlling atomic energy, were conceived more or less simultaneously in 1944-46, to be acclaimed for a few months and then rapidly forgotten. The time was doubtless favorable to the drafting of ambitious plans, but a study of these documents discloses a family resemblance that has not received sufficient notice. There is, on the one hand, the traditional emphasis on the elimination of barriers to peace and world trade: a rational framework is to be constructed within which all nations shall be free to pursue their legitimate aims. But the introduction of such bodies as the Security Council and the proposed, if stillborn, international atomic-control commission, strikes a new note. Here the accent is on planning, intervention, and a strong central authority. The old and the new liberalism—both meeting in the person of Keynes, who in some sense impressed his stamp upon the whole era— share the belief in a rational solution of the world's problems. But where the older school placed its trust in individual and national self-interest, the new hard-bitten generation of post-totalitarian liberals is distinguished by a reluctant acceptance of the need for more centralized power. This new liberalism no longer puts its entire faith in enlightened self-interest and the hidden hand: it has became "managerial." Hence the fashionable talk of "putting teeth into the Charter." Where its utopian character still shows is in its indifference to problems of social and political structure— *e.g.,* in the naïve assumption that all powers, including super-powers like the United States and the Soviet Union, can be trusted to subject themselves to a neutral agency actuated by a purely rational, *i.e.,* purely technocratic, conception of its duties; or in the belief that an international regime of free trade might have drawn the Soviet Union into its orbit and thus prevented the cold war from becoming really dangerous. The lawyers, scientists, economists and publicists who in 1945-46 brought this ideology into prominence were clearly unaware of its utopian character. They appear to have thought that, given a minimum of sanity and good will on the part of the politicians, these aims were easily attainable. It is one of the weaknesses of liberalism, considered as a general philosophy, that it encourages such notions. The Keynesian-New Dealish, or neo-liberal, utopia of 1945, like its Wilsonian predecessor, did at bottom reflect a rational impulse toward world organization; but its evasion of the main political issue made it certain that the advance would be halted long before the goal had been reached.

The liberal utopia—to which the British Labor government, for all its socialist protestations, was as firmly committed as the U. S. administration—rested upon the expectation of a prolonged era of peace, Anglo-American hegemony (with the aid of China) in the United Nations and in the world generally, free trade outside the Soviet orbit and gradual liberalization within, a weakened and profoundly pacific Russia far behind the Western powers in the utilization of atomic energy . . . What has become of these assumptions, which were then held by all the best-informed people? We have seen the world polarized between the Atlantic Community and the Eurasian bloc; China repudiating the traditional pro-American orientation of her intelligentsia and going through a Communist revolution; India vacillating and profoundly endangered by reason of her unsolved problems; the Western powers divided among themselves, with America and Europe drawing apart after a brief period of close co-operation; neutralism in Europe and nationalism in the United States growing apace, and large sections of the European working class in a state of what amounts to secession from the body politic; lastly, the Soviet Union, under rigid totalitarian leadership, developing her heavy industry, if not the whole of her economy, at a faster pace than most other countries and gradually exceeding the combined output of western Europe. In the light of these developments one can scarcely go on maintaining that the institutions set up in 1945 are adequate, or that they can be shored up by the establishment of a series of regional defense systems resting on nothing better than a combination of outdated nationalism and air-borne imperialism.

One can indeed argue that even in 1945 these dangers were foreseen and that a conscious attempt was made to guard against them. Was not one of the prime purposes of the United Nations Charter the integration of the Soviet Union into the framework of an international society, precisely because it was felt that failure in this respect would split the world in two? And did not the U. S. government's atomic-control proposals in 1946 spring from a similar perception? One can only say that in both instances the scheme assumed a balance of power which did not in fact exist, or which ceased to exist after China had passed through revolution and after Russia had recovered from the war and developed her own atomic weapons. It is no criticism of the planners to say that even their most idealistic schemes presupposed effective American control of the new world organization, including the projected international atomic-control commission. It is a simple tribute to their common sense to note that even at the height of enthusiasm they did not altogether overlook the fact that someone would have to make the new global machinery work. That someone, needless to say, was to be the United States, just as in the nineteenth century it had been Britain. There is no discredit in admitting this; indeed, it would have been better if it had been stated more plainly, instead of being concealed behind a great deal of rather spurious rhetoric about the new world society. What was wrong with the system was not that it contained a built-in device for keeping it in touch with politico-military reality, but that the calculation left out too many imponderables. These included the totalitarian character of Soviet society, the Stalinist drive to make capital investment in heavy industry prevail over all other considerations, Russian mastery of the atom bomb, the strength of Chinese Communism and its attraction for other Asian revolutionary movements, and the inadequacy of neo-liberal solutions in Europe, especially in countries like Italy, but also to some extent in France. Last but not least, the planners trusted too much to the continuance of liberal-labor influence in the United States—the only element which in this age can keep America in touch with the radical mass movements of Europe and Asia.

The relationship between the new world society and the emerging *Pax Americana* is neither simple nor free from contradictions. It requires some mutual adaptation, for the United States will in the foreseeable future not merely be more powerful but socially more conservative than the majority of her allies. The alliance demands from Americans tolerance for the world-wide growth of socialist tendencies, and from socialists in Europe and Asia a better understanding of the fact that America need not be a hindrance to progress, even though she is still wedded to capitalism. It requires the creation of common organs, such as an Atlantic Council and possibly a Pacific Council, to include like-minded nations—a function that the United Nations should never have been expected to fulfill and will become increasingly less capable of fulfilling as it becomes more truly universal. It demands common planning in the economic sphere, even at the cost of some distress to the fanatics of *laissez-faire*. It necessitates, in short, a genuine alliance between, or synthesis of, liberalism and socialism, freedom and planning, American and European-Asian thinking. There was a brief period after the war when this aim seemed to have been accepted on both sides of the Atlantic and in parts of Asia, but the opportunity was allowed to slip, and we are now witnessing the consequences of this retrogression. No doubt western Europe bears as much (or more) responsibility for this partial debacle as America. What matters

now is that both should recognize their common interest
and the need for another joint advance.

3: *Problems of Coexistence*

To DISCUSS THE QUESTION of
so-called "peaceful coexistence" in a world thus radically
divided into two incompatible halves evidently requires
something rather different from the kind of political analysis
appropriate down to 1914, and in some degree even down to
1939. Instead of the familiar "concert of powers," all pur-
suing limited aims, there are now two great politico-military centers, around which the remainder of the world tends
to organize itself. And while in the nineteenth century
affiliation to rival groups of powers did not, in the majority
of cases, involve basic issues of political loyalty, today every
such move is fraught with consequences of the most far-
reaching kind. In this sense it is true to say that we are living
in an age of world revolution. Not only is the disturbance
global in scope, but the nature of the upheaval renders
genuine neutrality impossible. The totalitarian reorganization of society unsuccessfully attempted by Germany in
1933-45, and currently undertaken on a vastly greater scale
by the Communist powers, is so radical as to turn every
political issue into a life-or-death matter. It is not surprising
that, in the face of such a challenge, talk of peaceful coexistence should sound hollow. Yet the technical developments
which have accompanied, and to some extent caused, this
situation are themselves so startling and unprecedented that
all traditional notions of legitimate self-defense will have to
be revised. If it is unrealistic to suppose that East and West
can at present dwell peacefully side by side, it is dangerous,

to say the least, to fashion policy on the tacit assumption that all-out war is a suitable way of resolving the issue. For it takes no great effort of the imagination to realize that, were such a catastrophe to occur, it would make an end of civilization as we have hitherto known it, and in the face of such a virtual certainty even the issue of global hegemony for one or the other side begins to look a trifle old-fashioned.[5]

Moreover, it is by no means certain, or even likely, that the issue can in fact be settled, even at the cost of destroying the world's centers of civilization. On the contrary, there is good ground for thinking that there exist no military means of breaking the fundamental deadlock, and that even a war waged with the latest weapons would merely result in a somewhat different kind of stalemate. The "cold war" remains cold precisely because neither side believes that the results to be expected from "hot" war would warrant the risks. It does not follow that this state of affairs will last. Quite likely the deadlock will at some point be broken. What should be clearly envisaged even now is the kind of world likely to emerge from an atomic "test of strength." In all probability it would be a world not differing fundamentally from that in which we are now living—except that it would be a great deal poorer and more savage. The thought of an atomic conflict which may flatten most of the world's

[5] "Compared with the cost of rebuilding, the cost of destruction has been very considerably reduced by the development of atomic weapons. In 1946 General Arnold estimated that with conventional bombs the cost of destruction was about one-fiftieth that of rebuilding, while with mass-produced atomic bombs the cost would be reduced by at least a factor of six. Senator McMahon told the American Senate in 1951 that the cost had become hundreds of times less with T.N.T. Hydrogen bombs may now reduce the cost by yet another factor of 10, if the speculations already quoted on the nature and cost of the thermonuclear explosive are substantially correct. Such considerations lend force to the belief that full-scale atomic war could bring about the end of civilization itself." *The World Today,* (Royal Institute of International Affairs publication) *November* 1954, Vol. 10, No. 11, p. 474.

centers of population cannot, unfortunately, be dismissed as too improbable or too terrible to be seriously considered; what can and should be said is that even such a global disaster would be unlikely to make much difference to the basic cleavage running through the present international society. There is something unreal about the notion that either the Western world or the Russo-Chinese bloc can be conclusively defeated and disarmed, let alone occupied or "liberated." But even if such a consummation were possible, neither the Communist movement nor the forces upholding the Western way of life would disappear. Least of all would the problem of organizing the world society have been solved. At bottom each side still believes that there can and should be one center instead of two, though neither is at present willing to take the risk of putting the issue to the ultimate test. What the real development of the cold war suggests is, on the contrary, that the world is irremediably split into two political halves and that this cleavage will continue in the foreseeable future. It does not follow that a third world war is therefore improbable; what does seem to follow is that it would be meaningless.

This conclusion is today challenged by a powerful school of thought which to all intents and purposes favors an all-out atomic war (whether "preventive" or camouflaged to look like defense against "Communist aggression") as the solution to all the world's ills. And doubtless there are similar tendencies on the other side of the Iron Curtain. It is against this background that one has to judge the current wave of "neutralism" in both Europe and Asia: a movement more powerful under the surface than above it. Those who hope and believe that their own particular nation or community can stand aside from the military conflict whose imminence they fear would admit that this attitude really amounts to acceptance of the worst as being likely to happen. Neutralism in fact, in so far as it is more than a simple desire to escape destruction, discloses a belief that there is no *via media* between peace and global catastrophe. It is a way of indicating that the world must either be wholly at peace or wholly at war. But is this true? Is it not rather probable that we are moving into a twilight zone of "neither peace nor war," in which the "cold war" and "coexistence" will increasingly appear to be merely two sides of the same medal?

Let us assume that either the Korean or the Indo-Chinese conflict had given rise to the employment of what are known as "tactical atomic weapons." By what logic is it supposed that their use would "automatically" have led, through various undefined intermediate stages, to a total world conflagration? That, in other words, the major powers would have become involved in the kind of war which, by general consent, can only end (or rather begin) with the destruction of the great urban centers of America, Russia, and Europe? It may indeed be "logical," but it is not in the least likely, that this would have happened. The mere availability of "absolute" weapons and other means of "total" destruction is no guarantee that they will be used—unless each side is secretly convinced that their use is planned by the other. On any realistic calculation of the probable effects of such a conflict, it is far more likely that "total" destruction would have been confined to the smallest possible area —just as, in the past, wars were fought on the tacit understanding that ordinary life was not to be disrupted. The lapse from these civilized standards during the confused period of the First and Second World Wars is no proof that the process must be carried to its final conclusion. It merely suggests that society has not yet adapted itself to the new technological level.

What these rules are likely to be emerges much more clearly from the actual course of events since 1945 than from the voluminous discussion on universal disarmament and/or international control of atomic weapons—a discussion whose futility should by now have become evident. Everything that has happened since the last world war suggests that the typical present-day conflict is one in which the belligerents stop short of going to the final extreme suggested by military logic in its purest—*i.e.*, most abstract —form. Precisely because it has now become possible to destroy civilization itself, the actual conduct of war tends to become once again a matter over which statesmanship exercises some control. Both sides are groping toward new forms of limited warfare; and since it is impossible, or at any rate impracticable, to limit armaments in type or in quantity, the need to limit the scope of destruction territorially asserts itself instead. If "total" war cannot be altogether prevented, statesmanship can at least make sure that it is confined to areas where no fundamental issues are involved. Thus the balance of power in Asia has been stabilized, for some time to come, on the battlefields of Korea; while the corresponding issue in Europe was settled, not by atomic bombardments, but by the bloodless blockade of Berlin and the equally bloodless Berlin air lift. It depends entirely upon the political direction on both sides, and not in the least on military logic, whether this kind of struggle shall go on, or whether we are due for a complete and universal breakdown. For short of a direct Soviet military advance into western Europe, or an "atomic Pearl Harbor" upon the cities of Europe and America, nothing will cause the democratically elected governments of the

Western world to send out air fleets laden with atomic bombs; and since both sides must be aware that this *will* occur on one of the above suppositions, it would seem that the urge for universal suicide would have to become very powerful before either side made a move calculated to bring about such results. This is not to say that it will not happen; it well may. But if it does, it will testify not to military logic, but to political fanaticism and the absence of rationality.

And conversely, there is nothing to prevent an age of "peaceful coexistence" from being also an era of cold war, and even of "real" wars, provided they are localized. It is a misunderstanding to talk of coexistence as though it precluded conflicts such as those which have taken place in Korea and Indo-China. On the contrary, the will to make coexistence possible manifests itself precisely in the occurrence and the conduct of such wars. They are the equivalent, in modern terms, of the nineteenth-century struggle between the British Empire and Russia along the Indian and Turkish border—a struggle that flared into large-scale war in 1854 and very nearly did so again in 1876. What is implied by the term coexistence is solely the desire to spare the world the catastrophe of all-out atomic war; more positively, the belief that in the last resort the world can and will stay divided for a very long time to come. To say that coexistence is possible and necessary is to say that the Communist powers will fail to conquer or overthrow the West, and that the West cannot hope to undo the Chinese Revolution or to overthrow the present regime in Russia. And the "cold war" for the allegiance of the intermediate areas—principally, though not entirely, the so-called backward or "undeveloped" countries—is the corollary of this state of affairs, for while both sides will naturally try to win over as many doubtful elements as possible, neither is compelled to use military means to this end. War, revolution, propaganda, and ordinary diplomacy are intermingled in the conflict, but its purpose is the imposition of a particular form of organization, not the annexation of territory or inhabitants. There is no inherent reason why, after a period of flux and reflux, the two "worlds" should not tacitly agree to abide by the eventual outcome, whatever it may be. That they will enter into formal treaties to this effect is just as unlikely as that they will consent to a mutually satisfactory limitation and control of armaments. It is sufficient that they should recognize the limits of their power.

What stands in the way of such an arrangement at present is the clash of mutually exclusive doctrines concerning the nature of the process in which we are all caught up. Just as there is a school of thought in the West which regards Communism as a temporary aberration from a supposedly fixed norm of development, so the Communists believe (even if they do not preach) that Western society is in decline, being irrevocably tied to a decaying economic system. On these suppositions, genuine coexistence is only practicable for brief, limited periods. If the non-Communist world is identified with "capitalism," or "bourgeois society," it becomes possible to project the image of an irrepressible conflict; and it does not greatly matter whether such predictions are confirmed by foolish talk in the West. If the Communist regimes are kept in power solely by terrorism, and not because Communism has exploited and travestied *one* particular solution of the modern problem of industrializing backward countries, there is a corresponding temptation to preach the inevitability of head-on conflict.

Paradoxically, both sides are at present restrained above all by their common fear of the very technical means they

are trying so hard to develop. But for the universal dread of
the consequences, it is not improbable that they would
already have put their respective notions to the test. But
while this mutual constraint lasts, there is at any rate a
chance for different views to make themselves felt, and perhaps for Western statesmanship to rise above the level of
parochial and melodramatic myth creation. For the heavier
responsibility lies with the West. The nature of the Communist system in its present form inhibits the process of
critical thinking that would enable the totalitarians to
get out of their mental strait-jacket. It is all the more important that Western statesmanship should recognize and pro-
claim the impossibility of either incorporating the Communist powers in our kind of world or destroying them by
force. However much they may dislike the prospect, the
Atlantic world and the Eurasian bloc are fated to live together, or at any rate alongside each other. When this realization has sunk in, our opponents may be compelled to revise
their concepts, and having taken the first step on the road to
sanity it is not inconceivable that they will in time shed
enough of their mental apparatus to make coexistence
genuinely workable. Yet to say this is merely to express a
hope, not to risk a prediction. Much may be credited to the
subterranean urge for self-preservation, which cannot fail
to be operative on both sides; but it is useless to deny that
there are forces at work which may yet carry the major
powers, and with them the world at large, "Through caverns
measureless to man, Down to a sunless sea."

CHAPTER II

ATLANTIC WORLD AND EURASIAN BLOC

1: *The Decline of Europe*

THE SETTLEMENT of 1945 was determined by the two great non-European powers, the United States and the Soviet Union, with the British Commonwealth nominally acting as a third and equal partner, but in effect increasingly reduced to the role of onlooker while the vital decisions were taken in Washington and Moscow. The justification for this state of affairs was the failure of the Versailles system, which had rested on an Anglo-French basis, and the subsequent disintegration of the entire European framework, until in 1941 Russia and America were needed to stop the onrush of Germany. *Mutatis mutandis,* the same applied in the Far East, where Japan had paralleled the role of Germany, after some initial encouragement from the West to seek a "sphere of influence" in China. What this arrangement meant was that the powers which between 1919 and 1939 acted the most prominent parts on the world stage were no longer able to manage Europe's and Asia's affairs. Italy, of course, had never been a power—the fiction that allotted her this status was one of the by-products of Anglo-French rivalry in the Mediterranean and the Balkans. But France had been the main prop of the Versailles system, and Britain had been responsible for the system's over-all functioning through her control of a world-wide trade and communications network which a Continental power like Germany could hope to disrupt only with the help of allies. When, therefore, Britain and France failed to prevent the outbreak of war in 1939, and then failed to prevent Germany and Japan from overrunning most of Europe and Asia, they wrote finis to their historic roles, a fact that no amount of rhetoric and heroism on the part of statesmen, soldiers, and underground movements could conceal. By the same token, however, they wrote finis to Europe's hegemony as such. For if Europe could no longer settle its own wars, or defend its own interests in the East, but required America and Russia to act as policemen, its traditional role was at an end. Thereafter it might still be possible to organize western Europe—if possible, plus Africa—as an economic and strategic unit, but the West's center of gravity had passed elsewhere. Viewed from Moscow, it now lay in the United States, as the strongest of the Western powers and the world citadel of capitalism—though only on the supposition that a genuine Atlantic Community could be brought into being.

Any interpretation that fastens on Europe's declining status after 1914 is doubtless in danger of yielding to one particular form of parochialism. It is at least arguable that the appropriate *terminus a quo* is 1917—the year of the Russian Revolution and of America's entry into the war. But in point of fact the two sets of circumstances were closely linked, and it matters little from which angle they are approached. After 1914 Europe lost its preeminence, though it remained the pivot of world politics. The war of 1914-18 can thus be regarded as a European conflict in which the United States belatedly intervened, or, alternatively, as America's first major foreign war, whose center of gravity happened to lie in Europe; but at least there is no doubt that it was wholly caused by European rivalries. In 1939 this framework was no longer fully applicable, and today it would be absurd to think of a possible third world war in European terms. Indeed, there are those who hold that it is possible as well as desirable for Europe to stay out of such a conflict. There could be no more striking sign of the change which has supervened in the last four decades than the existence, in the Europe of 1955, of a neutralism that regards the fate of the world as a matter to be settled between the United States and the Soviet Union.

The actual physical partition of the Continent, which in 1914 still harbored a number of great powers with world-wide interests and pretensions, has brought a forcible awareness of Europe's decline in status and simultaneously reminded Europeans that their common interests far outweigh their remaining conflicts and disagreements. That such a shift would take place, unless speedily counteracted, had indeed been increasingly regarded as probable toward the end of the nineteenth century, and it became the firm conviction of most leading European and some American statesmen at the beginning of the twentieth. The so-called imperialist era around 1900 had many aspects, but one of them undoubtedly was a growing belief that the coming age would put the nation-state to the test and that only the most powerful states would survive, on condition that they managed to transform themselves into empires with a modern economic foundation. This conviction was sharpened by the aggravation of traditional European rivalries via a new set of conflicts caused by intensified competition on a world scale. That the Anglo-German antagonism eventually became the central axis around which the others grouped themselves was due to accidental circumstances arising from Germany's belated unification and the political immaturity of her governing class. There was no inherent necessity in the timing of this particular conflict. There was, however, every reason why the German challenge to Britain should in the end have proved fatal to both. In the modern era Europe could not be made the theater of all-out war without being devastated on a scale for which the preceding century of limited wars and semi-developed industrial techniques supplied no model. That this was not perceived before 1914 gives the epoch its hybrid character, part modern, part belonging to the old nineteenth-century world of competing national, or even dynastic, systems. Symbolically the explosion was set off by the assassination of an Austrian archduke—a circumstance that by 1918 had already acquired a somewhat anachronistic look. Indeed, the war, which ended with the dissolution of the eastern empires, seemed in 1914 to be largely a continuation of the historic rivalries among Turkey, Russia, Austria, and Prussia. Before giving up the ghost, the nineteenth century indulged in a final orgy of traditionalism. The armies which marched into the field in 1914 literally did march, and they did so with equipment and uniforms altogether unrelated to the new techniques that evolved in the course of fighting. It took four years to bridge this gap, and by then millions had been slain and a new world had come into being, as different from its predecessor as the nineteenth century differed from the epoch preceding the American and French Revolutions. Compared with this upheaval, the 1939-45 war, although even more devastating and accompanied by the totalitarian innovations of genocide and mass deportation, appears less revolutionary in its general implications. It was already a conflict on the new technological and social level, whereas in 1914-18 society had to pass through a revolution in order to forge the technical means necessary to its destructive purpose.

The revolution was unleashed in the technological sphere, but the pattern it destroyed was political as well as social. It is a commonplace that between the end of the Napoleonic era and the outbreak of the first German war in 1914, the *Pax Britannica* operated so as to localize national conflicts and prevent them from becoming world-wide. The war that broke out in 1914 might still have conformed to the traditional model if Britain had not entered it—much to Germany's dismay. It was this intervention which turned it into a world war. But the British government's reluctant decision to intervene was itself a sign that the *Pax Britannica* was coming to an end. Before 1914 the mere threat of British action had been sufficient to localize any European conflict. By 1914 it was clear that nothing would stop the Germans from going to war, and that having defeated France and Russia—as in the absence of British intervention they were certain to do—they would construct their impregnable Mitteleuropa, build an even bigger navy, and finally challenge Britain—and after Britain, America—for the *imperium mundi*. The possibility of such a challenge meant that Britain had already in effect lost the predominant position that had been hers since the fall of Napoleon. The outcome of the 1914-18 war made this crystal-clear. Germany having been defeated, there emerged a new world system in which Britain and America were nominally equal, though America was in fact more powerful, but in which Britain still tried to exercise world-wide control, without having the means to back it up. The next twenty years were spent in elaborate efforts to camouflage this situation, until Hitler made an end of the fiction by going to war, although this time the British government had served advance notice of its intention to intervene. Finally, in 1945, America and Russia virtually determined the nature of the peace settlement, while not even a shadow was left of the *Pax Britannica* which in 1919 still conserved some reality behind the ample camouflage of the League. It was now clearly recognized that the only factor preventing Russia from overrunning all Europe was American power—specifically, American possession (then unchallenged) of the atom bomb; and by a final stroke of irony it was left to Winston Churchill, last surviving representative of the great liberal-imperialist school of 1900-14, to underline this fact in his Fulton speech of March 5, 1946, which can be regarded as the first public expression of Britain's still new and somewhat shaky faith in the effectiveness of the *Pax Americana*.

To measure the significance of this transfer it is necessary to bear in mind that the *Pax Britannica* never meant the absence of local wars. What it did mean was that such conflicts would not become global. It was the refusal of Germany and Japan to accept this limitation which drove Britain, and ultimately America, to war in 1914-18 and 1939-45. The paradox that a local conflict was thereby twice transformed into a world-wide one conceals a deeper meaning: America, Britain and France were the guarantors of the international order established in the nineteenth century, an order that in the last resort was designed to enable all political units, from the greatest empire to the smallest state, to compete in the world arena without destroying one another—the alternative to an Orwellian nightmare of unending conflict between rival empires. It would be absurd to pretend that the Western powers consciously elected to go to war on those grounds—no power ever fights for non-material aims, whatever utopians and propagandists may assert to the contrary. It is enough that their attitude was in accordance with the underlying reality of world-wide inter-dependence. As guardians of the *status quo,* they were also, in so far as the *status quo* expressed the existence of the world market and the world community, guardians of polit-ical rationality. Conversely, the Axis challenge (and the subsequent Soviet challenge) to Western hegemony were bound to endanger Europe's social institutions as well as its political framework. Throughout the nineteenth century all economic progress, and consequently all further social and political advance, depended on the functioning of the world-wide system of trade and communications that the vast network of British treaties, alliances, financial loans, naval bases, diplomatic agents, and political institutions existed to protect. Without this silent support, European liberal capitalism, and the political leadership of the liberal *bourgeoisie,* were doomed; the proof is that both came to an end when the *Pax Britannica* collapsed.

2: *The Imperialist Pattern*

THAT THIS COLLAPSE did not involve the permanent disappearance of west European society is due, as we all know, to the fact that by 1939 the United States, though with many hesitations and thanks in part to some expert political manipulation at the center, had been brought in to restore the threatened balance. But there was an interval during which it seemed possible that an Anglo-German combination would be formed, or, alterna-tively, that Britain would ward off the German threat without yielding her world hegemony. Because these issues, and the two wars fought to decide them, were intimately bound up with different interpretations of what was happening to the world as a whole, it is important to recall them here. We shall have occasion to suggest that the political and military upheavals of the period—roughly speaking, the forty years from 1914 to 1954—corresponded to the disintegration of the world market; and that the real task of the peacemakers, both in 1919 and in 1945, was to adapt the national economies of the principal European countries to the underlying change in the international division of labor. In anticipation of this theme, however, it is worth noting here that the struggle for European hegemony whose fruits were reaped in 1914, involved some basic decisions for the British Empire—at that time the greatest power in the world and the only power from whom America could learn how to manipulate the politics and economics of the globe.

It is common knowledge that on the eve of the First World War Germany's growing hostility, and the intensified competition British exports were encountering, combined to produce a drive to reconstruct the Empire on protectionist lines, with all its constituent members committed to a single foreign, military, and tariff policy. This project, of which Joseph Chamberlain became the principal spokesman, deserves all the more attention because in the end it failed, and because its failure involved the gradual conversion of the Empire into the present Commonwealth and the transformation of Britain's internal politics. Chamberlain's abortive scheme had a double aim: the retention by Britain of her former economic predominance through a better utilization of imperial resources and the maintenance of British naval hegemony in a world of competing powers, some of them better armed than Britain, and all of them less dependent upon imports.[1] The rejection of this program by the dominant Liberal party (and its Labor allies) did not mean a policy of abstention from the imperialist game as it was played by all the powers before 1914. What it meant was that the British government would continue to play the game according to rules no longer accepted by Britain's European rivals but still venerated in the United States. The chief of these rules was adherence to free trade: the principle that Chamberlain had challenged. Secondly, reliance upon the navy and a policy of limited involvement in Continental conflicts, although owing to the exigencies of the 1914-18 war this part of the program could not be sustained, and the consequent split within the Liberal party foreshadowed the latter's eventual disappearance; thirdly, and perhaps most decisive of all, the British government in 1917 committed itself to the acceptance of President Wilson's program—at any rate in broad outline—rather than conclude a compromise peace with Germany, as suggested by some leading Conservatives. This made it certain that the United States would be drawn into the postwar settlement, that American isolation would come to an end, and that Britain would have to yield an increasing share of her former position to her American ally.

The willingness to let this happen was perhaps the ultimate reason why Liberals and Conservatives could not find a common language during the interwar period, until Churchill eventually imposed his own Anglo-American outlook upon a Conservative party already remodeled to resem-

---

[1] "The essential element in the program was Imperial Preference, not protection per se; economists' arguments about the economic merits or demerits of protective duties thus failed entirely to meet the real—the imperialist—issue." J. A. Schumpeter, *History of Economic Analysis*, New York, London, 1954; p. 767.

ble its former Liberal rival. Until this had happened—*i.e.*, until Toryism had been partly reconstructed in the image of middle-class liberalism, high finance, and the exporting industries—there was always a danger that the Tory party might take the bit between its teeth and launch out on a genuinely imperialist campaign. Before 1914 this meant a policy of maintaining the *Pax Britannica* against all comers, building a preferential tariff wall around the Empire, and letting the workers share more generously in the proceeds as the price of gaining their help in upholding the *status quo*. To prominent Conservatives like Chamberlain, Amery, or Milner this seemed entirely feasible and indeed the only possible alternative to socialism at home and disintegration abroad. But even after 1919 such a policy had powerful support, and it is worth noting that in its advocacy political and economic motives were inextricably mixed: those who supported it did so in part because they saw, or believed they saw, that the world economy was being reorganized on a regional basis, in five or six great interdependent areas, and because they desired Britain to adapt herself to this trend. That in the end they failed to carry the day was doubtless due in considerable part to the unenthusiastic reception of their program in the British Commonwealth, notably in Canada; but at bottom it reflected the continuing strength of the liberal tradition among the British business class. After 1918 the temptation for Britain to embark upon a protectionist course was considerable, and the Ottawa tariff agreements of 1932, which successfully excluded Japanese and German exports from British colonial markets, showed how far the British government, under Conservative inspiration, was willing to go. But it never went far enough to satisfy the consistent imperialists, and indeed the Tory party never even became fully protectionist.

One is thus left with the curious result that British imperialism in its heyday not only lacked a consistent ideology —it did not even produce a major poet, *pace* Kipling's admirers—but was never wholly adopted as a policy. Indeed, what stands out very prominently from this record is the fact that the greatest empire of all was also the only one to reject a consistently imperialist solution of its problems, although it did annex as many colonies as it could. It was Germany, not Britain, that did commit itself wholeheartedly to imperialism—and failed! Highly protectionist, cartel-ridden, and governed by an unshakable alliance of great landowners and great industrialists, the Germany of 1914 (which in all essentials was also the Germany of 1939) was profoundly committed to military expansion, as was Japan. And precisely for this reason the two world wars turned into "ideological" struggles, in which the character of the world society was felt to be at stake. Whatever the failures of British diplomacy, the continuance of Liberal leadership down to 1914 did at least ensure for the gigantic free-trade empire the decisive support of the United States when the crisis finally came. Matters would have looked much blacker for Britain in 1917, the worst year of the war, had she entered the conflict as a tightly knit protectionist empire, with an imperialist ideology to match Germany's. Of the corresponding situation in 1939-45 it is unnecessary to speak.

But although it is a tribute to the political maturity of the British that they left it to the Germans (and the Japanese) to carry the tendencies inherent in the imperialist era to their logical conclusion, it cannot be denied that in the end Britain paid the price of letting the United States inherit a far greater share of her former world position than the original calculation had provided for. Most of our current troubles stem from the fact that this transfer has occurred too suddenly for American public opinion to become fully aware of its new responsibilities, and no country has suffered more than Britain from the relative immaturity of the new world power. Yet on balance the choice made early in this century has turned out to the advantage of the British Commonwealth—which, indeed, could not have come into existence in its present form but for the strength of the liberal tradition in the middle class and the readiness of the labor movement to step into the liberal inheritance. It was an amazing piece of good fortune that at a time when other powers were driven into the protectionist-imperialist impasse, Britain escaped with such minor blemishes as the Boer War and the poetry of Rudyard Kipling; and even the Boer War, now that it can be viewed in retrospect, turns out to have been a rearguard action, fought not in the full blaze of an imperialist high noon, but defensively, to safeguard a vast, sprawling, and decentralized empire on which even then the sun had already set.

3: *The New Power Balance*

IF THE GRADUAL REPLACEMENT of the *Pax Britannica* by the as yet imperfect and vulnerable *Pax Americana* has been the overriding event of the past half century so far as the Atlantic world is concerned, the substitution of Russian for German hegemony on the European continent has been no less marked, and even more revolutionary in its implications. The shift of power from London to Washington and New York merely displaced the West's center of gravity; the passing of Continental supremacy from Berlin to Moscow transformed eastern

Europe into an annex of the Eurasian bloc and threatened
western Europe with the same fate. For a brief period after
the war this consequence was obscured by speculation about
the fate of Germany. The defeat of 1945 had brought the
"German Century" to an end; outside a narrow circle it
was not immediately perceived that this conclusion threatened the inauguration of a "Russian Century," at least so
far as continental Europe was concerned. Yet to the Russians this seemed logical and inevitable, just as to some
Americans, at about the same time, it appeared incon-
testable that the "American Century" was about to dawn.
These formulations, after all, merely expressed the fact that
Germany and Britain had lost their respective hegemony on
land and sea (they had never possessed it in the air). Continental Europeans were quick to see the point, though not
necessarily eager to range themselves under these new ban-
ners, whose rivalry portended civil strife in addition to the
normal tension between great powers. The British were
slower to draw the inevitable conclusion. For some years
after 1945 the assumption that the British Commonwealth
counted as a unit equal in status to the two great extra-
European powers was carried over from wartime propaganda into peacetime political language. As late as the
summer of 1947, an official Labor Party publication[2] included a section, headed "The Big Three," which dwelt at
some length on Britain's traditional status in a world supposedly dependent on "Big Three Unity." Such fictions
were slow to disappear, as was the corresponding American
dream of a powerful and pro-Western China solidly linked
with the Atlantic powers in the United Nations and, by its
presence on the Security Council, condemning the Soviet

---

[2] *Cards on the Table—An Interpretation of Labour's Foreign Policy,*
published by the Labor Party, Transport House, London, 1947.

Union to impotence and isolation. In this as in other respects the eventual outcome bore no relation to the original prospectus.

A realistic assessment in 1945 would have compelled the admission that the Second World War had been fought in circumstances that ruled out a democratic triumph from the start, since the West was fundamentally on the defensive and could win only with Russian help.[8] It is true that a similar situation existed in 1914-17, but the embarrassment caused to the Western powers by their alliance with the ramshackle tsarist autocracy was as nothing compared to the risks they ran in 1941-45. In both cases the underlying geographic and military realities pointed to a choice between German and Russian hegemony on the European continent, though in 1917-19 the democracies were able to escape the logic of their choice, thanks to the simultaneous collapse of the three eastern empires, which temporarily caused a power vacuum in central and eastern Europe. Similarly, in the Far East the elimination of Japan could only mean that America and Russia would be left face to face, and here, too, the decision was postponed by the after-effects of the Russian Revolution, which forced a "withdrawal-and-return" pattern upon the activities of Russian imperialism in the period lasting from 1917 to 1945. The parallel is doubly significant because it shows how little the long-term trend was affected by temporary permutations: Japan was on the winning side in 1914-18, but that did not prevent her from being on the losing side in 1941-45, just as her alliance with the Western powers during the first war presented no obstacle to her subsequent switch to the Axis. The underlying fact in each case was that a medium-sized imperialist power, in the age of continental empires and larger eco-

[8] Cf. George Kennan, *American Diplomacy*, University of Chicago, 1951, Chapter V.

nomic agglomerations, tried to make a hurried bid for territorial expansion in order to stay in the race; but the Japan
that went down to defeat in 1945 had more in common with
the imperial Germany of 1918 than with the Third Reich.
Germany and Japan, it might be said, were struck by catastrophe in 1945 at different points in their own internal
development cycle, Germany having already passed through
the totalitarian stage that typically follows the breakdown of
traditional institutions, while in Japan this disintegration
dates only from 1945, with the consequent chance for a
Fascist or Communist mass movement to seize power and
thereafter practice upon the Japanese body politic all the
disillusionments which Germany underwent after 1933.
But in our present context this difference is less material
than the typically imperialist configuration of external and
internal factors which during the first half of this century
impelled Japanese and German statesmen to seek the expansion of their nation's territorial base by aggressive war.

The fact that both powers were late-comers in the game
explains the crudity of their methods. The relative backwardness of their political institutions reflected the late stage
at which they achieved their adaptation to the modern world
of sovereign nation-states—though in Germany's case the
time lag was of course far less pronounced than in that of
Japan. The failure of German, as of Japanese, imperialism
to develop a universal ideology, as a conscious or uncon-
scious justification of expansionist aims, had its roots in the
same awkward situation: smash-and-grab practiced deliberately by rising powers for the purpose of overcoming the
advantages possessed by older rivals—primarily Britain—
was in itself not a favorable theme for ideological rationaliza-
tion; but what really rendered the attempt hopeless was the
fact that aggressiveness went hand in hand with political

and social backwardness. In comparison with such opponents, America, Britain, and France had no difficulty in giving their own aims a universal character, while for the Soviet Union after 1917 this particular problem hardly existed at all. If it is a general rule that a successful imperialism requires, among other essential preconditions, an anti-imperialist ideology on the part of its governing class, one may say that both the Western powers and Russia were better served than the Axis, for all the talk about the "New Order" and the "Greater East Asia Co-prosperity Sphere." There is no sense in inquiring whether this particular handicap was more or less basic than the other disadvantages suffered by Japan and Germany, for in the last resort they were rooted in the peculiar blend of archaic and ultramodern features that made up their social pattern. Latecomers on the world stage because they had taken too long to modernize their economic life, they were by the same token condemned to enter the race with an unstable amalgam of political institutions which disintegrated at the shock of defeat. Similarly, their original lack of broad territorial and raw-material bases lent emphasis to that reliance upon efficiency, ruthlessness, and speed which in turn dictated their military strategy—much to their ultimate disadvantage. The development of a full-fledged imperialist ideology as the credo of the ruling class and the intelligentsia—Japan and Germany were the only major countries where imperialism not only was accepted but became fully respectable—was another source of apparent strength and real weakness, since it made a breach between the governing caste and the mass of the people that no amount of propaganda could bridge. The effects became visible in 1945, and for a brief moment the Western cause seemed triumphant. Then it was discovered that victory had been purchased by revolution in China and by letting the Soviet army advance to the gates of Vienna and the plains of Hungary.

Had the change been confined to a geographical displacement of the center of land within the Eurasian "heartland," it would have been revolutionary enough. What rendered it unbearable to the Western powers, as well as to the Germans, was the attendant subjection of much of central Europe to the rule of a power that was both backward and despotic—the kind of nightmare which had preoccupied European democrats and socialists throughout the nineteenth century. A Soviet Union dominant—though not physically present—in eastern Europe was just bearable from the Western viewpoint; it was in fact the real Anglo-American "war aim" from Teheran onward, as Churchill's account of the wartime conferences has made clear. A Soviet empire sprawling over half of Europe and firmly established in Berlin, Vienna, Prague, and Budapest was clearly intolerable. Yet, having once advanced beyond the limits of safety it was difficult for the Russians to draw back without a loss of prestige likely to affect the entire system of Soviet control in eastern Europe, and on the Western side the opportunity to bring about such a withdrawal by a mixture of discreet pressure and peaceful persuasion was missed during the first crucial postwar years. The outcome has been a stalemate, which at the moment no one—except the Germans—particularly wants to break. Yet the deadlock entails the artificial division of the most numerous and industrially most developed country in Europe. Neither side expects this state of affairs to last very long, and each seems determined to bring about unification on its own terms. This, of course, involves uncertain factors, such as the strength and tenacity of German nationalism, the potentialities of a German "neutralism" sustained by the prospect of lucrative trade relations with the East, and other imponderables. But it also involves at least one measurable factor—time.

It is often overlooked that the Soviet-American antagonism, of which the current arms race is merely one aspect, has had the effect of superseding the older pattern of international relations, which up to 1939 presented a fairly stable and calculable set of political factors. There was, on the one hand, a rough equality in world power and influence as between the United States and the British Commonwealth taken as a whole; and the corollary of this relationship on the land side was an approximate balance between Russia and Germany. This pattern came to an end in 1945, but unofficial attempts to conceal this fact were for long remarkably successful, at any rate in Europe. Thus, the notion that the U. S. A. and Britain were still in some sense equal partners survived the first postwar disillusionments, to be shattered only by the discovery that the U. S. A.'s over-all strategy—based on possession of the hydrogen bomb and willingness to utilize it, at least for purposes of political pressure on the Eurasian bloc—took no more account of British susceptibilities than of, say, popular alarm in Japan. Conversely, the belief that something like a potential balance still exists between the Soviet Union and Germany remains to this day an "unspoken major premise" of Western diplomacy. Although public opinion is not in step with actual developments, a change began to make itself felt in the spring of 1954, when the alarm over American test explosions of a type of fusion bomb in the Pacific brought a sudden realization that Britain, so far from being treated as an equal partner, was not even supplied with

relevant information, let alone consulted over future policy.[4]
The impact of Soviet developments has been slower and
subtler. Even today it cannot be said that Western policy-
makers have been weaned from the assumption that, given
a few years of rearmament and perhaps the unification of
the country, Germany is capable of "balancing" Russia in
eastern Europe. At most it is now conceded that effective
rearmament must be limited to the Federal Republic, Soviet
diplomacy being clearly unwilling to trade East Germany
for anything less than the neutralization of the whole country. Yet even on these revised assumptions there is room for
a great deal of thinking that must be classed as unrealistic.
The truth is that the picture of a Russo-German military
balance, parallel with, or corresponding to, the maritime
balance of America and the British Commonwealth, is a
relic of the Bismarckian era, which lasted from 1870
to 1945 and is now as dead as the epoch of French military hegemony was after 1815. No such balance exists or can be restored—if only because conventional
warfare is no longer possible: even a unified and heavily
rearmed Germany could not repeat the "drive to the
East" without risking total destruction. But the major reason
is quite simply that Germany has lost her old industrial
superiority over Russia, and having lost it cannot hope to

[4] Cf. the official account published in Hansard, April 6, 1954, of the
debate in the House of Commons on April 5, following Sir Winston
Churchill's disclosures, and editorial comment in *The Times* and elsewhere on the following day. The significance of the occasion was in part
veiled by an irrelevant dispute over the responsibility of successive British
postwar governments for surrendering the safeguards supposed to have
been contained in the so-called Quebec agreement of August, 1943,
drawn up in semiprivacy by President Roosevelt and the British Prime
Minister. The real, though suppressed, meaning of the emotional storm
aroused in this debate had more to do with the sudden realization that
there was no Anglo-American "partnership" in any effective sense of the
term, and that the United States government had not even troubled to
inform London of the impending tests.

compensate for her disadvantages by the strategy of the "lightning blow." In future the Germans will have to strive for peaceful relations with Russia, if not necessarily with all their neighbors. There is a very serious issue between Germany and Poland. There is no comparable issue between Germany and the Soviet Union, for the latter is now one of the two superpowers, whereas Germany cannot hope to be more than a middle-sized power on the scale of her former European rivals. Any rectification of the German frontier in the east can thus come about only with Soviet consent, or as a minor by-product of the Soviet-American antagonism, and the Germans know it. It is fantastic to assume that they can be unaware of it. Yet such assumptions are still quite common—though not in Germany.

To grasp the magnitude of the change in the relation between the U. S. S. R. and Germany, consider a few figures. In 1938, Greater Germany, with a production of over 20 million tons of steel, surpassed Soviet output by one-quarter. Production per head of population was higher in Germany than anywhere else in the world, and capital goods accounted for a larger share of domestic output than in any other country. In the later 1930's Germany not merely had geared her economy to yielding a higher war potential relatively than other countries, but her absolute striking power was considerably superior to that of the U. S. S. R. The disproportion was most strikingly reflected in the key sector of machine tool production. Soviet policy aimed at a reduction of tool imports, which was achieved after 1933, but the planned output of 40,000 metal-cutting machines in 1937 amounted to hardly a quarter of the corresponding German figure. Lastly, German armaments factories had only to be converted, while in the U. S. S. R. they had to be started from scratch. Germany's effective military strength therefore exceeded that of the U. S. S. R. by far more than the proportion of one-third suggested by a comparison of aggregate military expenditure.[5]

Nor was this great increase in German military strength accompanied by a fall in civilian consumption; it was rather the result of an expansion by about 20 percent in Germany's national output between 1929 and 1938. At the then existing level of military technique it was possible for Germany, within a few years, to rise from an almost defenceless state to a position of military eminence in Europe. Total German military expenditure between 1933 and 1938 equalled about £3,500 million. The equivalent expenditure today, so far from placing Germany in a position of military superiority over her neighbors—let alone the U. S. S. R.— would barely enable her to equip her projected NATO contingent.

Here is the key to Soviet policy in postwar Europe, and in particular to the somewhat more elastic tactics adopted since the demise of Stalin, whose belated disappearance from the scene may have come as a considerable relief to the more realistic planners in the Kremlin. The fundamental note of this policy is caution and avoidance of unnecessary risks, until such time as the balance will incline even more

[5] Cf. H. C. Hillmann, "Comparative Strength of the Great Powers," in *The World in March, 1939,* Royal Institute of International Affairs, Oxford, 1952. "Not only did Germany's output (of capital goods) in 1937 equal that of France and Britain combined, but it exceeded that of the U. S. S. R." (p. 446). Counting as capital goods industries the metal, engineering, shipbuilding, vehicles and chemical industries, as well as pig-iron and crude steel, their share in total manufacturing output in 1937 was about 51 per cent for Germany, against 39 per cent for the U. S. S. R. (*Ibid* p. 444). Even in absoute terms the Germans were far ahead. In 1941 German machine tool production had risen to 198,000. For the third quarter of that year, the Soviet Government planned an output of 22,000 tools, of which 14,000 were allocated to the arms industries (N. A. Voznesensky, *The Economy of the U. S. S. R. during World War II,* Public Affairs Press, Washington, 1948, p. 22; as quoted by Hillmann, *op. cit.,* p. 449.)

favorably toward the U. S. S. R. It is a policy which reckons in decades, remembers Germany's three-to-one industrial and military superiority over Russia in 1914 and her still formidable striking power in 1941, counts its present gains, and looks ahead with confidence to 1970 or thereabouts, when the Soviet Union's industrial output will have dwarfed that of central Europe and rendered the Soviet empire immune to threats from the European continent. The policy-makers are of course aware that East Germany is the weakest sector of the Soviet edifice, but they are equally conscious of the strength of their underlying position. Russia's aggregate industrial capacity is now between two and three times that of even a united Germany, and every year that passes diminishes the still existing gap in efficiency and mechanical saturation per individual. Simply by holding on to its present position in central Europe and delaying German unification and/or rearmament, the Soviet government is gaining the time necessary to bring its industrial revolution to the point where even a united Germany will have been hopelessly outclassed. At that point the Soviet Union will be able to offer Germany more than the West can ever hope to do: not merely unification, but revision of her eastern frontier *without war*. Whatever one may think of the possibilities of "Eastern" and "Western" orientations in Germany ten years hence, of the effectiveness of such slogans as "neutrality," or of the probability that Germany will content herself with a European existence not very different from that of Sweden, at least it should be recognized that this is going to be the stuff of German—and European —politics in the not very distant future. The partial re-arming of Federal Germany, and its inclusion in the Western defense system, are from the German view-point no more than provisional stages toward the unification of the country. Whether this aim is achieved peacefully or as a by-product of some global cataclysm does not depend on the Germans; but one can at least predict with certainty that they will place the physical survival of the nation above any political aims that Western statesmanship may associate with the prospect of including German divisions among the forces of the Atlantic Community. Germany in Europe, like Japan in the Far East, is obviously destined to make a political comeback, though this time under Anglo-American auspices; and doubtless the resulting shift in the world balance of power will become more noticeable if the peace is kept for a long time, and if "coexistence" becomes the settled aim of both the great power blocs. But it is somewhat fantastic to imagine that the shift will be great enough to restore the *status quo ante* 1939; just as it takes some degree of naïveté on the part of British publicists to suppose that London can place an effective brake on American foreign policy. The truth is that, having traded knockout blows for over a generation, Britain, Germany, and Japan have all, though in varying degrees, lost their former status vis-à-vis the only two great powers left in the contemporary world, and become spectators, or at most secondary figures, in a conflict transcending the old national and political boundaries.

CHAPTER III

DEFENSE OF THE WEST

1: *The Cold War*

THROUGHOUT THE GREATER part of the world the chief political issue today is Communist or non-Communist direction of revolutionary movements having for their aim a radical break with the pre-industrial past similar to that which western Europe and North America effected in the course of their history, and which eastern Europe has been trying to effect, with varying success, during the past century. In this struggle, ideas and values derived from Western experience are utilized, altered, inverted, and turned against their originators, so that we have the spectacle of Russians and Chinese conducting their anti-Western campaigns under the banner of Marxian socialism; Indian orators quoting Gladstone and the Webbs; Arab nationalists employing the vocabulary of the French Revolution to justify secession from France; and Latin-American demagogues appealing to Jefferson and Lincoln in support of the latest propaganda drive against the United States. The West's intellectual hegemony asserts itself most strikingly in the way in which it is being assailed.

There is a reason for this: the revolutionaries are themselves continuing Europe's historic work of reconstructing
traditional society. Consciously, at any rate, they are trying
to impose Western technology, Western organization, even
some aspects of Western thought, on people still living
under primitive conditions. But confronted as they are with
traditional, stagnant societies, impoverished peasantries,
corrupt bureaucracies, petrified cultures, they easily fall
prey to the myth of the October Revolution, which promises
a short cut through this tangle of obstacles. Democracy seems
to offer no comparable method of refashioning society,
while dictatorship holds no terrors for "professional revolutionaries" of the intelligentsia, cut off from the masses by
thick layers of ignorance, indifference, and cultural backwardness. Thus, the movement, from being revolutionary,
becomes dictatorial and finally totalitarian. And under
present circumstances this usually means joining the Soviet
camp.

The remote control of these movements is the principal
political aspect of what has come to be known as the cold
war. The United States and the Soviet Union being the two
main centers of power through which such influence can be
exercised, the struggle frequently assumes the character of
an ordinary conflict over spheres of interest. Yet the ideologies and the techniques of revolution are involved at
every step. Within the vast totalitarian orbit, serious political
conflicts are clearly concerned not with material stakes, but
with control over party organization and party ideology.
It is through this mechanism that rival centers of power are
established, collide with each other, and are "liquidated."
But a similar process is at work in the border regions between the two worlds. Where political expansion takes place
through the hold maintained by one totalitarian organiza-

tion over another, the defense likewise assumes a "total" character. The distinction between foreign and domestic policies tends in these circumstances to disappear. We seem to be back in the age of religious wars.

Notwithstanding its political and technical backwardness and the low level of its intellectual culture—by Marxist standards or any others—the Soviet regime is able to exploit the historic cleavage between Western and Eastern societies, which corresponds and runs parallel to the conflict of interest between industrial and agricultural countries. It is able to do this because it is itself the offspring of a revolution resulting from the impact of Western ideas and techniques upon a society closer in some respects to the East than to Europe. The breakdown of 1917 resulted from an abortive attempt to modernize traditional Russian society on Western lines, and the regime to which it has given rise combines modern techniques with the political methods of the great Oriental despotisms of the past. This outcome was not foreseen. In 1917, and for some time afterward, the collapse of the Russian state could be regarded either as the opening phase of a socialist world revolution—it was, of course, so regarded by the Bolshevik leaders and by Communists in the West—or as a belated "bourgeois" revolution confined to eastern Europe. In fact, it turned out to be the starting point of an entirely novel chain of events leading to the establishment of a totalitarian empire. In the historical perspective the Russian Revolution of 1917 is the successor, and the east European counterpart, of the French Revolution of 1789; much as the American Revolution of 1776 was a belated consequence of the Puritan Commonwealth of 1648-60. But the post-Stalinist regime, as it now exists, has no counterpart and no predecessor, though superficial analogies can be, and have been, drawn with the imperialism to which the French Revolution gave birth. It is an entirely new political and social formation, combining Eastern and Western features in an unprecedented manner, and it is capable of indefinite expansion into regions impervious to Western penetration. It is not a European formation, as the St. Petersburg regime on the whole was: it deliberately attempts to build up a Eurasian synthesis, and it persecutes the adherents of Europeanism even within the privileged Communist party. It hopes to overawe and incorporate Europe, after having revolutionized—and to some extent Europeanized—its own Asian hinterland; but it does not intend to amalgamate with Europe. It regards Europe as a mere adjunct in the expected trial of strength with America.

The appearance of a Eurasian empire in the place of the Russian state—which was a member of the European family, though a late-comer and in some respects not a full member—has changed the world balance of forces in the West's disfavor, and this change has been aggravated by the direction which the Chinese Revolution has taken under Communist leadership. The cold war, a technique for altering the balance of power without overt recourse to military means, is the outcome of a fundamental stalemate that has not been broken by the Korean conflict and cannot be broken by limited military campaigns, or even by unlimited ones, but only by an alteration in the basic relationship between Asia and the West. Whether this is going to take place depends on the West's ability to direct the technological and social changes which the impact of industrialism has let loose. The U. S. S. R. profits from the present state of international anarchy because it enables her to intervene between the Western centers of industrial civilization and the world's agrarian hinterland, which is also western Europe's and North America's Asian, African, and Latin-American hinterland. The effectiveness of this intervention is, in the final resort, a function of the world's need for a new form of the international division of labor. European predominance in the nineteenth century made possible a fleeting and precarious balance between advanced and backward countries, a balance maintained by uncontrolled migration and capital investment, and guaranteed in the last resort by the *Pax Britannica*. When the Bolsheviks after 1917 spoke of the capitalist system they had in mind not some textbook abstraction, but this historically conditioned nexus of international relationships, of which Britain happened to be the center. That international free trade, the gold standard, European control of primary producing areas in Asia and Africa ("imperialism"), and British naval and financial hegemony were in some sort linked together and formed a coherent pattern was perhaps more clearly understood in Moscow than elsewhere. The successive shocks sustained by this system in the 1914-18 war, in the world economic crisis of 1930-33, and in the war of 1939-45 (when it finally collapsed) gave rise in each case to utopian expectations of imminent world-wide social and political breakdown. But though the Kremlin consistently overrated the chances of revolution, and underestimated the West's capacity to reorganize itself under American leadership, it did perceive more clearly than its opponents the opportunities offered to a consistently anti-Western policy in Asia. Lenin had told his followers to look to agrarian revolution in China and India as a stimulus to proletarian revolution in America and Europe, on the grounds that Western capitalism maintained itself (and the high living standard of the "aristocracy of labor") only at the expense of the primary producing countries. His economics were crude, but they fitted the exigencies of Soviet foreign policy, as well as the anti-

Western prejudices the Bolsheviks had inherited from the Narodniks and the latter from the Slavophiles. In consequence, the anti-Western policy he laid down was continued and accentuated by the Stalinist regime long after most of the genuine innovations introduced by the Revolution had been "liquidated."

Despite its ideological overtones this line of approach laid bare a basic weakness in the international system of economic and political relationships of which Russia had after 1917 ceased to be a member. The economic nexus depended upon the free flow of capital and technical skill from highly developed to relatively primitive areas, which in consequence tended to fall under the political control of the great industrial centers—*i.e.*, the leading Western nations. The resulting imperialist rivalries might be thought to have in part provoked the catastrophe of 1914, and could in any case be used to mobilize working-class opposition in the West as well as nationalist movements in the dependent territories. Thus, Communist strategy took shape, under Soviet direction, in a manner agreeable to Russian interests as well as to Bolshevik preconceptions. There never was any basic conflict between "World Revolution" and "Socialism in One Country," for both expressed a fundamental determination to upset the existing pattern of international relationships. When the Kremlin denounced Western imperialism it thereby justified its own policy of repudiating tsarist debts and confiscating foreign holdings. When it identified colonialism with Western penetration in Africa and Asia—thus anticipating Professor Toynbee by at least a generation—it established an oblique defense of the tsarist achievement in colonizing Siberia and central Asia: an accomplishment it had no intention of surrendering. That the landlocked Russian Empire had been unable to practice overseas colonization, though it expanded overland until it reached the Pacific, was an additional reason for condemning all Western expansion as criminal. These naïve prejudices were rationalized by Lenin, who shared the traditional Russian view of Western history, into a doctrinaire system that his successors continue to employ, though they no longer feel bound by its logic. It is the theoretical foundation of Soviet propaganda in Asia, the Middle East, Africa, and even Latin America. What has rendered it intellectually respectable to European socialists and American liberals is its emphasis on the previously neglected role played by Western capital in hindering the economic and political development of backward countries. Soviet theorists do not feel bound to state in public that *some* form of imperialism is the inevitable consequence of "uneven development," though the entire policy of their government is based on this realization. That this policy is now consciously directed toward the replacement of Western by Soviet control need not be proclaimed from the housetops.

In principle, therefore, the Soviet Union and the West are competitors in a common task; and since there now exist two rival centers of power, there is no inherent reason why some backward countries should not be drawn to the quasi-revolutionary imperialism of Moscow. The trouble, from the Soviet viewpoint, is that the attractiveness of this solution has diminished *pari passu* with the improvement of its material chances of realization. Soviet prestige was high among anticolonial rebels in the decade following the Revolution, but at that time the program was flawed by Russia's military and economic weakness. Moscow might denounce imperialism as exploitation, but the primary producers needed machinery and manufactures, and were dependent upon markets in the industrialized countries.

Dissatisfaction with the terms of trade, or with Western political control, might stimulate nationalism, but could hardly induce a suicidal impulse to break away from the world market. This conflict of motivations underlay the Chinese Nationalist Revolution of the mid-twenties, which ended with a sharp defeat for the Chinese Communist party and the Comintern. Only after the Soviet Union had emerged as a world power rivaling the United States was it possible for Communist parties to take over the direction of national-revolutionary movements; and by that time the glory of the October rising had been tarnished by the Stalinist despotism. The pretense that the Soviet Union is not an imperialist power can hardly be maintained any longer, and Western spokesmen, having recovered some of their self-confidence, are now habituated to denouncing the enemy in the classic accents of democratic liberalism. To that extent the characteristic nineteenth-century relationship between the Russian Empire and the liberal West has latterly been restored.

Yet, on the whole the West remains on the defensive, and it is relevant to inquire into the reasons. Some of them are obvious: two world wars have discredited the notion that competing imperialisms can safely be entrusted with the task of "opening up" the world market and spreading the benefits of a civilization that has itself given rise to the monstrosities of European Fascism. On the economic side, the primary producers were all but ruined by the world crisis of the early 1930's which resulted from an industrial slump in the United States, and they have no guarantee that the disaster will not be repeated. These reminiscences, however, do not wholly account for the strength of anti-Western sentiment in regions freed from foreign control, such as India, or never subjected to it. The "anti-imperialist" campaign is running full blast in countries whose long-term interests clearly point toward closer association with the United States and western Europe. This is puzzling and disappointing to American liberals and British socialists who had been encouraged by the achievements of the Roosevelt regime, and by the British Labor government's successful Indian settlement, to hope for better relations. "Imperialism" had been solemnly buried; why then should anti-Western propaganda make so much headway? It was not perhaps sufficiently considered that the liquidation of imperial control by itself was no great benefit to the countries concerned, all suffering from the consequences of "uneven development" and crying out for massive capital investment as well as for radical internal changes. Nationalism had won a great victory; it was now confronted with the fact that backward areas can develop their wealth only if advanced countries are willing to invest some of their surplus capital. But foreign investment on a large scale, whether public or private, means some degree of foreign control, however camouflaged. Under the old liberal-imperialist scheme of things the whole process went forward more or less spontaneously, capital following the lure of profits, markets, and raw-material sources, and political control by the imperial metropolis establishing itself in its wake. The breakdown of this integration meant that a new mechanism had to be devised to enable capital to cross national frontiers. Bretton Woods, the Marshall Plan, Point Four, were efforts in this direction. But partly because their scale was inadequate, partly because they were not backed by popular movements able to compete with the Communist integration of imperialism and revolution, they never really touched the imagination of those key groups in the recipient countries whose co-operation was and remains essential. What little is being done along these lines by the United

States in Latin America and India, or by European countries in their remaining African and Asian dependencies,
cannot stem the Communist drive, which has behind it not
merely the resources of a great power, but a world-wide
totalitarian movement cemented by revolutionary myths.
That this movement is in part propelled by its own "internal
contradictions"—including the contradiction between a
revolutionary ideology and despotic practices—does not
lessen its immediate power to penetrate into the vacuum left
by the collapse of the liberal system. It is part of the irony
of the situation that the mechanism of imperial control via
popular revolution is better understood in Moscow than in
the capitals of the "imperialist" world.

The cold war in Southern Asia, Latin America, the Middle East, and North Africa must be viewed against this background. In form a conflict between two groups of powers, it
really concerns the political control of those regions which
the "uneven development" of the world economy has placed
in a position of inferiority toward the great metropolitan
centers. It therefore fits the "anti-imperialist" strategy that
the Soviet government has gradually elaborated. Success or
failure must in the long run depend on the West's ability to
replace the old division of labor by a system broadly
fulfilling similar economic functions, but better able to
satisfy national and social aspirations. Modernization, a mere
by-product of the old system, must be placed in the fore-
front and consciously expedited where the pace is too slow.
Conflicts between economic and social priorities must be
settled with a view to facilitating progress as a whole rather
than securing short-term economic advantages to foreign
investors and local property owners. Such changes may have
to be imposed on unwilling governments, even though overt
control is avoided. It is a mistake to think that non-interven-

tion can be practiced in a situation in which the ruling
oligarchies of newly emancipated countries will typically
shelter behind national myths to obstruct change. It is even
more fallacious to suppose that "politics" and "economics"
can be kept apart. The contest for the allegiance of the
would-be neutrals, notably in the so-called underdeveloped
areas, is steadily eliminating the distinction between war
and revolution, cold war and hot war, internal and external
politics, diplomacy and subversion, the Soviet drive proper
and the Communist movement. The challenge is total, and
the countermovement cannot afford to be less comprehen-
sive.

2: *Toward Atlantic Union*

AT THE POLITICAL LEVEL, which
concerns us here, the cold war takes the familiar form of
rivalry between two groups of powers. Increasingly compelled to organize itself into the Atlantic Community, the
Western world derives only the vaguest and most shadowy
kind of support from the moral authority of the United
Nations. But for the persistent lag in setting up common
political institutions, the Atlantic Community might by
now have reached the stage of being able to dispense with
the UN as a form of defense against centrifugal forces. By
clinging to the structure established in 1945, Western statesmanship has rendered unnecessarily difficult the essential
step forward. Yet the UN is today universally recognized as
not much more than an arena where the spokesmen of both
sides meet to exchange verbal blows, in the hope of impres-
sing the remaining neutrals. The true "world organization"
of the West is not the UN, but NATO, or rather the Atlantic
Community that may one day grow out of NATO. The na-

tions affiliated to the North Atlantic Treaty Organization, or having cordial relations with it, share common interests and "ideals," because they are committed to a common way of life. Within this orbit, political experiments are possible, ranging from full federation to loose Commonwealth ties. NATO is capable of development, though it could also degenerate into a mere assemblage of military staffs and bureaucratic committees, or into an unwilling instrument of the *Pax Americana*. The UN is incapable of development; its function, apart from the organization of a few technical services, is to provide a clearinghouse for the settlement of minor differences. If the Soviet bloc were to leave the UN, its supranational character might enable it in time to become a bridge between Western and Eastern countries, and an agency for drawing backward regions into the world economy, without impinging too obviously on their political status as sovereign entities. This was the original concept underlying the United Nations Charter, but Soviet obstruction has rendered it academic. The Soviet government obstructs the working of the UN, as it obstructs the work of any institution it cannot control, and the reason it cannot control the UN is not lack of military power, but social and political backwardness. It cannot compete on equal terms with the West, and it does not choose to have its despotic system of planning exposed to the light of day. Rather than face publicity and democratic control it prefers to paralyze the United Nations.

Can the emerging Atlantic Community replace the UN and overcome the centrifugal tendencies that at present are driving America and Europe apart? The question has for some time been overshadowed by the more urgent problems of military defense in Europe, the Middle East, and Southeast Asia, but it is now coming to the fore. The West's

firm defensive posture in Europe, coupled with military
stalemate in Southern Asia, represents a negative gain just
great enough to make long-term political planning possible.
Since the Korean and Indo-Chinese emergencies, the
capacity of the United Nations to function as a world government is no longer even an academic issue, while attention has shifted to military co-operation between western
Europe and the United States on the one hand, and between
the West as a whole and non-Communist Asia on the other.
The period of tentative experiments with political forms is
ending. We are moving into a situation in which great
regional alliances and associations will increasingly dominate the settlement of political conflicts. The Sino-Soviet
bloc, under one of its aspects, is itself such an alliance, and
there is no inherent reason why it should not in time be confronted by others—from the still shadowy association of
the so-called Colombo powers (India, Pakistan, Ceylon,
Burma, Indonesia) to the traditional assemblage of the
Latin-American republics. Indeed, this regrouping of all
the non-Communist forces on a regional rather than a
universal basis is already taking place, though with a slow-
ness characteristic of democratic processes. It is plain to all
that the United States is taking the lead in the formation of
a world-wide system of such regional associations for
mutual aid and mutual defense; but equally there are signs
that this initiative on the part of Washington is straining
its European and Asian political ties very nearly to the
breaking point. Handicapped by the inanities of its domestic
politics, committed to a policy vis-à-vis China that to most
Europeans and Asians appears not merely dangerous but
senseless, and increasingly tempted to rely on "massive
retaliation" in the unlikely event of a full-blown atomic
war, the United States government is in danger of losing
the leadership it had won by 1945. The issue is posed as

sharply in Asia as it is in Europe. Indeed, the danger of an Asian debacle is more urgent, for India and Japan are now exposed to the full impact of the Chinese Revolution, as well as its Russian parent. But while an organization for the defense of the Pacific area must primarily be an affair of military and economic ties, the co-operation of America and Europe within the Atlantic Community poses a more profound and subtle problem.

If in Asia and the Pacific it is enough for the United States, Britain, France, the Colombo Powers, Japan, Australia and the Philippines to pursue more or less coherent policies in order to establish a working organization for defense, in the Atlantic area more is required. America and Europe (which for this purpose includes Britain) cannot content themselves with the kind of loose arrangement for regional defense now under trial in the Pacific. Their ties are so close, and at the same time the centrifugal forces driving them apart are so powerful, that nothing less than a full-fledged Atlantic Union can hold them together. In our present context, at any rate, we are dealing with the defense of "the West"—not of the "free world" (however defined) generally. The distinction has become unpopular, and doubtless political prudence, and the exigencies of the cold war, will continue to blur it. But unless we are to relapse into the unreality that accompanied the construction of 1945, it must be kept in mind. The fact that Asians resent any display of Western exclusiveness cannot be made an argument for disclaiming the importance of Atlantic Union, as the center and the solid core of the world-wide association of all non-Communist countries. For the alternative—let there be no doubt about that—is simply the crudest kind of military power politics: the mechanical construction of an American empire with a ring of satellites in both hemispheres—and the prompt defection of these satellites at the

first sign of real danger. If the ideologists of American imperialism are blind to this danger, that is no reason why their
example should be followed. For the purpose of this discussion, therefore, it is assumed that the overriding aim of
Western democratic policy is neither American nor Anglo-
American world hegemony—both alike intolerable to
Europe and Asia, and certain to promote a nationalist and
neutralist reaction of appalling violence—but a genuinely
international system outside the Sino-Soviet orbit.

It goes without saying that, whatever its eventual political
structure, the effective power of the Atlantic Community
must for a long time to come rest upon that of the United
States. In this sense the Community might be described as
the political aspect of the *Pax Americana.* This is so not
merely because the United States at present produces about
forty per cent of the world's manufactures and has an overwhelming preponderance in those lines of production which
determine the fate of nations in modern war. There is the
further fact that its economy is by far the most dynamic, and
that, together with Canada, it obviously constitutes the main
reservoir of economic strength on which the rest of our
world depends. Moreover, it is comparatively well protected, even under modern conditions, against the immediate impact of war and can reasonably hope to survive
even an atomic holocaust. Lastly, it is able to intervene
directly in Asia, being a power with two continental frontiers, while its size, as well as its geographical location, pre-
disposes it toward all those forms of modern air transport
which are the effective basis of similar activities in wartime.
Compared with it, the European nation-state simply lacks
the size, let alone the strength, to sustain the shock of
modern war or to build a peacetime economy adapted to
mass production. If western Europe and North Africa

could be integrated into one political, economic, and strategic whole, there might be something of comparable weight in the contemporary world. But even a Eurafrican bloc would be dependent for a long time to come on American financial aid, to say nothing of the immediate military protection now increasingly afforded by U. S. air bases in France, Spain, North Africa, and elsewhere. The "Atlantic Union" concept thus represents a sharply defined advance beyond the notion of a western Europe vaguely associated with the United States, an advance which acknowledges the westward shift in the center of gravity that has taken place since the First World War. By recognizing both this shift and the growing interdependence of North America and western Europe it might succeed in overcoming the intra-European problems arising from the long-standing tradition of exclusive loyalty to the sovereign nation-state. For whatever the solution of its current problems—federal, confederal, or plainly national and traditional—western Europe as a whole would form part of a greater Atlantic grouping; and the real issue would be not European but Atlantic confederation—meaning an arrangement whereby all the Atlantic countries, from the United States to Iceland, would set up common institutions and, to some extent, pool their sovereignties. Such a larger whole, one can safely say after the experience of the past ten years, must make provision for a central authority strong enough to make binding decisions in the fields of defense, foreign affairs, and economics. Nothing less will do, for nothing less will stop the drift toward nationalism and neutralism that has latterly become so marked in Europe and America alike.

If the reaction from "one world" utopianism has not so far swung to the other extreme of reliance on "pure" power politics and old-fashioned alliances, the reason is that in the kind of world we live in these traditional methods cannot be made to work. Apart from the fact that all secondary arrangements are now dwarfed by the antagonism between the two great powers, there is the steady pull toward international forms of organization, a pull which even the absurdities perpetrated during and since the drafting of the United Nations Charter have been unable to discredit. If it is not exactly true to say that the world is steadily becoming more united—the constant repetition of this phrase was among the less attractive features of the utopian period just after the war—it is at least true that there is increasingly less scope for the kind of free-for-all that was practiced right up to 1914. Even the United States cannot act without regard for the interests and wishes of its associates in Latin America, Europe, the Middle East, and the Far East—where Japan has suddenly become an important bridgehead of "Western" civilization. There is, however, a constant danger that American policy will in practice override these wishes and interests, until brought up short by some disaster or by the danger of a permanent loss of influence. This nearly happened at one point during the Korean War, and the thought that it may happen again is a constant nightmare of European and Asian statesmanship. It is no consolation to say that in the long run such mistakes will be rectified; the process of trial and error through which the United States may have to pass before qualifying for leadership of the non-Communist world could prove extremely costly to its associates. It might conceivably entail disasters from which they would not recover, though from the American viewpoint these would be no more than incidents on the road to maturity as a world power.

Apart from the constant possibility of serious damage to

the weaker members of the association, there is the problem that American leadership presents to medium-sized powers like Britain, France, Federal Germany, or Japan, who can normally be trusted to look after themselves and are not without means of making their displeasure felt if their interests or their *amour-propre* are too patently disregarded. Relations between these countries and the United States have gone through a number of phases since the war, but on balance American influence may be said to have declined *pari passu* with the growth of American power—an odd paradox which is not simply due, as some Americans seem to think, to European and Asian fear of a third war. It is not just that there is at the moment little confidence in American leadership: there will never be much confidence as long as it is felt that Washington acts from nothing better than enlightened national self-interest. Hiroshima, it has been said, "scared hell out of America's allies." It did more: it convinced them that the *Pax Americana* is tolerable only if America agrees to surrender some of her sovereignty to a supranational body on which her allies have a vote.

The usual argument against such proposals is that they are unrealistic, since great powers cannot be expected to surrender their freedom of action to organizations in which minor nations have equal voting rights. It is interesting to note that this reasoning is put forward by "realists" who see nothing wrong with the Charter of the United Nations. Presumably it is felt that equality of voting rights in the UN does not matter a great deal in present circumstances. An Atlantic Council empowered to take binding decisions— political, military, and economic—for the Western world would be a different affair. It would, for example, oblige the United States to operate with the formal consent of its allies in drawing up treaties, securing military bases, carrying out atomic tests, or stock-piling raw materials; and generally would cause it to behave less like a superempire and more like the leader of a group of nations forming a community. On their side, America's associates would have to exercise their voting rights with due regard to the overriding importance of American leadership. Is such an arrangement impossible? Not if there is the will to make it work. If it were objected that it is unrealistic to give the United States and Iceland equal voting rights on the executive body of the Western world, the answer would have to be that it is precisely by such formal devices that overwhelming disparities in material weight are regulated in civilized society. They are not thereby canceled: it hardly requires proof that no legal provision will make the remainder of the Western world less dependent on American leadership and support. What such an arrangement would do lies on another plane. Primarily, it would give America's allies some guarantee against a further extension of the growing tendency in Washington to set up regional systems, co-ordinate them at the top in accordance with purely American interests and preconceptions, and treat other countries as expendable factors in a potential third world war that most Europeans regard as inevitable under such a system. If this tendency were to prevail, one can predict with certainty that it will be paralleled by a rapid growth of neutralism, and that in the end the United States will find itself in a condition of moral isolation culminating in actual political divorce from its present associates.

A program of this kind differs markedly from the post-1945 experiments, which combined universalist paper schemes with strictly regional planning for defense. Hitherto the only attempt to close this gap has been the illogical intervention of the United Nations as one "side" in the

Korean War—an expedient rendered possible by the Soviet government's failure to exercise its veto power: that is to say, by an accident. Even if the Charter were amended so as to make such intervention regularly possible in future against the opposition of one of the permanent members on the Security Council—and nothing is less likely—it would still be necessary to set up self-governing institutions for the Atlantic world, and eventually for that part of the Pacific world which is not under Communist rule. But in fact the tendency is for the United Nations to become that genuinely all-embracing, and consequently nonpolitical, world community which its founders undoubtedly had in mind when they drafted the Charter. And this process should be welcomed by internationalists.

It is the special curse of the post-war world that the utopianism of the peacemakers has driven it into an unreal choice between an empty universalism and a purely military regionalism unsupported by any wider considerations, indifferent to public support, and not based on genuine political or economic foundations: a choice between the UN and NATO. The solution lies midway between these extremes. Once the Atlantic Union takes shape at the political level, the military factor will fall into place, and so will NATO, which at present tries to fill a role for which it is not fitted. "Functional co-operation" has had its day, and so has the pretense that western Europe is full of great powers able and willing to co-operate on an equal footing with the United States. There is little point in contrasting the Atlantic Community and the *Pax Americana:* they are two sides of the same reality. If Americans enjoy this manifestation of their country's present hegemony, they are welcome to feel flattered, provided they bear in mind that without an effective Atlantic Union there can be no *Pax.*

CHAPTER IV

THE ECONOMICS OF A TRANSITION PERIOD

1: *The Dollar Gap*

ARGUMENTS IN SUPPORT of closer association among western Europe, the United States, and the British Commonwealth rarely encounter principled opposition at the political level. They are more likely to meet with doubts arising from the operation of the world economy since 1945. Leaving the Sino-Soviet bloc out of account, the international network of trade relations is articulated into three major monetary systems: the dollar area, the sterling area, and the European Payments Union. These intersect, and virtually every country that could be included in a politically defined Atlantic Union (with the unimportant exception of Spain) is a member of one or other of these monetary systems.[1] But it does not follow that a hypothetical Atlantic Union could easily comprehend any one, let alone all three of them. This is especially true of the members of the sterling area lying outside Eu-

[1] See *The Atlantic Community and the Dollar Gap*, by J. E. Meade, London, 1953. Published by Friends of Atlantic Union, Roxburghe House.

rope—Australia, New Zealand, India, Pakistan, Ceylon, and Malaya in the Pacific area, and their African counterparts; though the Union of South Africa might conceivably form an exception. Again the Latin-American subcontinent forms part of the dollar area, while on geographical principles its claim to be regarded as part of the Atlantic Community is no worse than that of North America; but it so happens that NATO—the organization through which western Europe and North America are linked—serves a specific purpose in which the Latin-American republics cannot be expected to have more than a marginal interest.

More important in suggesting doubt about the economic viability of Atlantic Union is the regional trend of world trade since the war. The technical problem of organizing international payments within the non-Soviet world is, broadly speaking, the same as that of organizing payments among the three great monetary systems, but its solution does not depend upon the progressive amalgamation of dollar and nondollar systems. In so far as the unbalance expressed in the "dollar gap" has tended to right itself in recent years, it has done so because dollar and nondollar areas have become less rather than more dependent upon one another. We are accustomed to hearing it said that Europe's share of world trade has steadily shrunk in recent decades. It is less generally understood that although the United States' share has grown considerably since 1939, the major part of this growth has been confined to U. S. trade with the other countries of the dollar area.[2] Again, half the sterling area's trade is between its own members, while of the remainder the area exports about equally to North America and to the west European NATO countries

[2] *Economic Survey of Europe Since the War*, Economic Commission for Europe, Geneva, 1953. Cf. Part I, Chapter 2

(other than Britain). The overseas sterling area takes nearly half the value of British exports and supplies two-fifths of Britain's imports. Lastly, Britain exports more to the Continental NATO countries than to North America, while Canada takes more of American exports than the entire sterling area, and also supplies more of American imports.[3] Thus, the tendency is for the dollar and non-dollar systems to become relatively less dependent on each other, despite the massive injection of U. S. aid and the growth of U. S. exports to a number of nondollar markets.

Indeed, the latter two phenomena are closely connected: while the European and Asian "dollar drive" for increased exports to North America has consistently failed to yield the desired results, the United States has proceeded to finance its export trade by gifts and loans to other countries.[4] Thus, in so far as it is at all possible to speak of closer interrelation of the three great monetary areas, it has been brought about by self-financed American exports rather than by any genuine growth of economic interdependence. The June, 1952 "Report of the President's Materials Policy Commission," generally known as the Paley Report, it is true, foresees a sharp rise in U. S. demand for metals produced outside the United States, but it also forecasts a decline in U. S. purchases of natural rubber and tin. On this assumption, Canada and South America are once more likely to benefit from greater U. S. imports of raw materials, while the sterling area can at best hope to

[3] *Economic Ties in the Free World,* by Majorie Deane, London, 1953; pp. 15-16.

[4] "Between the middle of 1945 and of 1952 the United States and Canada, in the postwar Anglo-American and Canadian loans, in Marshall Aid, and in economic aid under the Mutual Security Administration, have provided a net sum of no less than $31,000 million to the countries of western Europe, a sum which is equivalent to no less than twenty-nine per cent of all American and Canadian exports during these years" (Meade, *op. cit.,* p. 13).

maintain its present relative position. On the other hand there is no particular reason why U. S. imports of manufactures should increase in relation to the growth of the national income. Imports of manufactures into the United States before the war represented a little over three per cent of total consumer expenditure on nonfood goods; they have since shrunk to about two per cent.[5] Tariff concessions might effect some change, but hardly anything of the order suggested by the dollar gap.[6]

There is, in fact, only one means of overcoming the dollar gap—namely, that adopted by the U. S. Administration since the war: massive exports of American capital, through loans and grants, or, better still, through the purchase of goods and services not required by individual American firms or consumers, but by the United States as such. By these means the U. S. A. has since 1945 generally managed to inject a quantum of dollars sufficient to finance a slowly growing total volume of world trade. The size of these injections, broadly speaking, is determined by the American surplus on current account with the remainder of the world —a surplus that has grown from about $500 million in the later thirties to an average of ten times this figure since 1945 (except in 1947, when it was $11,500 million, and in 1950, when it temporarily fell to less than $2,500 million).

[5] Deane, *op. cit.*, p. 25.

[6] British gains from a more liberal American tariff policy would be considerable, since present policy discriminates more sharply against British than against other west European exports. But even on the unlikely assumption of a marked change for the better under the present U. S. Administration, western Europe's over-all dollar problem would still remain formidable, and British exporters might find new unofficial barriers raised against them. In general, the importance allotted to the tariff in the private mythology of British and European exporters is altogether out of proportion to its real significance. The fundamental barrier to the entry of European imports into North America is the self-sufficiency of that market and the greater productivity of American industry.

What lies behind this change is simply the fact that while
U. S. exports have risen even more sharply than production, imports have not kept pace:[7]

| | Average 1936-38 = 100 | | | | | |
	1947	1948	1949	1950	1951	1952
U. S. Industrial Output	185	190	174	198	218	217
U. S. Imports (by volume)	108	123	120	146	144	151
U. S. Exports (by volume)	275	214	219	193	247	251

While the resulting dollar shortage is world-wide, it has
been most acutely felt in western Europe, a point to which
we shall have to recur. Non-European countries have shown
greater resilience in meeting the repercussions of U. S. policy changes and economic fluctuations.[8] This is partly a
consequence of the regional development already referred
to: intra-Asian and British Commonwealth economic policies have to some extent overcome the barriers raised by
nationalism in the 1930's, without restoring the old multi-
lateral system. What has happened is best described as
growing independence from the American market, combined with increased dependence upon long-range U. S.
policies designed to supply the nondollar world with a certain quantum of dollars. A tendency to greater reliance upon
regional arrangements—typified by the sterling area and
EPU systems—is a necessary consequence of the continued
dollar shortage. Yet as long as world trade outside the dollar
area is growing, the exclusiveness of the North American

[7] Deane, op. cit., p. 17.
[8] Thus, Australia, having emerged from an internal crisis brought about
by a combination of inflationary policies and temporary high wool
prices in 1950-51, was throughout 1953-54 quite unaffected by the
recession in U. S. economic activity.

market is tolerable, and fortunately there has been such a growth, quite apart from the recent efforts to revive trade with the Sino-Soviet bloc. Conversely, the tendency for genuine U. S. exports of goods and capital to become increasingly centered upon the Western hemisphere signifies greater immunity of the nondollar world to the inevitable fluctuations in U. S. economic activity.

All this is wholly to the good, albeit not in accordance with some of the neoliberal expectations popular in 1945. The weakest link in the chain unfortunately is located in western Europe. There has in recent years been a spectacular growth of U. S. defense production orders to European industries, plus U. S. imports of European manufactures required indirectly for the American defense effort. Thanks to these transitory factors, western Europe's dollar problem has ceased for the moment to be unduly harassing—*i.e.,* Europe now subsists partly on its noneconomic function within NATO. In figures, this dependence on the military factor takes the following startling form:

Net Military Overseas Expenditure by the
United States
(in million dollars)

1952:	1806
1953:	2603
1954:	4216 (estimate)

This excludes military "end items"—*i.e.,* arms of U. S. manufacture, to a total of perhaps $3.5 billion in 1953/4 which are being supplied to the NATO forces. A sizeable proportion of the growing total of U. S. overseas defense expenditure represents offshore contracts, most of which go to western Europe. In 1954 payments on such contracts may have totalled $2 billion, according to the most authoritative estimate. In addition, there is direct U. S. economic aid, which, however, is declining, although still substantial: in 1953 Europe is estimated to have received $1.1 billion under this head. U. S. stock-piling, which in 1952 amounted to some $800 million (mostly from non-European countries), is also excluded from the above figures.

By contrast with these forms of income, Europe's commodity exports to the dollar area (United States, Canada, and some Latin-American countries) during a recent period of rapid growth—namely, from January to September, 1953—amounted to $2563 million, of which $1600 million went to the United States, $454 million to Canada, and $509 million to a group of South American countries "on dollar account." This unimpressive total actually constituted a new record.[9] Moreover commodity exports to the U. S. A. show a rising proportion of goods needed directly for the U. S. defense effort: "During the past three years there has been a marked shift in the structure of U. S. imports from Europe toward commodities which are, fairly evidently, closely related to American defense production."[10] The proportion, according to the *Survey*, was as follows:

[9] *Economic Survey of Europe in 1953*, published by the Economic Commission for Europe, Geneva, March, 1954; pp. 20-21. Even this is a considerable advance on the immediate postwar period. On December 10, 1949, *The Economist* described the lag in western Europe's exports to the dollar world as "one of the most baffling and intractable aspects of the entire dollar problem." Its calculations showed that while U. S. imports had risen from an average of $2.4 billion in 1936-38 to $7.1 billion in 1948, the total exports of the Marshall Plan countries—*i.e.*, western Europe—to the U. S. A. rose from an average of $600 million in 1936-38 to less than $1000 million in 1948—that is, proportionately they fell from one-quarter to one-seventh of U. S. imports. Compared with this picture, some progress has been made, but not much.

[10] *Economic Survey of Europe in 1953*, p. 22.

U. S. Imports from Europe (in percentages)

	First half of 1950	First half of 1953
Metals and Manufactures	15	26
Machinery	2	6
Vehicles	2	4
Chemicals	5	7
Subtotal	24	43
Food and Beverages	18	15
Textiles	19	13
All others	39	29
Total	100	100

Thus, Europe sells proportionately less food, textiles, and other consumer goods to the U. S. market, and more machinery, metals, and chemicals needed for the U. S. defense effort. Even so, the total of $1600 million over a representative nine-month period is not impressive. As has been shown, it compares unfavorably with the amount now spent directly in Europe by the U. S. defense authorities on offshore purchases and other forms of military aid.

With the help of these various expedients the dollar problem has for the moment been brought under control. "European countries taken together have accumulated gold and dollar assets from transactions with the United States without a break since the second quarter of 1952,"[11] mostly owing to the growth of offshore procurement, which, according to the *Survey*, is "likely to become the most important new source of dollar receipts for Europe."[12] How

[11] *Ibid.*, p. 16.

[12] *Ibid.*, p. 16: Some further implications of this singular pattern are brought out by the latest (March 1955) annual *Survey* of the United Nations Economic Commission for Europe, which notes that the 1953/54 American recession did not create additional difficulties for Europe, although between the first half of 1953 and the first half of 1954 the value of U.S. imports from Europe fell by some 12 per cent, while U. S. ex-

important a factor it already is appears from a simple comparison: commodity exports to the U. S. A. from seven leading European countries—Britain, France, West Germany, Italy, the Benelux group, and Sweden—during the first half of 1953 reached the record total of $1103 billion, or thirty-four per cent more than for the corresponding period of 1952, when trade suffered a setback. Even so, this unprecedented total amounted to considerably less than the United States was simultaneously spending on offshore procurement!

In the first half of 1954, there was a drop in European exports to the dollar area, compared with the latter half of 1953. During this period, eighteen West European countries exported 1,165 million dollars worth of goods to the USA and Canada, and 384 million dollars worth to the rest of the dollar area, a total of 1,549 million which percentagewise represented 89% of the total exported to the same area in the second half of 1953. Commenting on this drop, the ECE's *Economic Bulletin for Europe, Second Quarter, 1954* (Geneva, October 1954, Vol. 6, No. 3) observed that "the United States and Canada were, broadly speaking, the only weak spots in a picture which otherwise reflects sustained expansion" (p. 14). In comparison with the average for the whole of 1953, the first half of 1954 showed a 15% fall in West European exports to the United States alone, coupled with a slight increase in imports from that area. This was clearly one aspect of the U. S. recession during the period. But not all the news was bad. "This worsening of the trade balance was, however, largely compensated for by increased United States military expenditure,

---

ports rose by some 8 per cent. It so happened that the cyclical situation differed significantly in the two areas., but "the exceptional factor of high and increasing American disbursements abroad on defence account" (p. 36) was equally instrumental in warding off a payment crisis.

and the accumulation of gold and dollar reserves continued, although at a slower rate than during 1953" (op. cit., p. 16). Not surprisingly, the *Bulletin* concluded: "The prospective changes in Western Europe's dollar balance in the near future depend on the course of American military expenditure in Europe no less than on ordinary trade" (*ibid.*, p. 16).

Yet the period saw an upturn in Western European production, while the United States moved into recession. The dollar gap remained, but it seemed to be having no effect on Europe's prosperity. Towards the end of the year and the opening of 1955 there was indeed increasing talk of a "boom." More important, a belief gained ground that the dollar problem either did not matter very much, or was on the way toward being solved. It was pointed out that from the summer of 1952 to the autumn of 1953, the United States had actually lost gold and dollars to the rest of the world at a rate of $2½ billion per annum, while during the subsequent period, Europe had remained unaffected by the U. S. recession. The long-term trend also seemed encouraging, at least if one cared to project the post-1945 development into the future, on the assumption that matters would continue to improve in the same way as they had done since the war. The principal favorable changes were easily visible:

1) Industrial production in the free world outside the United States had by mid-1954 nearly doubled compared with 1946, and risen by about 50% over the pre-war level, while food production outside North America had during the same period increased by some 25%, although failing to catch up with the population rise in the most crucial regions of Asia.

2) Mainly as a result of this recovery, the dollar gap

had shrunk to what seemed to be manageable proportions. In 1946/7 "the rest of the world paid for only one-half of its purchases from the United States by earnings in that country."[18] In the following two years the fraction was still only two-thirds; by 1950/51 it had risen to six-sevenths, and in 1952/3 it stood at 95%. Even though this left out of account military goods and services supplied free by the U. S. government, it certainly represented spectacular progress.

Yet if the improvement had by 1954/5 almost established something like a dollar balance between North America and Western Europe, that balance still depended on $2 billion a year of U. S. grants and loans to the rest of the world; nearly $2½ billion a year of U. S. military expenditure abroad, much of it temporary and non-recurrent; and about $4 billion worth of military supplies given free by the United States government. The balance also depended on an important invisible factor, namely governmental restriction of demand for American goods in the non-dollar world: a demand difficult to measure, but presumably running into a good many billions of dollars. This seems to suggest that the "dollar gap" is going to remain with us for the rest of our lives. From the standpoint of the industrialized countries of Western Europe—notably Britain with its heavy food imports—there is the further interesting reflection that if the *world* dollar shortage were to disappear as a consequence of greatly enlarged American food and raw material imports in the coming 15 or 20 years, the net effect might be to price European importers out of the world market! The explosive potentialities of an American import surplus are indeed almost as great—from the standpoint of smaller

[18] Cf. Professor Donald MacDougall, in *Economica*, London, August 1954, No. 83, pp. 185 sqq.

national units in the outside world—as the impact of a continuous American export surplus. The United States is now a net importer of both food and raw materials. If the trend visible since the beginning of the century continues, American raw material imports may treble or quadruple by 1975, compared with 1950 (as forecast broadly by the Paley Commission), in which case other industrial countries will have difficulty in obtaining supplies at prices which do not unduly depress their own standard of living. In food this danger is less urgent, but it is not totally absent. In short, the solution of the dollar problem might—and probably would—inaugurate a trade problem, at any rate for Britain and Western Europe: the primary producing countries—especially those situated in the Western hemisphere—might well benefit. The net effect would be an extension of the dollar area, and some indirect advantage to countries outside that area through greater demand for their products, together with an aggravation of the problems of the (shrinking) non-dollar remainder of the "free" world.[14]

These, it may be said, are the problems of 1975, not of 1955. Let us then go back to the dollar problem in its narrower sense, the sense in which it is commonly understood today. In a general manner this can be described as

[14] Cf. T. Balogh, "The Dollar Crisis Revisited," *Oxford Economic Papers*, September, 1954, Vol. 6, No. 3, "The classical model seems to have misled writers into thinking of the area benefited by the progress of a single country as large, and that harmed as small. As each single country was thought of as insignificant, relatively to the rest of the world, and therefore rather specialized in its (potential) exports, this was only too natural. The phenomenon of the U. S. (which is equivalent in economic power to the whole of the rest of the non-Soviet world) could not be accommodated by this model" (p. 268). "Once America has become a balanced provider of manufactured products in exchange for food and raw materials at favorable terms despite her high wages, there will be no reason why the rest of the world should not prefer to trade with her in preference to trading with Western Europe or Japan. This would necessitate acceptance of a (possibly painful) readjustment in their standard of life by the manufacturing areas." (*Ibid.*, p. 282)

the problem caused by the persistent, though uneven, tendency for American exports to outrun American imports. There are grounds for thinking that the persistence of this tendency is linked to the higher productivity of the U. S. economy, its intense dynamism, the large scale on which it operates (in comparison with other national units among the *industrial* countries outside the Soviet sphere), its disproportionately high investment rate, and other factors which cannot be duplicated within measurable time outside the North American continent. The ensemble of these factors, and of the social-cultural elements historically linked with them, constitutes the real, as distinct from the monetary, aspect of the so-called dollar problem, which is a problem of Western Europe's relative loss of status in a world economy no longer geared to the pre-1914 division of labor. The fact that U. S. progress opens up new vistas of economic development in the primary producing countries (including the genuinely "backward" ones—the terms are by no means interchangeable) should not be allowed to obscure the fact that it simultaneously creates a problem for Western Europe. It is indeed arguable that the present disproportion between American and European productivity is largely adventitious, in the sense that it has been historically conditioned by two wars in which U. S. economic progress was accelerated, while Europe suffered through devastation and lack of investments. But there is small comfort in this argument, for once a sizeable disparity in investment rate and general productivity has taken place, for whatever fortuitous reasons, it becomes a self-sustaining feature of the global landscape which cannot be eliminated. Nothing succeeds like success; and the fact that American productivity since 1929 seems to have risen even faster in farming and mining than in manufacture[15] suggests that this unique multidimensional progress will continue in future.

In principle the ideal solution would consist in systematically redistributing the monetary income of the non-Communist world, so as to speed economic progress without unduly depressing living standards. Programs to this end, which would benefit both the industrial and the backward countries (the latter by enabling them to industrialize) have been elaborated without number, ever since the Marshall Plan of 1947/8 seemed to suggest that American public opinion was ripe for the systematic application of such a policy on an adequate scale. None of them clearly have a chance of being adopted under the present U. S. Administration, though it is conceivable that a semblance of such a policy may eventually be introduced to satisfy the most urgent political requirements of some of the most strategically exposed "undeveloped" areas, (in all probability with the addition of crippling amendments designed to exclude even the minimum degree of discrimination against U.S. imports that must be practised to give home industries a start). Insofar as the present Administration is committed to the outlook enshrined in the so-called Randall Report (though this commitment clearly does not amount to a very great deal) it is apparent that its weight, such as it is, will be placed behind trade liberalisation rather than the kind of planned international investment policy foreshadowed during the Marshall period. Yet an eventual return to that policy seems dictated both by economic logic and by the steady growth of social-political pressure in the non-dollar part of the non-Soviet world. The present experiment in

[15] Cf. *The President's Economic Report, January, 1953*, quoted by Balogh, l. c., p. 249.

liberalisation, for all its timidity, is at bottom no less utopian than the blueprints of 1945.

Of the various solutions proposed in recent years, the one that currently appears to enjoy the greatest favor in orthodox political and business quarters is, by a curious coincidence, least valued by competent economists: U. S. private investment abroad, it has frequently been observed, not merely offers no way out, but is positively calculated to have a deleterious effect on Europe's ailing economy. Fortunately, the high level of profits earned in the U. S. imposes a brake on large-scale capital exports for private investment. Indeed, the most striking single fact about private U. S. investment overseas in recent years is its small volume. During the six years 1947-52 the flow of private U. S. capital into the world amounted to less than $5500 million, or an average of about $900 million a year: not very substantial in relation to the total outlays by the U. S. in the world as a whole; again, over 1947-52 private investment accounted for less than five per cent of total U. S. expenditure on imports, aid, and government investment. When the role of private U. S. investment in Europe's dollar receipts is considered, its relative unimportance is even more marked. Less than ten per cent of postwar U. S. private long-term capital has been invested in western Europe. In relation to the dollar flow to OEEC countries and their dependencies, it has been of very minor significance—the 1954 total of $1400 million is dwarfed by the sum of more than $43,000 million that has been spent on U. S. imports of goods and services from, and unilateral transfers to, OEEC countries and dependencies. On the whole, this has been fortunate for Europe, for unlike defense aid the flow of U. S. capital involves the question of ultimate repayment, and Europe is at present already paying considerably more to the United States on existing obligations—public and private—than it is receiving by way of new investment.[16]

Thus, private investment holds more dangers than advantages for Europe. The only type of investment that will bring in more than the dollars involved in its amortization and service is an investment not of dollars but of productivity—technological improvement and skill. In this respect a large part of Europe can today be described as a "backward area."

2: *The New Division of Labor*

How HAS THIS STATE of affairs come about? The customary explanation emphasizes Europe's two suicidal wars in 1914-18 and 1939-45, plus the ravages of "economic nationalism" in the thirties. This analysis in turn serves to support the now familiar campaign for a common European market as the economic counterpart of a political union of western Europe. However important this aim may be, it is a mistake to urge it as a solution to the problem of Europe's trade relations with the remainder of the world. There are excellent reasons for promoting a closer union of west European countries *within the wider Atlantic Community*; there is no need to confuse the issue by claiming that the creation of a unified European market

---

[16] "At the end of 1953 some 2,000 United States corporations had subsidiaries or other direct investments abroad with a gross value of over $16,000 million. . . . By comparison with these large direct investments abroad, America's private long-term portfolio investments abroad are relatively small. They amounted to just under $6,000 million at the end of 1953, of which some $3,300 million was in Canada and $1,400 million in Western Europe." *Financial Times,* May 16, 1955.

will promptly take care of Europe's payments balance. For the fact is that Europe's economic decline between 1914 and 1954 owed very little to the Continent's articulation into a number of competing national states. Some of the smallest of these—Sweden and Switzerland, for example— are among the most prosperous and progressive in the world: not merely because they had the good fortune to stay out of both wars, but because they systematically developed lines of production adapted to the character of a rapidly changing world market. And just as their smallness has not hampered them in steadily raising their level of productivity, so the existence of the British Empire did not preserve the British economy from stagnation during the interwar period.[17] It could even be argued that the ability of British and French exporters to rely on protected markets was a factor in promoting technological conservatism, whereas the strictly competitive policies of the smaller countries have been beneficial to their economic health. On the other hand, one need only consider the case of Germany between the wars to realize that lack of preferential markets and raw-material sources by itself is no spur to success. Germany between 1919 and 1939 got into trouble for different reasons than Britain, and German society reacted in radically different ways; but from an economic standpoint the stagnation of Britain and the cataclysm in Germany were diverse responses to the same underlying trend.

[17] Cf. *Britain and Her Export Trade*, ed. Mark Abrams, Pilot Press, London, 1946; particularly Chapters I, II, and IV. Commenting on more recent trends, a team of authors associated with the Fabian Society makes the following significant observation: "From 1945 to 1951 . . . we averaged about £150 million net new investment in the overseas sterling area every year. But this was covered by American aid worth over £300 million a year, while our short-term borrowing, as reflected in the increase in sterling balances, amounted to over £100 million a year." Harvey Cole & Michael Shanks, *Policy for the Sterling Area*, Fabian Tract No. 293, London, 1953.

The economic histories of Europe and Britain since 1919 deserve close attention, for they provide the key to the present unbalance in world affairs. With the exception of a few years, it is a story of continued and accelerated decline, not in absolute terms—though there were years when even this was the case—but in terms of ability to sustain full employment and the requisite level of food and raw-material imports, without constant injections of dollar aid. Some of the smaller countries have remained unaffected by this trend, Sweden and Switzerland being the most notable examples. But the region as a whole is in permanent deficit with North America, primarily because it is dependent on a level of imports that can no longer be paid for by exports of the traditional kinds. In this respect there is no fundamental difference between Britain and Germany, although Germany has repeatedly gone through a boom phase (it witnessed one in 1925-29, which was followed by a catastrophic slump), whereas Britain has on the whole struggled against the adverse current in a less dramatic manner. Thus, in the 1920's, when on the surface there was a marked difference between the German turmoil and the British stagnation, the fundamental fact was that both countries had lost their place in the world market.[18]

	1913 %	1929 %	1937 %
Share of world exports			
United Kingdom	13.9	10.75	9.87
Germany	13.1	9.73	9.11
Quantum of exports			
United Kingdom	100	87	72
Germany	100	95	65

[18] The figures that follow are quoted from W. Arthur Lewis, *Economic Survey 1919-1939*, Allen and Unwin, London, 1949, pp. 90-94.

In both countries production throughout this period was growing (though only slightly in Britain), but trade was shrinking, and therewith the ability to import raw materials and sustain economic activity at a high level. In the U. K. the problem was temporarily solved, or at any rate veiled, by drawing on capital. Thus imports in 1937 were maintained at 109 per cent of the 1929 level, whereas Germany's imports declined by one-fifth during the same period. Germany's position was worse than Britain's, in that she had lost her sources of invisible income and had to live on foreign credits (mostly American), whose sudden withdrawal after 1929 caused an unprecedented collapse. On the other hand, the very starkness of the German dilemma gave rise to expedients which, until perverted for political purposes by the Hitler regime, held promise of an eventual solution: exchange control, planned internal investment, and stoppage of unnecessary imports. In Britain, thanks to the afterglow of pre-1914 prosperity, the evil day was put off, with the result that the reconstruction of the economy was not undertaken while there were still means to cushion the shock. Fundamentally, the British problem was and is caused by excessive reliance on a shrinking export trade: Britain had in the early nineteenth century obtained a volume of trade she could not possibly hope to hold, once her industrial competitors had caught up and the new countries had started to build their own industries. This situation first became visible in the 1870's, when the British rate of industrial growth began to fall, concurrently with a decline in the rate of export growth. It is significant that relative stagnation began in the export trades and spread from there to industry. From the beginning of the century until the 1870's, industrial production had been increasing at an annual rate of not much less than four per cent; thereafter until 1914 the rate was less than two per cent, while the rate of increase of British exports had by 1900 fallen to one per cent from an average of eight per cent in the sixties. At the same time, other countries were advancing more rapidly. The cumulative annual increase of manufacturing production from 1873 to 1913 was 4.8 per cent for the United States, 3.9 per cent for Germany, 3.7 per cent for the world as a whole, and only 1.8 per cent for Britain.[19]

The First World War accelerated the relative decline of Britain, and in some domains stagnation, from being relative, became absolute. The development of Britain's export trade illustrates the change:

	1913	1929	1937
World-trade quantum	100	133	128
U. K. exports, quantum	100	87	72
U. K. share of world exports, per cent	14	11	10

After 1929 exports no longer paid for imports, and in consequence Britain throughout the 1930's was living on her capital, while neglecting her industries.[20] The seriousness of the situation was masked by favorable movements in the terms of trade—*i.e.,* by the more rapid fall in the price of imported food and raw materials, compared with prices of manufactured goods. This, plus the retention

[19] Lewis, *op, cit.,* p. 74.
[20] *Ibid.,* p. 79. Britain's share of world industrial output had already fallen from 31.8 per cent in 1870 to 14 per cent in 1913, and declined further to 9.2 per cent in 1938. Yet her share of the global import total fell only from twenty-nine per cent in 1870 to seventeen per cent in 1938 (cf. André Philip, *L'Europe unie et sa place dans l'économie internationale,* Presses Universitaires de France, Strasbourg, 1954). Even today her import total is not far inferior to that of the United States, notwithstanding the latter's overwhelming share (48.5 per cent) of the non-Communist world's industrial production. But then U. S. imports represent only four per cent of the national revenue, or three per cent of gross domestic output.

by Britain of an inordinate share of "invisible" income from banking, shipping, and insurance, helped to create an illusory sense of well-being in the later thirties, though at the cost of heavy unemployment: but for the presence of two million permanently unemployed, whose consumption was effectively restricted, the British payments problem would have become unmanageable already before the war. As matters stood, Britain could still to some extent cover the export-import gap by drawing on her earnings from shipping, insurance, and overseas investments. By 1945 these had shrunk so far as to leave no further excuse for ignoring the real problem. The response was an "export drive," with the particular aim of capturing the "dollar market"—a fantastic gamble that need not detain us here. From the British standpoint the best opportunity was missed in the interwar period, when capital was available to reconstruct the country's basic industries. A policy of industrial re-equipment would have stimulated employment, generated purchasing power, and at the same time reduced real costs, thus easing the export problem. By 1939 a readjustment on these lines was under way, but on an insufficient scale; in any case, it was brought to a stop by the war, which thereafter intensified the relative backwardness of British industrial equipment compared to American.

The problem was not, however, confined to Britain, nor can it really be envisaged from a narrowly national standpoint. The stagnation of the British economy in the interwar period was a symptom of Europe's basic failure to adapt itself to the international division of labor that had emerged since 1914. The trouble was that western Europe had ceased to function as the highly industrialized center of a world still on the whole preoccupied with food and raw-material production. Britain before 1914 reaped the greatest advantage from this arrangement, but other countries were not far behind. Not merely Britain, but western Europe as a whole functioned as the "workshop of the world." Historically, this arrangement—which seemed "natural" to its beneficiaries—was due to Europe's temporary ability to exploit the advantage of having been first with the industrial revolution. Since modern industry is not dependent on the particular constellation of factors present in its historic birthplace (though they certainly helped western Europe to acquire a valuable head start), the whole system could last only until the outlying regions had begun to build up their own industries.[21] This process was inevitable, and the two world wars merely accelerated it. What was not inevitable was the British and European reaction, which mainly consisted in intensified national competition, plus a drive to exploit the dwindling colonial patrimony of the leading "imperial" nations. Germany, of course, as we all know to our cost, went to the extreme of trying to colonize the rest of Europe; but her frenzy was merely the final and most extravagant expression of tendencies inherent in the whole situation.

In this struggle, conservative and radical solutions crisscrossed to produce a pattern particularly confusing in the later thirties, when newcomers like Germany and Japan contributed their quantum of irrationality to the growing turmoil by trying to stake out new empires on the ruins of their rivals. But the latter had no constructive answer to the Axis challenge, since they were themselves committed

---

[21] Cf. Lewis, *op. cit.*, p. 187: "Taking 1913 as 100, the manufacturing indices in 1937 for the old countries stood well below those of the new: the United States stood at 186, Germany 138, U. K. 128, France 124; but the world index exceeded all these, standing at 196; and this was because new countries had increased at an enormous pace: U. S. S. R. 772 (the official figure), Japan 551, India 235, Sweden 229, Finland 300, and so on. The declining growth of old countries had been largely offset by the rapid progress of new countries."

to an anachronistic attempt to preserve the nineteenth-century division of labor, which had hopelessly collapsed. This clash between a criminal adventure that at least recognized the end of the old order, and a despairing effort to preserve a crumbling structure, underlay the Munich episode and the whole imbecile record of Western diplomacy in the thirties. In the last resort Britain and France were thrown on the defensive throughout this period because the world economic crisis of 1930-33 had undermined the international division of labor on which west European predominance had rested during the preceding epoch, and because democratic policy as yet held no answer to the twin challenge of industrial unemployment in the advanced, and rural poverty in the backward countries. If Fascism gave a deceptive impression of being more "modern" than democracy, the fault lay with the Western governments, committed to *laissez-faire* at home and colonialism abroad. Their nations had largely ceased to export capital and become *rentiers* dependent for their living standard upon the interest paid by non-European countries on capital formerly sunk in those areas. Their attitude in consequence tended to be defensive and timidly conservative, in political and military matters as in all others. The Maginot Line was the perfect symbol of this situation; it protected (or failed to protect) not merely a frontier but a state of mind.

By the time the war ended in 1945, a mental awakening had perforce taken place, and most governments were now ready for planning policies at home and greater realism in relation to the backward countries, which also for the most part happened to be colonies or semicolonies. At the same time, however, the inherited wealth that between 1919 and 1939 still cushioned the democracies from the worst economic shocks had for the most part been swallowed up by the war. Western Europe thus became aware of its own impoverishment at the precise moment when its former economic dependencies in eastern Europe disappeared behind the Iron Curtain. A few years later the victory of Communism in China set the seal on an epoch: Europe was now cut off from a large part of its former markets and raw-material sources by a political frontier that was also a geographic one. In the pre-1914 world, and to some extent after 1919, East and West had formed a complementary system, though the West had reaped most of the benefit. Now a highly industrialized western Europe, which had come to depend on outside sources for the bulk of its industrial raw materials and for a sizable proportion of its foodstuffs, at last found itself confronted with the problem it had for so long been trying to evade.

The point that concerns us here is that the Second World War accelerated long-term trends very inadequately summed up by the phrase "economic nationalism."[22] The most important of these was a tendency to reverse the process of increasing international specialization that had gone on all through the nineteenth century and enabled western Europe to exchange its manufactures for the surplus foodstuffs and raw materials of less developed regions. Investment opportunities in these areas had already begun to slacken before 1914, as the overseas primary producing countries began to build up their own industries. In the thirties another important factor intervened: the primary producers encountered growing difficulties in finding markets for their products, and consequently began to question the value of international specialization and to

---

[22] Cf. H. W. Arndt, *The Economic Lessons of the Nineteen-Thirties*, Oxford University Press, 1944; Chapter 1 and *passim*. T. Balogh, *The Dollar Crisis*, Oxford, 1949, especially Chapter I.

set greater store upon the development of their own internal markets. The British Dominions were as much affected by this trend as were South America and Southern Asia. At the same time, technological changes reduced the importance of international specialization in the industrial field.[28] It was an easy step from here to the belief that both city dwellers and agricultural producers would benefit from increased industrialization, and the step was in fact taken by almost every country in the Southern or Western Hemisphere, under a variety of political slogans whose extreme adaptability reflected the presence of an unusually strong underlying current. The Second World War, which once more cut the primary producers off from most of their European markets, gave additional momentum to the new policies: it is significant that Perónism installed itself in Argentina from 1943 onward, and that Argentine nationalism henceforth became associated with an ambitious drive to industrialize the economy. Once more, Britain was the chief sufferer, for the disappearance of Argentina's traditional meat surplus directly affected the living standard of Britain's industrial population, and the postwar adjustment was *pro tanto* rendered more difficult. Simultaneously Britain and the remainder of western Europe were feeling the effect of political changes in Southern Asia, hitherto an area under the control of European powers *and for that*

[28] Arndt, *op. cit.*, p. 12: "The development and diffusion of new power resources (oil and hydroelectric power) lessened the need for rigid localization of industry on the basis of coal supplies. The gradual replacement of steel by light metals altered the relative advantages of various countries as the producers of the most important industrial raw material. Mechanization widened the scope of industry based on cheap rather than skilled labor, and the growing importance of tertiary industry implicit in rising standards of living, coupled with decreasing transport costs, reinforced the tendency toward the localization of consumers' goods industries near their markets rather than near the supply of basic raw materials."

reason an important link in the global division of labor on which the predominance of the older manufacturing centers had been built. For the type of political control established throughout these regions under the system of "colonial imperialism" facilitated a development of international trade which took the form of an exchange of manufactured goods for food and raw materials, and the monetary arrangements arising from this trade were an important aspect of the international network of payments down to the Second World War. In this system, which was badly shaken by the depression of the thirties but nonetheless continued to operate, "the merchandise trade balances formed an interlocking network, where trade balances in one direction were offset by deficits in other directions. Secondly, capital movements and payments for "invisible" items generally offset remaining trade surpluses and deficits."[24] Thus Southern Asia had a consistent trade surplus with the United States, which in turn had a trade surplus with Britain; while Asia's export surplus with Continental Europe ran parallel to the latter group's export surplus with the United Kingdom. Both circuits were closed by Britain's consistent surplus with the Southern Asian region. The special beauty of this self-regulating system lay in the fact that it enabled Britain and Continental Europe to run a steady export deficit. In the late twenties these deficits were more than covered by receipts on "invisible" items, estimated at some 2,000 million dollars annually for Britain and about 1,000 million for Continental Europe. By 1938 the British figure had shrunk to about half, but the United Kingdom could still finance part of its import surplus through interest and dividend payments, shipping, insurance and other services; and a sub-

[24] *A Study of Trade Between Asia and Europe*, United Nations Dept. of Economic Affairs, Geneva, November, 1953; p. 6.

stantial share of this income was bound up with the historically conditioned relationship between metropolis and colonial dependency. To a lesser degree the same applied to France and Holland. It would be an exaggeration to say that the system has ceased to operate, but it is certainly not nearly as important as it was before 1939, and *a fortiori* before 1930. On the other hand, the Asian countries have since the war obtained about $9,000 million in grants and credits from the West, to help them finance their trade deficits and make a start on industrialization.[25]

It is not, on the whole, surprising that the British government showed rather less enthusiasm for this cause than certain more or less innocent bystanders. Although it participated in various plans for accelerating the economic development of formerly dependent territories, it did not conceal its belief that the countries in question would profit from better farming methods even more than from ambitious schemes of rapid over-all industrialization. If there was an element of self-interest in such advice, there was also greater realism than was to be found elsewhere. In addition, the existence of dependent or semidependent territories, such as Ceylon, Malaya, or Nigeria, whose wealth (considerable by Asian or African standards) was plainly due to the production of specialized crops and minerals for export (rubber, tin, tea, cocoa), suggested caution in condemning colonial methods of economic development *en bloc* as mere "imperialist exploitation." Specialization did create additional wealth in these areas, and this development was made possible by British control, as in the case of the Philippines it was brought about by the American

---

[25] *Op. cit.*, p. 7. The figure includes sterling balances released by Britain to India, Pakistan and Ceylon. Their release was in part made possible by United States aid to Britain, so that here as elsewhere the outflow of American capital is shown to be the overall conditioning factor.

connection.[26] By and large, however, no Western government today is likely to put its faith in the kind of colonialism that accompanied the former international division of
labor. Whether it is a question of Point Four allocations, of
the Colombo Plan adopted by the British Commonwealth,
or of the massive investment of publicly controlled capital
in the African territories of the French Union since 1945,
the emphasis has come to lie upon balanced development
of economic resources and public control of funds.

Whether one chooses to describe this as "socialism" or,
more accurately, as state capitalism, it certainly represents a break with former practices. To the extent that
such policies are consciously adopted and proclaimed, a
bond is established between advanced and backward countries, and specifically between democratic movements in
the former and nationalist ones in the latter. This rejection of
the primacy of profit—*i.e.*, of private investment—is the
real reply to the Communist attempt to fashion a lasting
alliance between nationalist movements and the Soviet
Union. Colonial imperialism, according to Lenin, is an aspect of monopolistic capitalism. Since the latter is assumed to
predominate in the Western world, it follows that backward
territories have nothing to expect from the West, save intensified exploitation. In reality, every departure from reliance
on market forces, every step toward a planned and regulated
economy, is potentially a step away from colonialism. The
difference between "liberal" and "monopolistic" practices

[26] Cf. W. A. Lewis, *Report on Industrialization and the Gold Coast*,
Gold Coast Government, Accra, 1954. "Whatever the foreigner's faults
may be, the fact remains that the Gold Coast needs him more than he
needs the Gold Coast" (quoted in *The Economist*, January 2, 1954).
Since Professor Lewis is a socialist and of West Indian descent, this
observation carries additional weight, as does his insistence that "African
enterprise cannot be built up simply by lending Africans money. To
lend money to entrepreneurs who lack managerial ability is simply to
throw it down the drain" (*ibid.*).

is in any case much smaller than Communists (and some non-Communists) are willing to admit. Nineteenth-century colonialism was a creation of the "liberal" era of free trade and *laissez-faire*. In contrast, today's semi-regulated economy has made it possible to direct *public* investment in the dependent and backward territories where it is most needed. There is, of course, no guarantee that this will always happen under state capitalism: it emphatically did not always happen under colonial rule. What is quite certain is that it *cannot* happen (except by accident) under *laissez-faire*.

3: *Economics of Democracy*

IN EUROPE, the structural unemployment of the thirties, which was an aspect of the global dislocation already described, gave rise to mass movements that either destroyed the democratic framework or caused the governments of the leading industrial countries to become more or less committed to the goal of full employment. The political expression of these movements has tended to alter with varying circumstances, running all the way from Fascism to Communism, via democratic socialism and New Dealism. What matters in our context is that in the world-wide disturbance caused by the collapse of the old system of international trade, the rise of revolutionary nationalism in Asia was the counterpart of the political and military upheavals that Europe has witnessed since 1930. If the symptoms were different, the cause was similar. In the East, unregulated capitalism had ceased to promote an expansion of wealth commensurate with population growth and pressure on the land. In the West, it had ceased to maintain full employment. From about 1930 onward the excuse that this failure was due to temporary after-effects of the First World War lost its power of enchantment over the minds of those affected by the continued idleness of resources, and there arose a variety of responses—some crude and naïve, some criminal like the National Socialist dictatorship in Germany, others constructive and democratic—that could no longer be fitted into the old framework of liberal politics and economics. This was true even of the United States; for a variety of reasons, however, the reaction was more violent in Europe, and since we are here concerned with the question whether western Europe and the United States can in the long run co-operate, we must try to understand in what respects the social scene in Europe has been permanently altered by the political upheaval of the thirties and forties.

The simplest way of summing up the change is to say that, as a result of their experiences in the great depression and the subsequent war, the great majority of people now regard the economic domain as capable of intelligent regulation. To that extent European opinion has become converted, if not to socialism, at any rate to something that is not the liberalism of the last century. One may call it state capitalism, the welfare state, the mixed economy—it is, at any rate, something distinct from totalitarian Communism, on the one hand, and unregulated private capitalism, on the other. Here is a source of "neutralism" as potent as any atom bomb, for to the extent that the United States is identified— through the fault of its official spokesmen rather than from any inherent necessity—with private capitalism, it inspires a medley of feelings running all the way from uneasiness through dislike and contempt to positive hatred—save, of course, among those dwindling sectors of opinion whose group interest conspires with their congenital shortsightedness to turn them into blind supporters of the Atlantic alliance in its most sterile and unprofitable form: that of a defense of social positions and policies associated in the minds of most Europeans with unemployment, governmental helplessness, and war. By supporting these forces, the present United States Administration has gone a long way toward wrecking the Atlantic cause. That cause is lost if it is not supported by European labor and socialist opinion —the latter by no means confined to the labor movement in the narrow sense, but powerful among the "managerial" stratum and the technical intelligentsia who, in Europe as in Asia, form the hard core of all revolutionary movements in our epoch. The picture must be viewed in the light of labor's much more prominent role since 1945 and, last but not least, in the light of Communist pressure in such countries as France and Italy. If western Europe could afford to go to sleep economically behind the protective shield of NATO-*cum*-dollar aid the present situation might be indefinitely tolerable for all save those most affected by economic stagnation. But the conjunction of labor pressure— by no means all of it Communist-inspired—and a high rate of growth in Soviet Europe renders such a solution impossible. Yet economic expansion in western Europe is not primarily a question of good intentions or of the adoption of Keynesian techniques. It is basically a question of being able to produce or import the necessary quantum of food and raw materials. Western Europe's permanent dollar deficit—taking the region as a whole and leaving out of account the relatively favorable position of some of the smaller countries with assured export markets—is linked as we have seen, to its inability to produce a larger share of the foodstuffs and raw materials required to feed its swollen industrial populations and keep them fully employed all the year round. This is now clearly perceived by representatives of the most varied political faiths.

If the future lies with large economic units, then the case for expanding rather than contracting the unities of the free world outside the dollar area becomes overwhelming. There is indeed only one radical remedy for our present endemic disease, and that is to build a trading area in which we can all breathe and live, and in which the Americans may find a profitable field of investment. Within this area there must be adequate supplies of raw materials, a high degree of productivity, and assured markets. Western Europe, as such, is not a viable economy. It is a dense industrial area, without visible means of support. Moreover, the national economies of the countries which comprise it are competitive rather than complementary, and their economic policies are sharply divergent. It is, therefore, an error to suppose that the creation of a single market in western Europe alone is the answer to the problem. . . .

In order to restore an economic balance to the free world we have, simultaneously, to maintain internal financial stability, to expand production, and to eliminate external deficits. To some extent these aims are contradictory. Any rapid increase in production must involve public expenditure, capital investment and an expansion of credit which, added together, can only increase the inflationary pressure. . . . Having outlined this dilemma . . . let me say that I believe the problem to be by no means insoluble. But it can be solved only by radical measures of international regulation, discrimination, co-ordination, and planning which are alien to European traditions, and which certainly have no part in the American experience.[27]

Whether such changes can be effected without a different distribution of political power is a question on which conservatives and socialists will continue to differ. What neither side to this debate can afford to disregard any longer—now that we have had the combined lesson of the great de-

[27] Sir Robert Boothby, in *The Twentieth Century,* London, August, 1952.

pression, the Hitler experience, the Second World War, and the Communist advance—is that another failure on the lines of the interwar experience would mean the end of Europe, and indeed of the free society to which socialists as well as liberals and conservatives are committed. It is as simple as that.

In a sense this is the fundamental problem that has dogged Western statesmanship since the beginning of the present century. The Germans tried to solve it by constructing their Mitteleuropa at the expense of everyone else; the British by clinging to free trade and hoping for the best— *i.e.*, for an American credit and tariff policy that would make it possible to continue in the old way. Both solutions have now failed, after jointly helping to bring about two world wars in which Europe's political predominance has been destroyed and her economic decline accelerated. They were bound to fail, for the *Pax Britannica* was losing its economic foundation, while its Germanic substitute (leaving aside its later and more fantastic aspects) only provided for central Europe and took no account of the rest of the world, except as a potential field for military experiments. Yet a vague realization that "larger economic units" had become necessary, and that the process of setting them up was incompatible with the traditional European nation-state, was fairly widespread in the decade before 1914. It produced a crop of rival theories, mostly concerned to explain the new phenomenon of imperialism. The First World War itself was in some quarters viewed as a clash between the new technological forces and the old political frontiers. This concept was common to the Pan-German ideologists who supported the imperial (and subsequently the Hitlerian) war effort, and to the more farsighted of their socialist opponents, from Kautsky and Hilferding to Rosa Luxemburg and Trotsky. There were even socialists—chiefly in Germany but equally among the Fabians in Britain—who saw some good in imperialism, or at least were fatalistically resigned to it.

Today we can see this period as a crisis in which European political institutions were shattered because neither her traditional political forces nor her revolutionaries were capable of rising to the height of the situation. In 1919 it was imagined that because Europe had been saved from German imperialism the road was now free for the triumph of liberal democracy. In fact, liberal democracy failed in the interwar years, and not only in eastern Europe, where it had never really struck root and where the unsolved problem of rural overpopulation held a special pitfall for any liberal regime. It failed in central Europe, with consequences disastrous to the world, because it could not guarantee full employment, and its failure in the latter respect was due to reliance on the world market—a world market in which western Europe and Britain had once enjoyed a specially favored status which they were beginning to lose. With the high American tariff and the closed Russian market before their eyes, the European governments, including the British, ought in the twenties and thirties to have taken those measures which they belatedly took, in very inadequate measure, after 1945. The interval was wasted; and it was wasted in part because America's great influence was employed to perpetuate the very discrepancy between the European political system and its economic foundation—between sovereignty and planning, the national state and the need for regional economics—out of which the First World War had arisen and the Second was presently to arise. Even today, when some, at least, of these illusions have vanished, and economists are no longer quite so sure that planning is sinful, there are influential Americans who seem to think that the world would be better off if western Europe were deprived of its economic hinterland in Africa and the Middle East, and that, for example, the Balkanization of French North Africa would contribute greatly to the happiness of its inhabitants.

One can only register such tendencies in the hope that they represent the last expiring flicker of a nineteenth-century orthodoxy about to give up the ghost even in its remaining stronghold. Were it to prove otherwise, all thought of genuine co-operation between the two halves of the Western world would have to be abandoned, for it is quite certain that Europe cannot and will not permanently live on American subsidies, while its own economic foundations are vaporized. Long before this process had reached its conclusion there would be a reaction against the United States, and against the whole concept of Atlantic solidarity, that no European government would have the power to stop. It would not take the Communist parties long to cash in on it, and one may be sure that they would receive effective backing from the U. S. S. R.; but it is more than likely that the reaction would in the first instance take a nationalist form: "nationalist" in the sense of a self-consciously "European" orientation as against an "Atlantic" one. If one believes that a "third-force" Europeanism of this kind is not in fact practicable or desirable, one can only hope that the Atlantic Community will provide room for a planned economy linking western Europe and the British Commonwealth with the United States, just as, on political grounds, one must hope that it will enable socialists and liberals to work together. In the perspective of classical liberalism such arguments no doubt suggest a sacrilegious attempt to lay hands upon the ark of the covenant—namely, upon the historic link between democracy and free trade. But surely the operative term in this context is "historic." It cannot be assumed that a free-trade policy is always and everywhere desirable from a democratic standpoint. Weighed against the disruptive effects of mass unemployment, unused resources, and shrinking national incomes, its advantages must seem academic. And we now have the experience of the Hitler era to draw upon. In the early thirties, the effects of orthodox economic policy proved too much for the stability of democracy on the European continent. Since then, the need to maintain something like full employment has impressed itself upon the consciousness of most governments responsible for the conduct of policy in industrialized countries—there is, of course, a totally different problem of unused resources in backward areas. These two must not be confused; neither must one confuse the pre-1930 controversy over protection with the post-1930 argument over planning. Here is the point where the new liberalism to some extent parts company with the old; here, too, is the explanation of European labor's gradual shift from liberalism to socialism—an irreversible movement that no amount of scolding or propaganda from Washington will affect.

It is seldom realized how recent this shift is. Until about 1930 the older generation of European labor leaders were still firmly wedded to free trade, and this was especially true of the two most important areas, Britain and Germany. In both countries, labor's struggle against protectionism and its political corollary, imperialism, had been part of the general struggle for democracy, with the important difference that in Britain a peaceful victory was gained before 1914, while in Germany the change came violently in 1918. Thereafter, for a few years, all seemed plain sailing. In 1923-24 the British Labor party even won office for the first time on a free-trade platform, in close alliance with the Liberals, and as late as 1929-31 this constellation was the dominant factor in British politics. The great depression killed all that. After the electoral debacle of 1931, when the rump of the old free-trade Labor party, abandoned by its leaders, went down to disaster in an atmosphere of national panic, the political battle lines were redrawn between a "National" coalition of Tories and former Liberals won over to protection and a Labor opposition that increasingly looked to economic planning as the foundation of full employment, hailed the New Deal, adopted Keynesian theorizing, and for a time took a friendly interest in the Soviet "experiment" until its real character became evident. In Germany, where the Social Democrats, for all their verbal loyalty to socialism, had clung to *laissez-faire* in practice and surreptitiously supported Brüning's disastrous deflationary policy, which reduced the country to the lowest depths of misery, the advent of Hitler performed an even more radical operation upon the consciousness of organized labor. The new generation of Social Democratic leaders who after 1945 emerged from the concentration camps had been cured for all time of the notion that mass unemployment is tolerable in a modern industrialized society.

These shattering experiences of the thirties and forties have had a far more profound effect upon the political outlook of Europe's democratic labor movement—Communism does not enter this context—than any amount of "Marxist" teaching. Indeed, in a sense they may be said to have run counter to the influence of classical Marxism, especially where it was strongest on the Continent—*i.e.*, in Germany. The old pre-1933 German Social Democratic movement had taken over from Marx a bias in favor of free trade that fitted admirably into its sectional defense of consumer interest.[28] If it was not always very clear to what extent this attitude was grounded in conviction and how far it merely expressed a policy of championing the urban electorate, there was at any rate no doubt that, in so far as the movement was Marxian, it tended toward liberalism in its short-range economic policies: socialism was something for the distant future, not a practical program for today and tomorrow. Before 1914 such an attitude was indeed virtually compulsory, since the struggle for democracy was at the same time a struggle against the protectionist bloc of great landowners and heavy industrialists. After 1918 this obstinate attachment to *laissez-faire* became an anachronism thinly veiled by the continued employment of socialist incantations on May Day and similar ceremonial occasions. During the depression years, when the National Socialists clamored for full employment and a planned economy, Social Democracy became easily the most conservative political force in Germany. As such it inevitably took the blame for the prevailing mass unemployment, notwithstanding the desperate efforts of a small group of trade-union leaders and economists, with a pre-Keynesian faith in planning for full employment, to rouse the party leadership from its somnolence before catastrophe overwhelmed the Republic and the labor movement alike. Since then a great deal of water has flowed down the Rhine, and one must be extremely naïve to imagine that German socialism will ever go back to the state of mind it cherished in 1930, when to be in favor of planning was to be frowned upon by the high command of a movement that in all seriousness regarded itself as socialist. Superficial observers who from time to time congratulate the German Social Democrats on their emancipa-

[28] Cf. A. Gerschenkron, *Bread and Democracy in Germany*, Berkeley, California, 1943.

tion from Marxism (whatever that may mean) are less inclined to broadcast the fact that this alleged emancipation has gone hand in hand with a decided conversion to the principle of a planned economy, full employment, and state intervention.[29]

In Britain, where the old guard of the Labor party took its economic doctrine not from Marx, but straight from Adam Smith, the debacle of 1930-31 had similar, though less dramatic, consequences, capped in subsequent years by the Keynesian revolution in economic thought, and finally confirmed by the experience of wartime planning under a coalition government headed by Churchill. Sweden did not need this example—it had witnessed economic expansion under a socialist government since 1932. These lessons have sunk in. It does not, of course, follow that there is substantial agreement among the major political forces in Britain and Europe on the importance of maintaining full employment: if there were, political rivalry would be at an end. The choice lies, broadly speaking, between a policy of planned internal investment and one that relies on capturing a larger slice of a presumably expanding total world trade. For highly industrialized countries like Britain, Germany, Sweden, and Belgium, there is always a temptation to

[29] A full-employment program backed by some of the leading trade-unionists was, in fact, turned down by the party leaders in 1932 (less than a year before Hitler arrived to demonstrate his own solution) on the grounds that, under capitalism, pump-priming policies could only result in inflation and would have no effect on the level of employment. This view was successfully maintained, against the "statist" opposition, by German Social Democracy's chief theorist, the distinguished economist and veteran Marxist, Rudolf Hilferding, author of the classic Marxist study of imperialism, *Das Finanzkapital*. On the subject of state intervention, Hilferding, in fact, was as conservative as Herbert Hoover. Both lived to see their party swept from power by a mass movement of revolt against unemployment, though the consequences in Germany's case were of course utterly different politically (and infinitely more tragic for the honorable men who in 1932 held the leadership of Europe's strongest socialist movement).

suppose that the national problem can be solved by cutting costs and subsidizing exports through all-round deflation and the deliberate creation of "moderate" unemployment at home. Such tendencies can be countered only if labor is politically strong and well organized. It is *not* true that full employment is a nonpolitical issue. It implies a conscious choice among basic social priorities—*i.e.*, a decision about the character of society.[30]

The record of the 1945-51 British Labor government is not entirely conclusive in this respect. The government did, it is true, achieve some control over the economy during the difficult postwar transition period, but lost it as soon as the apparatus of wartime rationing had been dismantled, and currently there is considerable doubt whether similar machinery could be reassembled rapidly enough to prevent a wholesale flight of capital during the first weeks or months of another Labor administration. If it should prove that this problem is insoluble by present-day methods one would have to conclude that the institution of a planned economy in Britain calls for emergency action of a hitherto unfamiliar type. Again, in 1945 full employment became the basis of

[30] "What is needed to secure stability and greater social justice is not the mitigation or counterbalancing of business cycles, but their elimination. There is no reason to doubt that if the steady increase in the basic minimum standard of life were to be the first charge on economic progress, that is to say, if mass consuming power were to be always kept high enough to cause a slight inflationary tension, and if this inflationary tension were kept in check by direct controls, this object could be fulfilled" (T. Balogh, *The Dollar Crisis*, p. 102). "The resistance of the entrepreneurial class to state measures calculated to maintain full employment is based on their correct intuition that such measures, while they safeguard their short-run profits, would in fact undermine their ultimate source of power, the power to decide the level of business activity and thus their relative bargaining power as a class. . . . Once the power of inflicting slumps is removed, the entrepreneurial classes lose their role as absolute rulers; a balance is established which will force deliberate measures and decisions on matters of economic policy which were hitherto their sole prerogative" (*ibid.*, p. 105).

social policy because it guaranteed political stability; yet in
so far as it tended to make labor immobile it interfered with
the second aim of policy, which was to adapt the British economic structure to the changing requirements of the world
market. The Labor government perhaps had a fleeting
chance to bring about the necessary adjustment in the guise
of planning policies that would have had the twofold effect of
eliminating economic deadweights and making socialism
truly "national" by associating it with the essential task of national reconstruction. The opportunity was not altogether
missed, but neither was it really taken. A more rational
direction of capital investment has become possible with the
nationalization of some basic industries, and the expansion
of food production was pressed with commendable energy.
But in general the Labor government, true to its basic trade-
union orientation, concentrated on the establishment of the
welfare state, while Sir Stafford Cripps ruined his health in
a superhuman (and, unfortunately, in part successful) attempt to revive Lancashire's dying export industries, which
had mercifully shrunk during the war and should have been
further contracted in 1945.

Since nothing really drastic was done in Britain under a
soi-disant socialist government, it is hardly surprising that
the remainder of western Europe has shown even greater
reluctance to face realities. And yet the plain fact emerges
that the issue of full employment is now so closely bound up
with that of state control over the economy as to constitute
the main battleground between the parties. Compared with
it, the old controversy over protectionism versus free trade
has no more than historical interest. If anything is certain
today it is that British and European labor cannot be de-
flected from regarding full employment as the basic issue,
and that all national and international policies will have to

be measured by this yardstick. In northern and western Europe this particular fight has largely been won, as has the closely related struggle to make society and the state more democratic; in the economically and socially backward southern regions of Europe and *a fortiori* in the vast "underdeveloped" areas of Asia, the situation is very different. What this means for the political aspect of the cold war will become clearer when attention has been given to the link between the growth of Communism and the impact of the planned industrial revolution in the Soviet Union.

CHAPTER V

THE PLAN ERA

1: *The Permanent Revolution*

TO THE STUDENT of history, it has been said with reason, the most baffling thing about the Russian Revolution is that it is still going on. Other revolutions have after a while come to terms with their environment—the regime that issued from the 1917 upheaval has not. Internal crises notwithstanding, it continues to display the dynamic that in a generation has transformed the U. S. S. R. into a first-class power, drawn eastern Europe into its orbit, and assisted Communism to victory in China. It has weathered the transition from popular upheaval to autocratic rule, from utopian leveling to a new hierarchical society, from internationalism to imperialism—and yet it has maintained its hold upon the loyalty of Communists the world over. It represents revolution and counter-revolution in one, the ideology of the October rising and the practice of despotism, socialist slogans and technocratic reality, slave-labor camps and industrial progress, imperial conquest and world-revolutionary rhetoric. The motor that drives it may have slowed a little, but the mechanism still churns up the living body of society in a manner unheard of in earlier revolutions. It seems incapable of halting, and since 1945 it has engulfed large parts of Asia. There is no sign that it can be brought to a stop, or that the ruling group is willing to lessen the pace in response to internal difficulties and popular demands for a respite. Communism seems to have discovered the secret of making the revolution permanent.

All this is quite unprecedented, and it is not surprising that the outside world has repeatedly been taken in by spurious analogies with earlier revolutionary epochs. The traditional cycle is one in which a popular upheaval exhausts its impetus with the defeat of the movement's radical wing, after which a new ruling class makes its peace with the remnants of the old order. Ever since Lenin introduced the New Economic Policy in 1921, this familiar schema has again and again suggested itself to foreign observers, and on each occasion they have, after a brief interval, been confronted with another upward turn of the revolutionary spiral. Nor has this experience been confined to conservatives, liberals, and democratic socialists. Within the Communist orbit itself one dissident group after another has been baffled by the operation of a system apparently immune to the laws governing earlier revolutions. Trotsky was not alone in predicting a "Soviet Thermidor" in the later 1920's, just as his opponents were not entirely disingenuous in treating the Army he commanded as a potential source of Bonapartist tendencies. In actual fact, the regime had at that time already carried out its own controlled Thermidor after the Kronstadt rising and the introduction of NEP, while the Bonapartist function was at first neutralized by police terrorism and later successfully usurped by Stalin himself. Even the destruction of the Bolshevik old guard in the 1936-38 "purge" was accomplished without any real alteration in the political control exercised at the center by the remnant of the victorious faction. And to this day, notwithstanding the more prominent position occupied by the leaders of the military hierarchy since Stalin's demise and particularly since the governmental reshuffle of February 8-9, 1955, no serious challenge has been offered to the hegemony of the party machine, or to the concentration within that machine of ultimate power in the hands of a small group of men stemming from the original Bolshevik movement.

So far as its mechanics are at present understood, the Soviet regime presents itself as an autocracy superimposed upon an exceedingly dynamic industrial economy, which in some of its branches, at any rate, is developing at an unparalleled rate. The "internal contradictions" of a society so constituted must necessarily revolve around the issue of political control over the planning apparatus. This follows from the logic of a system that assigns to the central authority the task of determining not merely the broad lines of economic and social development, but the rate of progress for each and every branch of activity, as well as the means proper to the achievement of the various goals. An authority which habitually makes decisions of this kind clearly is something radically different from a government—socialist or liberal—operating under democratic restraints within the confines of a predominantly uncontrolled economy. The ability to make such decisions (and, of course, to see to it that they are carried out) is the central feature of the dictatorship—much more so than concentration camps, which could conceivably be abolished without altering the essential character of the system. It is the distinguishing mark of this kind of regime that there is nowhere any firm distinction between the state and the rest of society, so that the individual is nowhere firmly protected against invasion of his rights. But conversely, the state machine itself also lacks that relative immunity which in our kind of society is conferred upon it by the fact that the state's functions are sharply circumscribed and differentiated from the free, spontaneous, uncontrolled activity of social groups or individuals. Instead of this clear-cut legal and practical division of society into two distinct spheres, there is in the Soviet Union a forcible amalgamation of both under the aegis of the party. For the ultimate authority that presides over this shotgun marriage is the party, not the government as such. The latter functions as an organ of the party—if it failed or refused to do so, the system would collapse and the U. S. S. R. would, by Western standards, become a "normal" country—*i.e.*, one in which the political authority is clearly distinguishable from the remainder of society. To the extent that this is currently impossible, the state can, in a sense not intended by Communists, be said to have "withered away," although this feat has been performed only at the cost of merging state and society.

What this merger means in practice, under a "permanent revolution from above" which is also a permanent industrial revolution, is difficult to picture because we are used to thinking of autocracy as something static and remote, whereas the Soviet autocracy is dynamic and pervasive in the highest degree. The social stratum most exposed to its impact is apparently the managerial one, which provides the party with the bulk of its cadres—and the secret police with the greater number of its victims. "To try to understand the atmosphere in which the upper stratum of Soviet society has lived since 1928," it has been said, "one must imagine the Spanish Inquisition of Philip II established in a Californian town during the gold rush." That such a system should function at all, let alone that it should yield remarkable results in the production sphere, seems hardly credible. And indeed it has never been easy for the ruling group to decide how far Communist slogans can safely be taken seriously. There is always the danger that they will prove explosive even under an autocracy—they may, for example, be used to rationalize either a demand for rapid improvement in living standards or a camouflaged attempt to upset the internal political balance by placing more power in the hands of people outside the inner circle of party leaders.[1] In a stationary society this would not matter, but the Soviet regime is dedicated to the task of revolutionizing the country's economy, and to this end popular energies have constantly to be mobilized for the unpopular task of depriving the people of the consumer goods they have been promised since about 1930. The whole process lurches forward under the weight of its own internal contradictions, of which the chief is that between an unprecedented rate of growth and an equally unprecedented distortion of the economy in the interest of heavy industry and arms production—a disproportion which the changes introduced since 1953 have not fundamentally affected. Thus, it has been said with good reason that a systematic effort to "distort the evolution of society into a pattern which is unnatural but not impossible" lies at the heart of the entire system.[2]

[1] Cf. Stalin's diatribe against Yaroshenko's proposals for giving a new formulation to the basic aims of Communist policy (*Economic Problems of Socialism in the U.S.S.R.*, Moscow, 1952; pp. 65-92). These proposals were clearly intended to give the planning bureaucracy greater scope.

[2] Cf. Richard Lowenthal, in *The Twentieth Century*, London, March, 1953, p. 188: "It is unnatural in the sense that without the constant application of force from above, society would not evolve in that direction; it is not impossible in the sense that it does not simply run counter to the technical and organizational data which impose certain common features on all major societies of our time, to the state of the 'productive forces,' and hence the requirements of physical survival in the modern world. That it is 'not impossible,' or more positively, that it is one of the possible variants of social organization in the twentieth century, saves it from failure. That it is unnatural serves to provide ever new justification for the totalitarian power that called it into being."

The party's functions under such a regime include the mobilization of popular support for the official policy of superinvestment, as well as the constant maintenance of a balance between the privileged stratum and the masses. Because these functions are conflicting and in a sense contradictory, they impose upon the leadership a very high degree of independence from democratic processes of opinion formation. A party that has to justify the exclusive rule of a privileged caste, in the name of a revolutionary ideology originally derived from the radical wing of a popular movement, can function only if it is permitted to make up its ideology as it goes along. Internal democratization is out of the question while the gap between reality and fiction remains as wide as it is. One may speculate upon the possibility of a totalitarian organization permitting genuine, if restricted, freedom of opinion among the upper stratum of its members—provided it is socially homogeneous. But there is no easy steppingstone from this to a democratization of society. On the contrary: the more the party becomes identified with the actual ruling class, the greater the temptation to govern autocratically and to fob the populace off with elaborately contrived fabrications about external perils and domestic "enemies of the people."

Because this topic has of late become so familiar to readers of political literature, there is some danger of forgetting how little we know in fact about the internal mechanics of totalitarian rule. Far more is known about the economic results of what may briefly be called the plan era. Since 1945 we have, moreover, been able to watch the introduction of the Soviet system in the countries of eastern Europe. Thus, however great our uncertainty about the eventual outcome of internal political struggles which reached a provisional climax in the opening months of 1955, we have at any rate been provided with a yardstick for measuring the relative effects of Communist planning policies in the economic sphere. The outcome of the Second World War has forced Communist and non-Communist members of the European family to live side by side, and in the case of Yugoslavia there has even been a spectacular defection from the Communist camp, which, however, has not led to a total repudiation of Communist planning concepts. Thus, if we wish to discover how "coexistence" operates at the economic level, and which side has the better chances in the long pull, it is advisable to consider the part of Europe that is either under Soviet control or directly exposed to the influence of the Soviet bloc. And as a preliminary we cannot do better than begin with the Soviet economy itself.

2: *Rates of Growth*

LET IT BE CLEAR that under this head we are concerned not with consumption but with the growth of the total national income. There is no point in dwelling upon the gap between west European and Russian living standards, and, conversely, it is not particularly relevant that the non-European regions of the Soviet Union may have a higher standard of personal income than much of Asia and the Middle East; for in principle this state of affairs could be reversed. The crucial question is whether the Soviet economy is or is not developing fast enough to outstrip, both absolutely and relatively, the Soviet Union's European and non-European neighbors, while leaving a margin for the industrialization of China. The answer seems to be that it is doing so—at any rate, in the domain of heavy industry. There is nothing to suggest that the system need fear comparison with the West in terms of investment or the rate of industrial progress. In fact, the evidence points in the other direction,[3] notwithstanding recent official admissions of a serious lag, amounting very nearly to a partial breakdown, in agriculture,[4] and notwithstanding, too, the generally fraudulent character of official price and output statistics. It is quite possible for the official indices to be generally untrustworthy without thereby invalidating the claimed achievement of certain definite, and very startling, production targets. The element of fraud appears to be located in claims relating to the net national product rather than in the absolute figures of output for selected industries. Thus, the real increase in industrial production between 1928 and 1937 probably was below 200 per cent, instead of the 338 per cent claimed officially; and the growth of the entire net national product between 1928 and 1948 has been authoritatively measured by the figures of 25 and 60 billion rubles, respectively, as against the official claim to have raised the base figure of 25 million to nearly six times its amount, or 143 billion.[5] But even so, the rate of progress is remarkable, and, when translated into absolute output quantities for heavy industry, very startling indeed.

[3] Cf. N. Jasny, *The Soviet Economy During the Plan Era*, Stanford, 1952; also *Soviet Economic Growth*, ed. Abram Bergson, Row-Peterson, Evanston, Ill., 1953.

[4] *E.g.*, in Malenkov's Report to the Supreme Soviet of August 8, 1953, and in Khrushchev's Report to the Party Central Committee's plenary session, September 3-7, 1953. Cf. also Malenkov's letter of resignation of February 8, 1955, whose terms were clearly dictated by growing concern among the ruling caste over the failure of the Government's farm program, however little Malenkov himself may have had to do with the miscarriage of policies presumably advocated by Khrushchev.

[5] For detailed estimates, see Jasny, *op. cit.*, p. 85. For Soviet industry alone—*i.e.*, ignoring farming, transport, services, etc—Donald R. Hodgman arrives at an annual average growth rate of 15.7 per cent for the period from 1927-28 to 1937, 4.7 per cent for 1937-40, when military preparations were interfering, and 20.5 per cent for 1946-50. For the entire period of 1927-28 to 1950 his index shows a growth rate of 8.9 per cent annually (cf. *Soviet Economic Growth*, p. 242).

The most reliable computations indicate that, since the opening of the plan era, the share of net investment in the national product has quadrupled, with an ever-increasing proportion (at least up to 1953) going into industry, and a steadily increasing proportion of *that* devoted to the producer-goods industries. An extrapolation of some necessarily abstract figures of industrial growth since 1928—inadequate though such a procedure is, for obvious reasons—suggests disquieting comparisons with economic growth in the West. It has been calculated that, over the past quarter century, Soviet industrial progress—despite famines, purges, and war—has continued at an average rate of eight per cent per annum.[6] Such rates of increase are not entirely unprecedented,[7] but the Soviet emphasis on basic industries and producer goods has introduced a new factor. On the whole, it seems probable that the rate will tend to fall with the disappearance of certain temporary features characteristic of the early plan period—*i.e.*, the impact of borrowed Western technology, the availability of an untapped reservoir of agricultural surplus labor, etc. Yet the gross industrial product may well continue for a while to increase at an annual rate of between six and seven per cent. At 6.5 per cent, compounded, the growth is to almost double in ten years, or to more than three times in twenty years. It is a remarkable thought that Soviet industrial output in 1970 may be three, or three and a half, times what it was in 1950

---

[6] *Soviet Economic Growth,* Chapter VII.

[7] From 1900 to 1906 the annual increase in manufacturing production in the United States averaged nine per cent; from 1906 to 1913 in Japan it even averaged eleven per cent. Cf. W. Arthur Lewis, Chapter X, *Economic Survey 1919-1939,* Allen and Unwin, London, 1949. For the period from 1929 to 1950, the rise of the U. S. gross national product at constant prices has been estimated at just below three per cent annually (cf. Gregory Grossman, in *Soviet Economic Growth,* pp. 1-23). The same author suggests that Soviet national product from 1928 to 1937, and again from 1948 to 1950, grew from 6.5 to seven per cent annually.

—and this without the remainder of eastern Europe. On this supposition the Soviet Union would in 1970 have more or less attained the U. S. national product of 1950, though in view of her much larger population (an estimated 260 million by 1970), output per head would be less than half the American figure, while personal consumption would of course be far lower, owing to the continued investment in heavy industry and military preparedness of the bulk of the available funds. Still, at the end of such a period of growth, the U. S. S. R. would be from three to four times more powerful, in terms of heavy industrial output, than in 1950, after the victory over Germany. It is assumed that capital investment and defense would still have priority over consumption, atomic energy would to some extent have been added to other sources of power for military and industrial use, and the systematic conditioning of the population to an austere existence—though with certain alleviations for the managerial class, and perhaps for the consumer generally—would have been continued. The outcome would be a vastly more powerful military and industrial machine on a social foundation no longer marked by extreme shortages of basic goods, but still bleakly puritanical and rigidly regimented. It is perhaps worth adding that this forecast says nothing about the ability of the U. S. S. R. to "overtake" the United States, whose net national product per head was probably three and a half times that of the Soviet Union in 1940, and by 1950 had risen to about four times the Soviet figure.[8]

[8] Jasny, *op. cit.*, p. 14. By the end of 1954 the population of the Soviet Union had attained an estimated 216 million and was rising at an annual rate of over three million. The urban population increased between 1926 and 1953 from 26 to 81 million, i.e. from 18 to 38 percent of the total. Over approximately the same period—from 1928 to 1954—the number of workers in the "national economy" increased from less than 11 to 47 millions. (Cf. *Economic Survey of Europe in 1954*, published by Economic Commission for Europe, Geneva, March 1955; pp. 65/66)

But such comparisons are irrelevant for political purposes —just as it is not strictly relevant that in 1950 the U. S. S. R. was perhaps spending the equivalent of $22.5 billion on all forms of "defense," and therefore considerably less than the United States spent in the same period. The Soviet Union can make war on fewer dollars than the United States, and, generally speaking, the effective value of the various factors entering into the national product is very different in a highly developed and in a relatively primitive society. For the same reason, the application of atomic energy to industry may have more revolutionary consequences in the Soviet Union than in the West.

What, then, does all this mean in terms of military strength? Due allowance being made for the peculiarities of Soviet pricing and official budgeting, it is commonly estimated that something like one-fifth of the U. S. S. R.'s net national income is directly devoted to military purposes. There have been fluctuations since 1946, but taking into account both the post-Korean rearmament wave all over the world and the subsequent tendency to level off (until early 1955, when there was a partial return to the earlier policy) twenty per cent seems a safe estimate.[9] What this signifies in real terms is not easy to say, since recent technical developments in aerial and atomic warfare have upset the bases of previous calculations, but in relation to conventional war-

[9] The 1952 defense budget came to 23.9 per cent of all budgeted expenditure. It has been reliably estimated that this may have represented over a quarter of the national income, in real terms as distinct from ruble values. Such estimates are necessarily tentative, but they permit certain general conclusions. (See, for example, *The Times*, London, October 6-8, 1952.) On the other hand, the 12 per cent rise in military expenditure announced at the February, 1955, session of the Supreme Soviet—specially called to sanction the official return to a "tough" policy at home and abroad—need not be taken at face value. It may well have been notional rather than real.

fare, at least, some conclusions can be drawn. It is worth recalling that in 1944 the Soviet Union produced a mass of armaments roughly comparable to the output of Germany and German-controlled Europe, although her territory was then much reduced by invasion.[10] Indeed, there is reason to believe that she then produced as many aircraft as Germany, and forty per cent more than Britain, and that her output of armored fighting vehicles in that year was about two-thirds larger than the total German output. The amount of steel needed for this peak wartime production has been put at about eight to eight and a half million tons. By comparison, the tonnages required to supply the enormous peacetime forces maintained by the U. S. S. R. are much smaller, though the increased weight of modern weapons has naturally made itself felt. It has been estimated by competent authorities that about a million and a quarter ingot tons of steel are sufficient for the output of all the aircraft, armored vehicles, guns, shells, and mortar bombs required by the Soviet forces in peacetime,[11] while another million tons would provide for mechanized transport and engineering requirements. The tonnage of steel consumed by the Soviet armaments industry trebled in the thirties, but even so this consumption did not rise much above three million, construction of new plants included. This sufficed for the war against Germany. Steel production is, of course, only one index to over-all military capacity, but it is noteworthy that the quantities required for large-scale warfare represent only a small proportion of current Soviet output.

These wartime achievements were made possible by

[10] *Ibid.* The calculation rests upon a comparison of official Soviet disclosures with what is known of German output during the latter part of the war.

[11] *Ibid.*

single-minded concentration of a temporarily reduced total output upon the sole aim of war production, and by a comparatively high standard of technical and scientific skill in the heavy industries. In all these respects, progress since then has been considerable. Something is known, too, about the priority accorded such matters from the evidence contained in the *Supplement* to the 1941 Plan, a seven-hundred-page secret document that was captured by the Germans, later came into Allied hands, and is now available in photographic reproduction. From this and other evidence it appears that even before the outbreak of war with Germany, the Soviet government had allotted to the armaments industries investment funds sufficient to employ upward of two million workers, or as many as those in the coal, iron, steel, and engineering industries combined. There is no point in comparing absolute figures for this or subsequent years. Doubtless the aggregate military expenditure of the NATO powers is larger than that of the Soviet bloc. It is not, however, so overwhelmingly great—even if nuclear weapons are taken into account—as to constitute the kind of deterrent to aggression that Western statesmanship has been aiming at. In fact, it appears more than likely that, taking into account the present relationship of forces in both manpower and technical proficiency, no such deterrent is practicable, or rather, that the only effective deterrent lies in the threat of atomic warfare; and this obviously cuts both ways.

To return to the more general topic of Soviet production, the following figures compiled by the Secretariat of the Economic Commission for Europe, from Soviet sources, in its *Survey*[12] for 1953 (p. 46), give a graphic picture of the current rate of growth in the U. S. S. R.'s heavy industry:

[12] Geneva, 1954.

Output of Soviet Industry and Certain Producer Goods

	1950	1952	1953	1955
Gross industrial output (Index Nos. 1950=100)	Actual 100	Actual 131	Estimate 144.5	Plan 170
Of which:				
Producer goods	100	131	146	180
Consumer goods	100	130	140	165
Coal and lignite (million tons)	260	300.7	320	372
Crude oil (million tons)	37.8	47.4	52	70
Electric power (billion kw.h.)	90.3	116.4	133	162.5
Crude steel (million tons)	27.3	34.5	38	44.2
Cement (million tons)	10.3	14.1	16	22.7
Engineering (Index Nos.)	100	140	165	200
Chemicals (Index Nos.)	100	—	167	200 (approx.)

3: *The Cost of Stalinism*

SUCH RESULTS clearly could not have been achieved under any other political system, which of course is merely to say that no other political system could have starved the population quite so effectively. But although this consideration will not recommend the regime to Western democrats, it is implausible to suppose that opposition to it on this score is widespread among the managerial caste and the Soviet intelligentsia generally. These groups have come into being as a result of the Soviet industrial revolution and are presumably as philosophical about its cost as Victorian entrepreneurs were about child labor. If they have substantial grievances against the autocracy it is for denying them the per-

sonal and political elbowroom to which they now consider themselves entitled. The real problem lies elsewhere.
It is gradually becoming evident that the weakness of the
system is to be found in its mismanagement of agriculture.[18]
There is evidence that farm output has either stagnated or
risen only very slightly, and that the net effect of mechanization in the countryside has hitherto been confined to releasing surplus labor for industry—part of which was and is
being wasted in forced-labor camps. If Soviet planning
eventually comes to grief it will be owing to its failure to
break the resulting food bottleneck. In the face of continued
shortages the planners hitherto have ruthlessly opted in
favor of maximum industrial investment, at the cost of
holding consumption down to the barest level compatible
with the need to improve productivity. As industrialization
gradually creates a more differentiated urban environment,
dependent for its efficiency on a multitude of ancillary
services and a gradual rise in living standards, the cruder
methods of the Stalin epoch are likely to become unserviceable and to give way to various refinements—from emphasis
on quality production to a slightly improved deal for the
consumer; indeed, there are signs that this process has
already begun. But, failing a solution of the farm problem,
these improvements must stay within narrow limits, and
a rational policy seems unlikely under the present regime:
it would affect too many vested interests, including the
kolkhoz bureaucracy and the apparatus of political control
in the countryside. How long these institutional "fetters on
the productive forces of society" will be tolerated is a ques-

[18] "At the cost of several million lives, the Communists dispossessed
close to a hundred million peasants, compelling them to give up their
entrepreneurial independence and to work much more than formerly, and
this without compensation in the form of even slightly improved consumption levels" (Jasny, *op. cit.*, p. 90).

tion to which an exact answer is obviously impossible. One may, however, hazard the guess that any slowing down in the rate of industrial advance owing to a lag in farm output will cause serious tension between supporters of more stringent collectivization and "revisionists" inclined to allow the peasants more latitude; and that the proponents of "hard" and "soft" solutions will eventually look for support to the "public opinion" of the party and the managerial class as a whole. These are mere guesses; the tendencies already observable do, however, underline the importance of attending to the collective consciousness of the new Soviet elite rather than the inchoate stirrings of the masses, and of avoiding anything that looks like doctrinaire hostility to the planned economy as such. There is no inherent reason why a differently planned system should not live at peace with the outside world and with its own citizens. Any suggestion that the achievement of this aim requires a counter-revolution and the restoration of private capitalism is likely to confirm the Soviet elite in its contemptuous attitude toward the West.

This is not to say that democratic criticism of the Soviet social hierarchy and planning system should be stifled in the interest of winning the cold war. In the *long run* the issue within Soviet society is certain to lie between the autocratic planning bureaucracy and the producers. Indeed, it may well be thought that the world will eventually be offered the spectacle of a political struggle to decide whether the means of production should belong to the "associated producers" (the kolkhoz members, for example) or to the state. A faint foretaste of this coming struggle—which is certain to be reflected within the Communist party—may be traced in *Economic Problems of Socialism in the U. S. S. R.,* notably in Stalin's strictures upon the proposal made by two hitherto unknown Soviet economists, Sanina and Venzher, to let the collective settlements become the owners of the machine-tractor stations and other essential farm equipment. It would indeed be remarkable if in a nominally socialist economy this issue should not eventually come to the fore. But whatever its long-range importance, it is clearly impossible at the current stage for an effective opposition against the autocracy to crystallize around a radical program of this kind. The only stratum in Soviet society that can at present be appealed to by the West is the managerial one, and the only program that fits its needs is one which takes the hierarchical structure of Soviet society for granted and merely seeks to rid it of the monstrosities accumulated during the Stalinist epoch. Anything that goes beyond this, in the direction of creating something which democratic socialists might regard as an approximation to their ideals, must necessarily be the outcome of a lengthy process on which Western policy can hardly have much influence. The most that can be said is that Western democrats, if they take their professions at all seriously, will naturally welcome any movement to transfer effective control of Soviet industry and agriculture to the real producers in town and country, much as they have welcomed the tentative experiments with works councils and the like in Yugoslavia. And, needless to say, any influence they possess should be exerted to prevent the adoption of imbecile proposals for associating the democratic cause with the restoration of private property in the basic industries.

This topic is inevitably loaded with political dynamite. Ever since the cold war became really serious, a determined effort has been made, notably in the United States, to turn it into a crusade on behalf of "free enterprise" and other market-economy slogans, and to detach from the crusading army all those who adhere to democratic socialism, or even to the principles and practices of the New Deal. The net effect has been to isolate the United States from most of its potential allies in Europe and Asia, and to reaffirm the Kremlin's grip upon the more critical elements of the Soviet intelligentsia. It is significant that such unfavorable results have in no way disturbed or disconcerted those who are loudest in proclaiming the need to assemble a grand alliance against the Communist bloc. One sometimes suspects that socialism at home seems a greater threat to them than Stalinism in the U. S. S. R. Be that as it may, the atmosphere has become decidedly unfavorable to a dispassionate weighing of the evidence for and against the economic efficacy of planning methods, whether in the U. S. S. R. or elsewhere. And yet the question has to be faced. We know that the entire Soviet economy is completely distorted by the Stalinist policy of building up heavy industry at all cost—building steel plants to turn out steel for the construction of more steel plants, in fact. Why has this distortion not hitherto interfered with an unparalleled rate of economic growth? It is no answer to say that it is precisely the tempo of industrial advance that constitutes the distortion, for in theory at least most of the abnormal investment could have been wasted. There is no simple correlation between maximum exploitation and maximum rise in productivity. The Pharaohs invested Egypt's surplus labor in the construction of pyramids, at great cost and inconvenience to the ordinary Egyptian, but there is no evidence that productivity benefited from the effort to provide Cheops with a suitable tomb. There must be something in the Soviet mechanism that not only insures an unparalleled rate of capital investment in heavy industry, but also a consequent rise in total industrial output. That something cannot be the dictatorship as such —*i.e.*, the system of terror and propaganda. However essen-

tial it may have been during the transition period, something steadier and less haphazard is required to explain a
fairly continuous economic performance. It does not seem
unreasonable to suggest that the factor we are looking for
is to be found in the institutional arrangements surrounding the operation of the planned economy. One may in
particular mention two: the great inequality in earned
incomes, and a social setting favorable to the emergence of
a competent class of technicians. It is unnecessary to dwell
at length on these two related but distinct factors. The
phenomenon itself has frequently been noted and has not
been denied by apologists of the regime. It is, indeed, one of
its less detestable features—compared, for example, with
the institution of "labor camps," or the treatment of strikes
as crimes against the state. A non-Stalinist government
might do away with forced labor and restore some of
the worker's elementary rights, which have been filched
away from him on the pretense that he is now laboring for
the public good and not for some exploiter. But even a
greatly liberalized regime would in all likelihood have to
preserve something like the present scale of earned incomes,
and the corresponding tax rates, for a long time to come.

In a country which is still relatively poor in comparison
with most other industrialized societies, the scarcity of consumer goods obviously necessitates the introduction of
special monetary privileges for the managerial stratum and
all those willing to acquire special skills. But quite generally
it should be obvious that, under any form of planned economy, managers and technicians must be given encourage-
ments similar to, though not identical with, those obtained
by the entrepreneurs in a capitalist society. The kind of
egalitarian sentimentality that denies this, although widespread among Western socialists, has really nothing to

commend it, except the obvious advantage of being popular. It is one of the heaviest counts against democratic socialism that it has consistently evaded this issue, from fear of antagonizing its labor allies and going against the egalitarian sentiment historically bound up with the democratic labor movement. This intellectual dishonesty has earned the usual reward of early popularity and subsequent disillusionment —a pattern most conspicuously displayed by the almost total failure, from a production viewpoint, of the British Labor experiment in 1945-51. For here a democratic movement with an egalitarian ideology came up against the problem of making socialism synonymous with efficiency— and promptly shirked it.[14] Under the very special conditions obtaining in the U. S. S. R. any indifference to this key issue was, of course, ruled out altogether by elementary considerations of security and self-preservation. If the planned economy was to develop at a pace commensurate with the political aims of the regime, something had to be done to counteract the deadening effect of police terror upon the new intelligentsia, and that something could only be the granting of very substantial material and social privileges. There is nothing immoral about this; it is, on the contrary, immoral to pretend that it could have been otherwise, or that any modern economy can dispense with a high degree of social stratification. To the extent that criticism refuses

---

[14] There were, of course, other factors as well. The structure of British society is reflected in a labor-management relationship that is probably the greatest single hindrance to Britain's industrial advance. But the democratization of management (which was equally shirked by the Labor government) could have gone hand in hand with a policy of raising the technical intelligentsia—and the professional class generally— above the wretched level to which it had been condemned by the fall in the effective purchasing power of the national currency. Nothing of the kind was done, or even dreamed of—it would have gone against the leveling ideology that serves British labor as a substitute for socialism.

to acknowledge these facts it simply disqualifies itself from being taken seriously.

The real cost of Stalinism, economically speaking, appears elsewhere: primarily, in the creation of disproportions—between production and consumption, industry and agriculture and within industry itself—so immense that their correction would entail a complete reversal of previous policies. It is the peculiar nemesis of planning that, just because it is so effective in changing the "natural" shape of the economy, it is capable of distorting that shape to a degree which runs counter to the basic aims of the plan. Thus, it is probably no exaggeration to say that the calamitous state of Soviet farming is related to the fact that the share of the product left to the peasants, after meeting the claims of the government and the kolkhoz, is so small as to undermine not merely their willingness but their sheer physical ability to produce more. This startling result could certainly not have been achieved by any regime which exposed itself, in however slight a degree, to democratic control. But that is the consequence of absolutism, not of planning as such. It does not suggest that economic planning is wasteful, but that it must be placed under public control if the colossal disproportions incurred during the Stalinist epoch (to say nothing of its massacres, purges, deportations, and forced-labor camps) are to be avoided. There is good reason for describing this side of the system as "Asian"—and for reminding ourselves that it is historically related to the great Asian despotisms of the past, with their immense, centrally controlled irrigation systems and their authoritarian bureaucracies: features which, significantly enough, have promptly appeared in Communist China. But there is no reason for closing one's eyes to its startling achievements in the industrial sphere, all the more so since these achievements are now being duplicated throughout eastern Europe. Everything we know points to the conclusion that, in terms of over-all economic growth, "Soviet Europe" is gaining on its immediate neighbors. This subject is worth more emphasis than it has customarily received.

4: *Soviet Europe*

IN A SENSE it is misleading to talk of "Europe." There are at least three Europes: (1) Soviet Europe, of which little need be said in this context; (2) western Europe, which is the best known and of course the most important part of the area; and (3) southern Europe, less well understood and saddled with problems radically different from those of the western region, while in some ways closely related to the pattern of the area at present under Soviet control. These distinctions call for some elaboration.

There is obviously no difficulty about defining Soviet Europe. It coincides with eastern Europe (except for Yugoslavia), but also includes the highly industrialized regions of Czechoslovakia and East Germany, which until recently would have been described as central European. Owing to the Sovietization of these two countries, on the one hand, and the rapid industrialization of Poland, on the other, differences in class structure, social outlook, and living standards between these two subregions of Soviet Europe are being leveled, but there still remain considerable variations within a group of countries stretching from the Baltic to the Black Sea and comprising some 90 million inhabitants. The special defining characteristic of the whole area— East Germany, Czechoslovakia, Poland, Hungary, Rumania,

Bulgaria, and Albania—is, of course, the exercise of control by the Soviet Union. What matters here is that the economies of these countries are centrally planned, both nationally and in relation to the U. S. S. R., with whom they exchange the bulk of their surplus product. But in addition there are more long-standing links: cultural in the case of Poland, Czechoslovakia, and Bulgaria; economic as between the predominantly agricultural countries, which are only now undergoing the kind of industrial revolution already achieved in, for example, prewar Czechoslovakia. Thus, Poland has links in both directions, being Slav in culture (unlike Hungary and Rumania) and engaged in transforming her economy. The odd member of the group is East Germany, which has some economic contact with Czechoslovakia and the industrial regions of Poland, but differs in social and political type from the other Sovietized countries, has no traditional cultural relations with any of them, and was included purely as a result of military conquest and the enlightened statesmanship displayed at Potsdam. Not surprisingly, it is the weakest link in the chain and the one most liable to snap in an emergency.

Now, of all these satellites, Poland has clearly made the most rapid progress, owing, of course, largely to postwar acquisition of new industrial resources and a better balance of population consequent on the redrawing of frontiers. According to the 1950 census, forty-six per cent of the population was then dependent on agriculture for its livelihood, compared with sixty-two per cent in 1930. In 1952 the proportion of nonfarmers was given as about sixty per cent.[15] The rate of progress in industry can be deduced from

[15] *Zycie Warsovy*, August 19, 1952, quoted in *The World Today*, monthly publication of the Royal Institute of International Affairs, Chatham House, London, Vol. 10, No. 3, March, 1954.

data published in the annual reports of the Economic Commission for Europe. Such computations, for what they are worth, show the following changes in net industrial production:

Country	1938			1952 (1938 prices)		
	Aggregate $ billion	p. cap. $	p. cap. ratio to Poland	Aggregate $ billion	p. cap. $	p. cap. ratio to Poland
Poland	0.71	20.5	1.0	2.5	89.6	1.0
France	3.2	75.7	3.7	4.4	104.3	1.16
Italy	1.8	41.0	2.0	2.5	52.1	0.6

Commenting on these estimates, a writer adds: "Even when making all necessary reservations as to the criteria and methods of calculation involved, the claim that net industrial production reached a value of $2500 million (1938 prices), as compared with the prewar figure of $700 million, is not without significance. While even stronger reservations of the same nature are justified in any country-to-country comparisons across the Iron Curtain, there may also be some truth in the claim that in his per capita industrial output the Pole has overtaken and left far behind the Italian, and is in fact already approaching the French in the industrial race."[16]

It is one of the minor ironies of the situation that the intensive industrialization of Poland started under German control during the war, when the Upper Silesian coal fields were intensively modernized with the latest German equipment, as was the Moravská Ostrava coal field of present-day Czechoslovakia. In consequence of the postwar partitions and the over-all Soviet control of the area, the coal-steel complex formed by the Moravská Ostrava coal field, Polish Upper Silesia, and the district between Cracow

[16] *The World Today, loc. cit.,* p. 123.

and Czestochowa has developed into a "Little Ruhr" that is beginning to cause concern to West German economists and technicians.[17] To its original coal-steel resources there have been added, since the war, the synthetic-oil plants, steel works, and other enterprises that are developing in Poland, and to some extent in Czechoslovakia, with Russian technical aid and equipment. The entire Moravian-Upper Silesian-Polish heavy industrial complex is organized as one unit, and its development is linked to the Soviet industrial plan, with the aim of creating a "combine" or vertical trust uniting the iron ore of the Ukraine with the coal and steel industry of the "Little Ruhr." East Germany's surviving heavy industries, notably the great chemical works of Saxony, although lying outside this particular complex, are equally linked to the Soviet plan, whose over-all aim may be defined as the achievement of technical integration— which also happens to be the ideal of West German technicians in the Ruhr! Thus, in this particular instance, not only is investment centrally directed into an industrial complex that may in time come to rival the coal-steel community in western Europe, but the elimination of private ownership has actually hastened the tendency to form vertical trusts—which under present political and social conditions are rightly thought dangerous in the Ruhr, but which technicians and managers happen to regard as important to further technical progress. This is an extreme instance, though not the only one, of a dilemma that confronts

[17] Cf. *The Economist*, July 10, 1954. See also Jean Bird, *East-West Trade*, Batchworth Press, London, 1954, p. 14: "What was once an integral part of the German economy has become an appendage of the Soviet economy, a unit in which heavy industry is being developed so rapidly that it will shortly act more as a competitor than as a complement to Western Germany. Even if tomorrow all trade barriers between the two halves of Germany were to be abolished, it would be found that the old channels and the old bases of exchange had been destroyed."

Western policy-making almost everywhere. In this case, although eastern Europe's present steel output is only about a third of that of the west European coal-steel union, and hard-coal output about half, the writing is already on the wall. Nor is there any doubt that East Germany, until lately the stepchild of the plan, is beginning to reap appreciable results from the drive to expand its heavy industries—at the consumer's expense, needless to say, but that does not detract from the significance of the fact.

The case of Poland is, however, more interesting than that of Czechoslovakia or East Germany, because agriculture was still dominant until the war, whereas by now its share has slipped from nearly one-half to one-quarter, while industry's share of the national income has risen from thirty per cent to more than half the total.[18] The reverse side of this picture is the fall in living standards. A rough figure derived for 1952 from United Nations computations[19] would put the national income per head of population in Poland at $450. Since it is estimated that consumption's share in the total is less than half, the individual is left with something like four dollars' worth of consumer spending power per week—a figure that gives some idea of the sacrifices demanded from the present generation. An ever-increasing proportion of the nation's manpower, equipment, and raw materials is diverted to building factories, mines, shipyards, power stations, railways, etc., and to creating export surpluses to serve as payment to foreign countries for new machinery and raw materials. To induce the popu-

[18] According to official computations, quoted, with some reserve, in *The World Today*, Vol. 10, No. 4, April, 1954. There seems little reason to question the trend illustrated by these percentage figures, especially since they are accompanied by official admissions that roughly three-quarters of all investments have been channeled into heavy industry, and only one-fourth allotted to industries that serve the consumer.

[19] *Ibid.*, p. 174.

lation to put up with this state of affairs is one of the main problems raised by this kind of economic policy. Large armies of workers have to be drafted into factories, their working hours lengthened and their productivity raised, while on the other hand their wages in terms of consumer goods must be kept low. It is, however, the peasantry that has to foot the largest part of the bill, if for no other reason than that it is the most numerous class. The general tendency is to extract from the peasant the greatest possible quantum of produce at the cost of the lowest possible food consumption; to make him surrender as much as possible of his produce for the towns, in exchange for as little as possible in the way of manufactured goods. The regime is, in fact, more interested in the marketable produce than in the aggregate of farm output as such, there being a close relation between this policy and the aim of collectivization; for it is only when the peasant no longer has a say as to the ratio between his production and his consumption that the plan can extract a sufficiently large proportion of the agricultural produce.

It might seem that this state of affairs must be intolerable to all classes alike; it does, indeed, necessitate a dictatorship, but there is every reason to distrust the easy conclusion that the regime is only tolerated because there are at the moment no physical means of removing it. The fact is that economic expansion, however heavily paid for, creates a vested interest on the part of the minority privileged to direct the process. After what has been said earlier, there is no need to stress that it is precisely this fact which constitutes the link between the Communist regime and the technical intelligentsia. It generally supplies the state-party with the prestige it requires to maintain its hold on the bureaucracy and, last but not least, it is essential for keeping up the morale of its members: if Italian Fascism had not bogged down at this crucial point—if, that is to say, the social relations prevalent in Italy under Mussolini had permitted a genuine industrialization drive, instead of the lopsided development of a few monopolistic concerns wedded to restricted output and high profits—the subsequent history of the Fascist regime would have been very different. It is, of course, just here that Communist planning (being genuinely "total" and unhampered by regard for property rights) scores over its Fascist imitation. The real alternative, however, is not "free enterprise" (which in backward countries does not exist, or is a positive hindrance to development), but a different kind of planning. It is for lack of such an alternative that considerable areas of non-Soviet Europe are in danger of falling into the Communist grip.

5: *The Perils of Retardation*

IT IS CUSTOMARY to contrast Soviet Europe with "free" or western Europe as a whole, and this pernicious habit has become more firmly ingrained since the inclusion of Greece and Turkey in NATO. Whatever the strictly military merits of this arrangement, it has led to confusion in the political and social fields. As we are here concerned with the cold war, not with the apocalyptic prospect of its becoming hot, the military structure of NATO can be ignored. For long-term purposes, Greece and Turkey form a natural whole, together with Yugoslavia (with which they are now linked by political and military treaties), southern (but not northern) Italy, Portugal, and Spain. These countries, or areas, constitute an indissoluble geographical, social, and economic unit, despite the fact that

Yugoslavia is predominantly Slav in culture and also differs from the others in having a planned economy. The regions most closely related to them are Cyprus, Lebanon, and Israel, the last of which is not an Oriental country (whatever its ideologists may affirm to the contrary), but a Mediterranean one. For present purposes they can be ignored, as being unlikely to form part of a European system in the near future, although in the long run they ought to be included in it. Spain, however, cannot be ignored, despite the fact that it has the misfortune of being governed autocratically (like Yugoslavia). It is too important to be left out, and too typical of the south European structure, which differs sharply from the west European one. There are, in fact, two different societies, and consequently two different cultures, living side by side in western and southern Europe —in the case of Italy, under the same national roof. These differences are so strongly accentuated, and their long-term political significance is so great, that some attention must be devoted to them.

A glance at the Continent's population structure tells one a good deal about the social barriers drawn by history to separate the three Europes. As against the 90 million inhabitants of Soviet Europe, and the 100 million of southern Europe,[20] the west European group counts 225 million concentrated in the relatively small and densely populated areas of northern Italy, France, Switzerland, Austria, West Germany, Belgium, Holland, Britain, Ireland, and Scandinavia. There is no need to dwell upon the fact that this tightly packed region is the cradle of what is commonly known as Western civilization: it has become the favorite theme of historians, sociologists, political theorists, and

[20] Southern Italy, 18 million; Spain, 28 million; Portugal, 8 million; Greece, 8 million; Yugoslavia, 16 million; Turkey, 22 million.

advocates of European federalism. Here it is more to the point to note that it is also the birthplace of modern industrial civilization in its various institutional forms, including liberal capitalism and democratic socialism (both unknown in the remainder of Europe). These tendencies have, of course, at different times radiated into the surrounding eastern and southern regions, but the gulf remains startlingly large. Now, as already noted, Soviet Europe in some ways occupies a position about halfway between the west and the south. This is true, for example, of such indicators of industrial activity as energy consumption, electricity output, or industrial consumption of steel, in all of which southern Europe lags considerably behind the Soviet-controlled area (taken as a whole—*i.e.,* including East Germany and Czechoslovakia). Of the three great economic regions, the south is the most backward, a fact that cannot fail to have growing political importance as time goes on and these disparities become more accentuated. It is of crucial significance that, compared with Poland, Italy as a whole is falling behind. That, of course, is due to the economic and social dead weight represented by the backward southern part of the country, but such explanations are small comfort to Italians. As the planned industrial revolution proceeds in Soviet Europe, at whatever cost in hardships to peasants and workers, the effect of the Soviet example upon the more backward regions of southern Europe is bound to become stronger, unless countered by alternative methods of stimulating progress. In the case of Italy one can almost calculate the point in time when, combined with internal Communist pressure and rural overcrowding, it will be sufficient to topple the present political structure.

Leaving Soviet Europe out of account, and looking merely

at the disparities between west and south, one cannot avoid the conclusion that they amount to a contrast between two different types of civilizations, both covered rather inadequately by the "European" label. That wheat yields throughout the south average only about half the corresponding figures for the west can to some extent be put down to differences in soil and climate. But when one sees that commodity exports from southern Europe per head of inhabitant come to only one-eighth of the west European average, one obtains a glimpse of the gap separating the two regions. Moreover, such figures are national averages which cancel the differences in income distribution between town and country. These are considerably more pronounced in the south than in the west. The poverty of the rural areas is indeed the basic economic and social problem throughout the south, and it is worth noting that the rural population accounts for over half the total in Greece, southern Italy, Spain, and Portugal, and near to seventy per cent in Turkey and Yugoslavia, as against thirty per cent in France, the least advanced of the west European countries. Partly as a by-product of this situation, rates of infant mortality in the south are more than double the corresponding figures for the west, while illiteracy, virtually unknown in the west, reaches almost Oriental levels in Turkey—and in Spain—with only half of all children going to school. (Significantly, Spain is the only country in the group that since 1939 has shown no progress in this respect.)[21] Lastly, there is in all these countries a problem of rural unemployment which has no counterpart in the west, but is uncomfortably reminiscent of the state of affairs in eastern Europe during the interwar period: a period of slowly growing Communist strength throughout that area. Not only is the percentage of

[21] Cf. *Economic Survey of Europe in 1953*, p. 80.

male workers actively employed in agriculture almost three times the west European average (fifty-seven against twenty-one per cent in 1950), but there is, in addition, increasing pressure upon the available cultivable land and an absolute growth in the numbers of the rural population, despite a small percentage fall (from sixty-five to fifty-seven per cent since 1920). Owing partly to the high birth rate, and partly to the slow development of industry, the current natural increase cannot be absorbed by the towns. The exceptions to this picture are Turkey and Yugoslavia: Turkey because there are reserves of cultivable land not yet settled, Yugoslavia because its planned economy, whatever its faults, at least gives promise of rapid industrial growth. In the remainder of the area, growing pressure upon the land goes parallel with an inadequate rate of capital investment in industry. What this means in terms of human suffering is obvious even to the casual visitor. What it portends in terms of social pressure and political explosiveness can be deduced from the dispassionate judgment of the ECE's *Economic Survey*:

"Thus, despite efforts in all of the countries to promote industrialization, the phenomenon of surplus manpower in agriculture—the characteristic of most underdeveloped countries—has taken on even more serious proportions. Suffice it to say that in Greece, southern Italy, and Spain, the degree of underemployment in agriculture has been roughly estimated to be around one-third."[22]

This is not the place to discuss the politics of "underdevelopment." Something will have to be said about it later on. Here it is relevant to note that, unlike the Asian countries, southern Europe represents the relatively backward part of a geographical and cultural unit—the European con-

[22] *Op. cit.*, p. 82.

tinent—which as a whole is highly developed. This circumstance is responsible both for the more favorable long-term prospects of the region, compared with, for example, southern Asia, and for its even higher degree of political consciousness and latent political tension. Societies that have before their eyes the existence of much higher standards— a Neapolitan, after all, has only to board a train to see the very different conditions north of Rome—are even less likely to remain sunk in apathy than populations who have only vaguely begun to sense the possibility of another kind of existence. The disparity between north and south is at the root of Italy's social and political problems, just as the continued impact of France upon Spain has been a factor in the internal convulsions of that tortured country since the early nineteenth century. With the emergency of supranational patterns, such as the Marshall Plan, the Council of Europe, and the various inter-European economic bodies, this type of relationship has become continental rather than national, so that it is no great exaggeration to say that southern Europe as a whole stands in the same relation to western Europe as the *Mezzogiorno* to the prosperous northern half of Italy. The stresses likely to arise in a hypothetical European Confederation can easily be imagined, especially if attempts were made to tax the wealthier countries in favor of the poorer ones. Americans, for so long familiar with this type of problem, are perhaps unduly optimistic about the chances of a federal or confederate solution, but they are certainly right to doubt the capacity of these countries to raise themselves by their own bootstraps. South European income levels average about forty per cent of the French standard, which may be regarded as typical for western Europe. It has been calculated that in order to reduce this gap by half, over a period of thirty years, it would be necessary for the countries in question to maintain an annual rate of economic growth of 3.5 per cent, which in turn demands a rate of capital investment equivalent to between ten and fifteen per cent of their national income.[23] This is considerably above their current achievements—with the significant exception of Yugoslavia. Even in Italy, where the situation is eased by the presence under the same national roof of a second and relatively prosperous section, the funds available to the postwar *Cassa del Mezzogiorno* for land reform and industrialization in the south are now recognized to be entirely inadequate.[24]

It is of course a truism that poverty is self-perpetuating. On the national level any advance must in the end be financed by savings, for which no adequate margin exists if consumption has already fallen below a certain level. Hence the familiar vicious circle of capital shortage, low living standards, and lack of investment funds. But in backward countries this problem is typically aggravated by a system of taxation which, for example, in the case of Greece has enabled the propertied classes to double their real income since the war, at the expense of everyone else.[25] Such unequal distribution is sometimes justified on the grounds that, in the absence of efficient administrations able to enforce a regime of "austerity," a wide disparity in incomes is the only means of encouraging some degree of voluntary saving. But this argument is badly adapted to situations where entrepreneurial activity is notoriously weak. It is significant that even in post-Civil War Spain, the government has had to take the initiative in whatever industrial progress has been achieved.

The case of Spain indeed epitomizes all that is most per-

[23] *Economic Survey* of Europe in 1953, p. 187.
[24] Cf. *The Economist*, July 10, 1954.
[25] *Economic Survey*, p. 97.

verse and intractable about the southern maladjustment, and the alarming thing is that, by comparison with her partners in misfortune, Spain is in a relatively favorable situation. Her economic structure is more diversified than that of any other member of the group; electricity output is more than double that of Portugal, southern Italy, or Yugoslavia, and three or four times as high as that of Greece or Turkey; and industrial skill is more widespread. The country was neutral during both world wars and able to reap corresponding profits from exports of strategic raw materials. Yet the Spanish economy is so seriously unbalanced that some of the main branches of industry have still not recovered their 1929 level, electricity output is totally inadequate to the rate of industrialization necessary to absorb the growing population, and the latter's twenty per cent increase since 1920 has been accompanied by almost complete stagnation in agriculture. No wonder real wages, including social payments, in 1952 were estimated to be from ten to thirty per cent below the inadequate 1935 level.[26] How little the Franco regime has done to correct the underlying distortions can be gathered from the fact that between 1940 and 1950 there was no advance whatever in farm output, while simultaneously the rural population rose by ten per cent—most of them joining the army of landless seasonal laborers. Surplus labor on the land is now estimated at one-third of the rural population. Grotesquely enough, the pre-1936 republican regime had tried in 1932 to stem the consequent rise in urban unemployment by forbidding rural workers to leave their villages, and by taking measures to *prevent* the mechanization of farming. This shows, at any rate, that in the matter of competing for the prize in absurdity the present autocratic regime has noth-

[26] *Economic Survey,* p. 141.

ing to learn from its "liberal" predecessor. If anything, economic policy since 1939 has been slightly more realistic, in that it has at least recognized the need for state intervention to correct the "natural" flow of capital to where it is least needed—*e.g.*, to the already industrialized and fairly prosperous regions around Barcelona and Bilbao. (In the perspective of the private investor, such choices are of course highly rational; that they happen to be irrational when viewed in the perspective of society's needs is only another proof that market economics are not suited to the problems of undeveloped countries.) But a regime so heavily dependent on the good will of landowners and industrialists is unlikely to go far in the right direction. Spanish Fascism, unlike Yugoslav Communism, supplies no adequate basis for a planned economy—to the great and growing misfortune of Spain.

These remarks are merely intended to correct the mistaken impression that all of Spain's troubles date from the Civil War of 1936-39. It would be truer to say that the Civil War was caused by the country's continuing economic and social maladjustment. Between 1920 and 1935, in the words of the *Economic Survey*,[27] "industrial expansion, increased output of power, and the improvement of the transport system were only just sufficient to maintain the average standard of living in the face of a stagnating agriculture and a rapidly increasing population." Since 1939, whatever the political and cultural sterility of the regime, Spain has at least been delivered to some degree from the curse of *laissez-faire*. But although the Franco regime declared its intention of speeding industrialization, absorbing the rural surplus manpower, and generally correcting structural maladjustments, its achievements in all these domains have been

[27] P. 146.

exceedingly small. Nor is this surprising: planning is impossible in the absence of an efficient administrative machine; moreover, under modern conditions the rapid industrialization of backward countries demands a degree of popular response that can be generated only by a quasi-revolutionary movement. In both respects the existing regime is seriously deficient. The Falange is ludicrously ineffective, compared with, for example, the Yugoslav Communist party (which, of course, fulfills similar functions), and the success of the Spanish bureaucracy in administering the intricate network of controls necessitated by physical shortages and halfhearted planning experiments is, to put it mildly, not outstanding. Thus, there has grown up a very striking contrast between the scale of ambitious, long-term planning for industrial investment and the extremely modest results actually achieved. Administrative inefficiency, and disappointment over the results of planning policies, in turn have stimulated a growing demand for a return to *laissez-faire*—a demand which the United States government is, of course, doing its best to encourage. Yet to believe that the elimination of structural distortions can be left to the free play of market forces is to show a quite remarkable degree of blindness. What is needed—and not only in Spain—is, on the contrary, the establishment of a rigid order of economic priorities, and the strengthening of such policy instruments as public investment and import control; secondly, social and educational policies designed to raise living standards and improve industrial skills; thirdly, a determined drive to alter the social structure of agriculture, which at present stands in the way of greater output.

In various forms this is the pattern in the south as a whole.[28] Throughout the region, farming units are either

[28] *Economic Survey,* pp. 156-163.

much too large or much too small, being either latifundia or poverty-stricken peasant holdings. Together with the technical inertia of a largely illiterate and undernourished rural population, this factor makes it impossible to raise output. Not only are the smallholders thus left with no surplus enabling them to transcend the narrow framework of subsistence farming, but further industrial advance is blocked as well. Any attempt to help these countries to industrialize beyond the narrow limits set by the availability of foreign currency must begin with the creation of a food surplus for urban consumption and foreign export. The obstacles to such progress are social, not physical—there is plenty of scope for irrigation and mechanization! What is lacking is the will or the ability to break out of the vicious circle. As matters stand, the solution is at present being sought throughout the area—Yugoslavia excepted—by the well-tried method of stimulating private enterprise, along with a meager and diminishing amount of state-supported investment in Spain, Portugal, and Turkey. That the resulting distribution of activities will both maximize private profits *and* lead to an allocation of resources desirable from the community's viewpoint is so utterly improbable in the light of past experience that no government is willing to place its full trust in private entrepreneurship. Even so, enough harm is being caused to prejudice the future. Given the absence of planning and "austerity"—*i.e.*, collective saving under state direction—the necessary capital, or at least a fraction of it, can be raised only through the familiar mechanism of allowing the propertied minority to acquire a disproportionate amount of the national income. This system, in turn, helps to perpetuate a social pattern that is (1) unfavorable to economic progress, (2) incompatible with democracy as understood in the West, (3) subversive of the authoritarian or semiauthoritarian regimes actually installed. Whether and how fast revolutionary movements will progress under these circumstances depends of course on a variety of social and political factors. Obviously, their task is most difficult in Yugoslavia, if for purposes of this analysis one equates "Communist" with "Moscow-controlled" and allows the claim of the Belgrade regime to represent a new political variety. Turkey is still regarded as immune, though with the current tendency for the wealthier farmers to monopolize the fruits of technical progress at the expense of the hitherto stable village community, this state of affairs may not last very long. At any rate, it should be clear that there is no reason for complacency while the long-term trend throughout most of the area has not been corrected. In backward countries, successful Communist movements are a function of failing capitalist progress—a point to which we shall have to return. The special urgency of the south European case results from the area's close connection with the other two "Europes": the highly industrialized countries of the west and the Soviet-controlled bloc to the east. The competitive pull of these conflicting examples is probably going to be the major problem of the next ten or twenty years, and if one believes that it is the business of democratic statesmanship to develop alternatives to Stalinist surgery, one must hope that southern Europe will be spared the experiences that countries like Poland or Rumania underwent in the interwar period.

6: *The Market and the Plan*

How LIKELY is it that this will happen? On our analysis the effective answer to Communist planning is not the encouragement of "free enterprise," but

planning of a different kind—*i.e.*, one that aims at the harmonious development of all branches of the economy, and
not at maximum investment in heavy industry. Unfortunately no isolated effort in this direction can go very far without effective American support. There was a brief period
after the war when the United States government seemed
ready to accept the view that economic planning is compatible with political freedom—indeed, a necessary precondition of it. The discovery was blotted out in the general
backwash of obscurantism that carried the Republican party
to power in 1952, amidst the plaudits of the business community. Even so, the lessons of the Roosevelt-Truman period
have not been wholly forgotten. One must indeed be remarkably indifferent to the experience of the interwar years to
imagine that the kind of statesmanship we have been getting
in recent years can cope with the problems of our epoch.
The matter has been well put by Mr. Averell Harriman, who
will not be suspected of indifference to the democratic cause:

> The prevailing philosophy of the administration appears to
> be to rely largely upon the automatic functioning of the market
> to bring about economic growth in the free world. But the
> market is not doing the job. Social and political progress in the
> underdeveloped countries is likewise being left to the market at
> a time when Communist pressure and penetration is increasing.
> But only a more rapid advance than the market provides toward
> socially strong, democratic, national states can provide a success-
> ful defense.[29]

"The market is not doing the job." Mr. Harriman, fortunately is immune to the charge of subversiveness, but he
and those who think like him are clearly guilty of advocating
"creeping socialism." One can only hope that they will
recover their former influence before the house of cards

[29] *"Foreign Affairs,"* Vol. 32, No. 4, July, 1954, p. 530.

built by their successors comes tumbling down upon our heads.

Since a preoccupation with the cold war is never very far removed from the discussion of this subject, it is worth considering the impact of Communist thinking upon those non-Communist elements who represent the last fragile barrier against the flood over much of Europe, Latin America, and southern Asia. The impact is of two kinds, constructive and critical. On the positive side, every conceivable brand or species of nationalism and/or socialism has been affected by the Soviet plan era, although most representatives of these movements would dissociate themselves from the cruder aspects of Stalinism and are still hopeful that Western (and especially United States) support will eventually enable them to tackle the job without recourse to totalitarian "frightfulness." Negatively, socialists of every political stripe have, since Marx, been critical of the kind of unplanned "development" that typically occurs when the entrepreneurs and their political friends are given their head. Marx, however, was careful to distinguish between the effect of unhampered capitalist progress in a thoroughly "bourgeois" environment, such as nineteenth-century America, and the very different results of the same process when let loose in a country like Russia; and although this distinction is customarily blurred in Communist propaganda, it is crucial to the understanding of Communist tactics. While Western writers monotonously repeat that Marxism has no relevance to situations different from that of nineteenth-century England,[30] the Russian Marxists and their successors—the present rulers of the Soviet Union and China—have developed that side of Marx's theorizing which

[30] Cf. Eugene Staley, *The Future of Underdeveloped Countries*, Harper and Brothers, New York, 1954; Chapter 6, pp. 102 *sqq.*

emerged from his profound study of Russia's political and social disintegration during the last stages of the tsarist regime.[31] The point emerges with considerable clarity from a letter of his to a Russian Populist Socialist prominent during the period when industrialization in Russia got into full stride and the prospects of unhindered "development" seemed eminently fair to bankers, businessmen, and orthodox economists:[32]

On the other hand, the appearance of the railway system in the leading capitalist states allowed, and even forced, states where capitalism was confined to a few summits of society, to suddenly create and enlarge their capitalist superstructure in dimensions altogether disproportionate to the bulk of the social body, carrying on the great work of production in the traditional modes. There is, therefore, not the least doubt that in those states the railway creation has accelerated the social and political disintegration, as in the more advanced states it hastened the final development . . . of capitalistic production. . . .

Generally, the railways gave of course an immense impulse to the development of foreign commerce, but this commerce in countries which export primarily raw produce, increased the misery of the masses. Not only that the new indebtedness, contracted by the governments on account of the railways, increased the bulk of imposts weighing upon them, but from the moment every local production could be converted into cosmopolitan

[31] Cf. his correspondence with N. F. Danielson in the late 1870's and early 1880's, and the lengthy drafts for his letter to Vera Zasulich of March 8, 1881, first published in full by Ryazanov, in *Marx-Engels Archiv*, Vol. 1, Frankfurt am Main, 1926. Since it has become the fashion to assert that the Russian Revolution developed contrary to all Marxian prognostications, it may be as well to restate, what is indeed known to all competent scholars, namely, that Marx expected its outbreak, and predicted its general course, from the 1870's onward. The point is relevant because present-day Communist thinking is still to some extent guided by Marx's repeated assertion that the posthaste industrialization of a backward agrarian country, under the political and social conditions prevalent in tsarist Russia, was bound to result in catastrophe.

[32] Marx to N. F. Danielson, April 10, 1879 (*Ausgewählte Briefe*, Berlin, 1953, pp. 375-6).

gold, many articles formerly cheap, because invendible to a great degree . . . became dear and were withdrawn from the consumption of the people, while on the other hand production itself, I mean the special sort of produce, was changed according to its greater or minor suitableness for export, whereas formerly it was principally adapted to its consumption *in loco*. Thus, for instance, in Schleswig-Holstein agricultural land was converted into pasture, because the export of cattle was more profitable, but at the same time the agricultural population was driven away. All the changes very useful indeed for the great landed proprietor, the usurer, the merchant, the railways, the bankers and so forth, but very dismal for the real producer!

It is . . . impossible to find real analogies between the United States and Russia. . . . In the former the concentration of capital and the gradual expropriation of the masses is not only the vehicle but also the natural offspring (though artificially accelerated by the Civil War) of an unprecedented rapid industrial development, agricultural progress, etc.; the latter reminds you rather of the times of Louis XIV and Louis XV, where the financial, commercial, industrial superstructure, or rather the façades of the social edifice, looked (although they had a much more solid foundation than in Russia) like a satire upon the stagnant state of the bulk of production (the agricultural one) and the famine of the producers.

This warning against the potentially disastrous effect of superimposing industrialization upon primitive economic foundations has not lost its relevance after seventy-five years. While the fantastic disproportions created by Stalinist planning in Russia necessitate the totalitarian apparatus of repression, the problem clearly presents itself in a different form in those backward countries, whether European, Asian, or Latin American, where modernization is going forward on capitalist lines; but at bottom it is the same. And whereas Communism can at least claim to have accelerated the rate of growth to an extent comparable with the achievement of *modern* capitalism in western Europe and the United States

—though at a cost these more fortunate countries have been spared—there is nothing to suggest that market forces can by themselves overcome the stagnation of the "backward" areas properly so called, while there is every reason to believe that uncontrolled "development" may in fact produce social results akin to those witnessed in late-nineteenth-century Russia. As between the market and the plan, the former functions with maximum effectiveness only in a social milieu of a very special kind. Where "bourgeois society" has not prepared the ground for it, the industrialization drive tends to bog down, or to accentuate the social tensions of a disintegrating precapitalist milieu. Because Communism—as a doctrine and as a movement—has arisen from a breakdown of precisely this kind, it is comparatively well equipped to cope with similar situations elsewhere, while the feebleness of the current Western response stems in the last resort from a commitment to policies whose inadequacy is veiled by grandiose but vague talk about "development" and "technical aid." Implicit in this kind of talk there is an assumption that, given the requisite economic impetus, the social milieu will look after itself. But this is not so; taken by themselves, market forces do not promote *modern* capitalism, any more than they help to strengthen liberal democracy (or democratic socialism, for that matter). In quarters not wedded to the naïve economic determinism of the school, this is beginning to be realized. Thus Mr. Averell Harriman, in the article already quoted, is at pains to emphasize the need for simultaneous advance along the whole front:[88]

One always comes back to the necessity for a high rate of economic growth in the free world, accompanied by measures designed to assure that that growth shall result in social advance-

[88] *Foreign Affairs*, Vol. 32, No. 4, pp. 531-32.

ment and satisfaction, political stability through democratic institutions, and national dignity and strength. This last point is important. History shows that rapid economic growth in itself does not necessarily produce stable democratic societies. Unless economic growth is accompanied by growth of democratic attitudes, methods, and institutions, as well as social justice, the result may not be an asset to free-world strength. The West has much to offer to underdeveloped countries in the way of assistance that will increase the likelihood of over-all development along solid democratic lines.

Even this is rather too optimistic a view. As matters stand, the West has little to offer except the hope of economic expansion in the United States as an essential precondition of world expansion—a point rightly stressed by the same author.[84] The institutional difficulties in the way of economic development in backward countries today are much greater than they ever were in the West. "In viewing the economic history of Europe in the nineteenth century," it has been said by an economic historian,[85] "the impression is very strong that only when industrial development could commence on a large scale did the tension between the pre-industrialization conditions and the benefits that may be expected from industrialization become sufficiently strong to overcome the existing obstacles and to liberate the forces that made for industrial progress." Yet Europe was far better prepared for this kind of transformation than most of the countries now subjected to the competitive pull between East and West. Bourgeois society was fully developed, and liberal democracy with it. Russia was the great exception, and even in Russia there was a close race between the

[84] *Ibid.*, p. 532: "With ten per cent of the free world's population, the United States accounts for more than half its combined gross national product."

[85] Alexander Gerschenkron, "Economic Backwardness in Historical Perspective," in *The Progress of Underdeveloped Areas,* ed. Bert F. Hoselitz, University of Chicago Press, 1952; p. 9.

forces making for "normal" progress and those which rejected the Western pattern. The Russian case, in fact, exemplifies one of the most important lessons of the whole
catastrophic period through which we have been passing:

> To break through the barriers of stagnation in a backward
> country, to ignite the imaginations of men, and to place their
> energies in the service of economic development, a stronger
> medicine is needed than the promise of better allocation of
> resources or even of the lower price of bread. Under such con-
> ditions even the businessman, even the classical daring and
> innovating entrepreneur, needs a more powerful stimulus than
> the prospect of high profits. What is needed to move the moun-
> tains of routine and prejudice is faith—faith, in the words of
> Saint-Simon, that the golden age lies not behind but ahead of
> mankind.[86]

Such faith is not easily kindled by reliance upon market
forces or by the liberal ideology that sufficed for the enter-
prising middle class of nineteenth-century Europe and
America. Whichever way one looks at it, the coming of the
industrial revolution is bound to subject the backward
countries to an ordeal unparalleled in the comparatively
gradual and organic development of our own society.
Whether they will turn East or West for guidance must
depend in large degree upon our awareness of this fact.
One thing is certain: as long as freedom is identified with
"free enterprise"—*i.e.*, with the untrammeled rule of market forces—no amount of propaganda will halt the march
of totalitarianism.

[86] Gerschenkron, *op. cit.*, p. 23.

7: *The Poverty of Nations*

It is necessary to stop and pause here, in order to ask what is meant by "backward countries." The term has occurred several times already in this discussion and will inevitably occur again; yet its meaning is clearly disputable, according to whether one applies social or economic criteria. There is the further difficulty that countries may seem backward to themselves, *i.e.*, to their more ambitious citizens, without necessarily being so from a more general viewpoint.

Is backward synonymous with "underdeveloped" or "undeveloped?" It is the fashion to assert this, but there are logical difficulties in the way, even if the discussion is restricted to economic life, and every suggestion of "cultural backwardness" is ruled out.[37] It is clear that no one would refer to "backward resources," though some writers might be tempted to speak of "undeveloped people." The current fashion is to lump "human" and "natural" resources together, and to describe as "backward" or "undeveloped" any country which has not achieved the fullest use of the potential wealth it is assumed to possess. Yet "underdevelopment" of natural resources and "backwardness" of people are entirely distinct phenomena; in fact, some countries inhabited by "backward" people are also notoriously overdeveloped from

[37] Cf. H. Myint: "An Interpretation of Economic Backwardness," *Oxford Economic Papers,* June, 1954, Vol. 6, No. 2, pp. 132-64. It is perhaps unnecessary in this context to discuss the theoretical status of the absurd term "underprivileged," which seems to have been invented for the express purpose of bringing rational argument to a stop. Whatever may be said, "privilege" is not an economic but a social category, and even in the social sphere its importance in the modern world is rapidly dwindling. With the exception of film stars, hereditary noblemen and Hindu Brahmins, there are precious few genuinely privileged groups of people left.

the viewpoint of their inadequate natural resources. Moreover, economic development may well aggravate social
backwardness. ". . . the problem of economic backwardness
in many countries has been made more acute, not because
the natural resources have remained 'underdeveloped,' but
because they have been as fully and rapidly developed as
market conditions permitted, while the inhabitants have
been left out, being either unable or unwilling or both to
participate fully in the process."[88] This is typically the case
in colonial development and it constitutes one of the most
serious charges against the imperialist system; but in principle it is an ever-present danger where the impact of market
forces is not corrected by the community. National governments anxious to stimulate private (foreign) investment can
stand comparison with any colonial administration in their
proved capacity for inflicting the maximum possible harm
on the people under their control; for under *laissez-faire*
such investments will typically tend to be concentrated in a
few extractive industries working for export, leaving the
native population to make whatever adjustment it can. In
some important cases, e.g. over most of southeast Asia, this
adjustment has taken the form of a rapid growth in numbers,
thus adding the new phenomenon of "overpopulation" to the
already deplorably long list of calamities associated with
"backwardness." Some of these countries initially started
from sparse populations which swelled to their present
unmanageable dimensions after they had been "opened up";
partly because their death rate fell, and partly because there
was additional demand for unskilled labor in some specialized lines of production whose profits went abroad or were
monopolized by the ruling oligarchy.[89]

[88] Myint, l.c., p. 135.
[89] It is not of course denied that in some countries overpopulation may
be a genuine cause of backwardness; in others progress is clearly hampered

It should be evident from these examples that the "underdevelopment" approach cuts at right angles across the discussion of "backwardness." The latter is both a social and an historical phenomenon, while "underdevelopment" is at best a criterion for the discussion of optimum allocation of capital resources. Such criteria are necessarily abstract, and the kind of technological enthusiasm that derives from the gospel of maximum development of "natural and human resources," has something lifeless and repellent about it. In comparison with the appeal made by national-social movements within a "backward" community striving for the harmonious development of the (frequently very inadequate) resources at the disposal of people struggling with their environment, it bears all the familiar hallmarks of a neoliberal "managerial" ideology for the elect.

If there is no simple definition of backwardness, it is even more difficult to state exactly what constitutes "development," if one omits to take account of the relative position of a given country within the world economy. Attempts to define such concepts in isolation from the total world picture are bound to result in paradox:

Taking the words literally, there is the obvious interpretation of underdeveloped—that natural resources have not been developed to the full extent possible. The greatest of all natural resources is land, and there are parts of the world, in the Yangtze delta for example, where the produce of a single square mile is sufficient to support several thousand human beings. There are some parts of India where a rural density of 1000 a square mile prevails. Can we possibly class such lands as underdeveloped,

---

by lack of population rather than by excess. In any case the real question is why in "backward" countries the population has in the past grown without a corresponding rise in productivity, while the Western nations have managed to absorb a huge population growth alongside a sharp rise in productivity and living standards.

though the people may live in conditions approaching misery, handicapped in every direction by poverty?

Well-farmed European lands support one person or more an acre, 640 or more to the square mile; yet lands we think of as "developed" by our modern Western methods, in the U. S. A., Canada, and Argentina, produce only enough food on a square mile to support some 200 or 240 persons. On the basis of output per acre we find the familiar mid-latitude or temperate lands of North America amongst the most underdeveloped lands in the world.[40]

Output per unit area is not, of course, the only possible test of "development" or "efficiency," but in a world short of food it seems natural to regard the actual amount of food produced as the criterion of economic progress. On this assumption, the United States, Canada, Argentina, and Australia, in their capacity as wheat producers, are a long way behind Denmark, Holland, Belgium, and Britain, if one regards output per acre (with some allowance for quality) as the test of productivity.[41] The same applies, as we have seen, if the standard of measurement is the ability of a given area to support the maximum number of people. The irrelevance of such technological criteria to an understanding of present world tensions becomes evident when one learns that, on a comparative basis and using computations based on output per acre of nine representative crops, a list compiled for 1946 showed Belgium, Denmark, Holland, New Zealand, Britain, and Ireland at the top, followed by *Egypt*, Germany, the United States, France, Canada, Argentina, China, Italy, Japan, Spain, India, and Australia![42] The prominent place here occupied by Egypt with its intensive monoculture, the juxtaposing of China and Italy, and the

[40] L. Dudley Stamp, *Our Undeveloped World*, London, 1953, p. 19.
[41] Stamp, *op. cit.*, pp. 90-92.
[42] *Ibid.*, p. 95.

presence of Australia among the "also-rans" reflect the deliberate omission of all save purely technological criteria—and even in this respect the approach is defective, since it treats input of labor as immaterial compared with output per unit. In fact, the relative success of Egypt, China, and the monsoon countries of southern Asia in making food available for large numbers of people is due to the unexampled intensity with which the land is worked, an intensity that probably reaches its highest level in the more favored parts of China. This unremitting activity, this constant expenditure of almost the entire available quantum of human labor (that of women and children included) upon the primary task of growing a minimum of food to sustain the population, may be "efficient" in some abstract sense, but in social terms it comes very close to being the reverse.[43]

[43] "What strikes the observer, of course, is the unceasing toil, the never-ending slavery, of the work involved" (Stamp, *op. cit.*, p. 96). Cf. also John Marlowe, *Anglo-Egyptian Relations 1800-1953,* Cresset Press, London, 1954; pp. 256-57: "It is on the benefits and advantages of perennial irrigation that Great Britain's contribution to Egypt must primarily be judged. . . . It is doubtful whether either Mohammed Ali's French engineers or the British engineers who followed them realized the far-reaching consequences that were to spring from perennial irrigation. They saw only increased efficiency, increased productivity, increased wealth. . . . There were other things which they did not see. They did not see that the perennial fructifying presence of water on the land set a veil between the land and the cleansing power of the sun, which dried out the basin lands during the season of low Nile. They did not see that the continual cropping made possible by perennial water would exhaust the soil and make its continued fertility dependent on the application of ever-increasing quantities of artificial fertilizers. . . . They did not see the ravages of the bilharzia snail, which the perennial water brought to nearly every village household in Egypt. They did not foresee the debilitating effect of a change from a usually dry climate to a perennially damp one. . . . As it was, Egypt was saddled with social and technical problems with which she was unable to deal. . . . It is difficult to escape the conclusion that what might be termed the bookkeeping approach to the rehabilitation of Egypt resulted in increasing wealth for the few, accompanied by increasing misery for the many." Here the usual consequences of "development" under the control of market forces were intensified by foreign influence and pressure, the combined result being a great deal worse than anything a native despotism would have been

Even if one starts from the fact that two-thirds of the world's population are still engaged in the production of food (for the most part inadequate even for the needs of the immediate producer), there is something appalling about the picture presented by the more backward countries. Yet within its own terms the Asian system is rational—more rational than is realized by efficiency experts who contend that the present world food output could be maintained with the use of far less labor. In North America, where land is abundant and labor expensive, such a viewpoint appears natural, but economy in manpower would not by itself solve the problems of India, Japan, Indo-China, or Java; for here it is land that is scarce and human labor that is plentiful. The short-run effect of mechanization would, therefore, be to aggravate rural unemployment, destroy what remains of the village community, and probably bring about a social explosion. The problem of simultaneously increasing yields and absorbing surplus manpower has by now impressed itself upon the consciousness of Asian governments, largely owing to fear of the Chinese example being followed. Its solution is, however, blocked by social and institutional obstacles that may yet prove strong enough to bring about another cataclysm on the scale of China's. In the meantime most of these countries have become net importers of food, while the world's hope for better farming supplies is coming to rest increasingly upon the genuinely "underdeveloped" areas—Canada, the U. S. A., and Argentina. It is here, if anywhere, that agricultural surpluses can still be tapped through the application of modern methods and without a ruinous expenditure of labor per unit. Here, too, popula-

---

able to accomplish. It is this kind of pattern which supplies the critics of colonial imperialism with their most telling arguments—provided they are not content with facile denunciations of foreign control, but are willing to probe beneath the political surface.

tions are still rapidly growing,[44] though considerably less fast than national wealth. Thus, instead of looking to the overpopulated and climatically handicapped countries of tropical and subtropical Asia for a dramatic increase in yields and living standards, we had best resign ourselves to the thought that these regions will, at most, manage to subsist at a somewhat less inhuman level, and that they may (if we are not careful) disappear behind the Iron Curtain. The opportunity (and the responsibility) of making significant progress in supplying the human family with basic necessities lies not with the "teeming millions" of Asia, but with the advanced nations of the West.[45] All this need not in

[44] "Owing to the much higher survival rate, the American population is growing at a faster rate than India's 'teeming millions.' The addition of 19 millions from 1940 to 1950 in the U. S. A. is at the rate of 1.36, against India's 1.26 or Pakistan's 0.75" (Stamp, *op. cit.,* p. 27). In absolute figures, of course, the Indian population growth has been immense, and in view of India's poverty this growth constitutes one of her chief problems. In 1951 the combined population of India and Pakistan was estimated at 437 million, and by 1981 it may well pass the 520 million mark (cf. *Financial Times,* London, February 26, 1954). Even so, there is nothing particularly remarkable about the *rate* of growth.

[45] "If we take the actual cultivated area of Canada at 90 million acres, and presume this to be capable of the same level of production as northwestern Europe, Canada could support 90 million people instead of 14. On the same basis, the existing farmlands in the U. S. A. could easily support 500 million people, and Russia perhaps treble the present 200 million" (Stamp. *op. cit.,* p. 181). Compare this with the following statement: "The plain fact . . . is that India began to be a net importer of food about 1921. . . . We have already seen that cultivation per capita has declined by twenty per cent in the last twenty years, and in the quinquennium ended 1952 arithmetical considerations would have implied an import of 10 m. tons of food grain annually. Shri Gopalaswami explains the fact that imports did not reach this level by saying that 'when population grows in number in conditions of growing food shortage, the average level of consumption does tend to fall.' In other words, many people in the towns are forced to eat less than they used to" (*Financial Times,* London, February 26, 1954). The writer's conclusion is that Indians must learn to practice birth control, while simultaneously stepping up production. He does not indicate whether he believes the present government of India to be adequate to this twofold task. Food production has indeed risen in recent years, and Mr. Nehru's slogan, "self-sufficiency in 1952," seemed close to realization two or three years later, with the help of some unusually good harvests. But it must be borne in

principle conflict with the viewpoint of the "underdevelop-ment" school. It is true that its spokesmen continue to lay great stress on the expected rise in the world demand for primary products, especially raw materials.[46] But no one knows better than they that the primary producers are not identical with the "underdeveloped" areas, just as the latter cannot simply be equated with the "backward" countries. "The industrialized nations actually produce more primary products than the underdeveloped nations do, and their total exports of such products bulk somewhat larger in international trade. . . . The underdeveloped economies may properly be referred to as 'the primary producers' only in the sense that a disproportionately large share of their total economic effort is devoted to the production of foods and industrial raw materials."[47] It is rather a substantial "only."

Taking the term "underdeveloped" in its crude sense, to refer to the non-industrialized countries of Latin America, Southern and Southeastern Asia, the Middle East, and

---

mind that "effective demand" is held down by poverty. That India has recently been able to dispense with food imports says little about the way in which her people are being fed.

[46] Cf. Stacy May, "Folklore and Fact about Underdeveloped Areas," *Foreign Affairs,* January, 1955, Vol. 33, No. 2, pp. 212-224. "Upon a reasonable estimate from past trends, we can say that the free world consumption of industrial raw materials may increase from about 46 billion dollars in 1950 to about 80 billion (at 1950 price levels) by 1975-80. The international trade in these commodities may increase from about 27 billion dollars to about 50 billion in the same period. Such an increase in consumption should afford presently underdeveloped areas an opportunity to increase their combined production of industrial raw materials from the 14.5 billion dollars of 1950 to something like 31.5 billion within 25 years, and their exports in this field from 13.5 billion dollars to about 28.5 billion. Increases of this magnitude, almost double the expected population increases, would exert a markedly stimulating effect upon the underdeveloped economies." (p. 223) They might also, as has been suggested earlier, result in a unilateral growth of the dollar area at the expense of other industrialized countries, though that is no reason for regarding the basic trend as unfortunate.

[47] Stacy May, l. c., p. 217.

Africa, with a total population of about one thousand
million human beings, we find, still according to the same
author, that in 1952 the United States, Canada, and Western
Europe drew 50 per cent of their combined imports of
industrial raw materials and 48 per cent of their imports of
crude foodstuffs from these regions,[48] while the latter obtained about 90 per cent of their "Western" foreign exchange
earnings from this trade.[49] This gives the measure of
the interdependence between the industrial and non-
industrial segments of the non-Soviet world, though it is
worth noting that the former produced over two-thirds of
that "world" 's total of raw materials, and its industries
processed more than 90 per cent of the free world total. Still
retaining the same definition of what constitutes "underdevelopment," the areas commonly so described in 1952
provided outlets for one-third of North America's and Western Europe's combined exports.[50] There is thus every reason,
strategy apart, why the West cannot afford to be indifferent
to their political fate. In this manner one is led back to the
cold war and the prospect of "peaceful coexistence," and one
begins to suspect that coexistence will be anything but
peaceful if the West fails to provide the kind of leadership
that will maximize not just "development" in general but
all-round economic and social "development." Although
political and economic considerations are inextricably interwoven at this point, the red thread of state control ("socialism") is clearly discernible. From the strictly economic
standpoint, two considerations are worth mentioning:
(1) there has already been enough experience with United
Nations and United States technical-assistance programs

[48] *Ibid.*, p. 213.
[49] P. 217.
[50] P. 212.

to show that technique by itself can do very little without massive capital investment, which in the nature of the case must come from the West—or be raised internally by the dictatorial methods made familiar by Soviet experience; (2) such investment cannot, in the main, be private. If provided by the West, directly or through the United Nations, "aid" must take the form of direct grants to public authorities, if only to obviate a new cycle of imperial colonization and nationalist rebellion. But there are also solid economic grounds for avoiding reliance upon private capital, whether local or foreign: in poor and static societies, where habits are fixed and margins over subsistence small, the classical doctrine that investment generates its own demand may still be true in the long run, but not in the short; and we are here concerned with runs of at most one or two decades. In the short run, the individual entrepreneur can only conform to the prevailing trend, which in backward countries favors investment in unproductive enterprise, or in a few undertakings that have ready-made markets in countries already developed—*e.g.*, oil extraction. This form of "enterprise" does not assist general progress.[51]

For reasons which should no longer constitute a mystery to the non-specialist, this point is of crucial importance to an understanding of the peculiar political tensions associated with the "development" of "backward" countries. Given the fact that all the "underdeveloped" regions will tend to diversify their economies—and the reasonableness of this aim is not disputed even by the most resolute defenders of

[51] The now familiar "vicious circle" of poverty and stagnation is most fully discussed in *Problems of Capital Formation in Underdeveloped Countries*, by Professor Ragnar Nurkse, Oxford University Press, 1953. Cf. also K. Mandelbaum, *The Industrialization of Backward Areas*, Oxford, 1945.

global specialization[52]—the investment rate is bound to assume a quite crucial importance. The chief problem in the theory of economic development, it has been pointed out, is to understand how a community which traditionally saved and invested 4 or 5 per cent of its income, steps up this rate to 12 or 15 per cent.[53] How this is done is more often than not a mystery to the economist, but it is quite clearly the central element of what is called "development." It is generally conceded that the rapid accumulation of capital (including industrial skills) depends on a sudden sharp rise in savings relatively to national income, and that the major source of such savings must be profits of one kind or another, the great majority of people in a pre-industrial economy being too poor to do any significant saving. This issue gives rise to many delightful social and psychological problems, not excluding attempts to define economic growth in terms of national "character." But in general, it is admitted that the stagnation prevalent in an economy of this type must be broken by a particular kind of economic action at some point.[54] The question what it is that breaks the deadlock in backward countries properly so called has puzzled economists and sociologists for years, and may well continue to form a bone of contention. But it can be assumed that, given some understanding of the economic mechanism involved, those in charge of the destinies of a backward

[52] Stacy May, l. c. p., 224. "They should exploit these advantages to increase the initial processing stages of raw materials in their own countries, and thus promote industrial development in the field where they have the clearest competitive advantage. . . . Above all, they should use the increased foreign exchange earnings obtainable in this field to buy the equipment needed to broaden their domestic industrial base."

[53] Cf. W. A. Lewis, "Economic Development With Unlimited Supplies of Labor." *The Manchester School of Economic and Social Studies,* May, 1954, Vol. XXII, No. 2, pp. 139-191.

[54] Nurkse, *op. cit.,* p. 10: "Economic progress is not a spontaneous or automatic affair. On the contrary, it is evident that there are automatic forces within the system tending to keep it moored to a given level."

country will under present-day conditions try more or less energetically to set the process in motion. For practical purposes this means trying to expand the non-subsistence sector of the economy, *i.e.*, the capitalist sector (including such elements of state capitalism as there may be).[55] Inflation may be used to help the process along, *i.e.*, to bridge the monetary gap until profits (or government receipts, as in the USSR) have risen so much relatively to national income that they are adequate to finance the new rate of investment. At a somewhat later stage the national income may be imagined to have grown sufficiently for the new rate of savings to be compatible with a rise in living standards, but during the interim period the real income of all classes outside the expanding capitalist (or state capitalist) sector is clearly bound to suffer a rather drastic shrinkage.

Now it is evident that in the real world of conflicting social purposes these abstractions can come to life only via the most drastic kind of political surgery.[56] This has been true even in Western Europe, although the "industrial revo-

[55] Cf. Lewis, l. c., p. 159: "If we ask, 'why do they save so little?', the truthful answer is not 'because they are so poor,' as we might be tempted to conclude from the pathbreaking and praiseworthy correlations of Mr. Colin Clark. The truthful answer is 'because their capitalist sector is so small.' . . . If they had a larger capitalist sector, profits would be a greater part of their national income, and saving and investment would also be relatively larger. (The state capitalist can accumulate capital even faster than the private capitalist, since he can use for the purpose not only the profits of the capitalist sector, but also what he can force or tax out of the subsistence sector.)"

[56] At this point modern post-Keynesian theory leaves us in the lurch. Cf. Lewis, 1 c., p. 139-40: "The classics, from Smith to Marx, all assumed, or argued, that an unlimited supply of labor was available at subsistence wages. They then inquired how production grows through time. They found the answer in capital accumulation, which they explained in terms of their analysis of the distribution of income. . . . Given the Keynesian remedies, the neo-classical system comes into its own again. Hence, from the point of view of countries with surplus labor, Keynesianism is only a footnote to neo-classicism—albeit a long, important and fascinating footnote."

lution" there took place in a comparatively slow and organic fashion. It has been demonstrated with startling clarity in the case of Japan during the past century, and it is of course a commonplace of political discussion throughout Asia, the Middle East and Latin America at the present time. For our purpose we need merely note that the problem subdivides itself neatly into a choice between following the example set by the USSR (where the government during the formative period raised the investment rate from about 5 to about 20 per cent, mainly through artificial price inflation, *i.e.*, deliberate depression of the national income of all classes), or trying to develop an indigenous capitalist class. The latter is clearly a social rather than an economic problem. The ruling groups of a pre-industrial society—landlords, merchants, moneylenders, soldiers, officials, priests—do not normally show entrepreneurial ability, or willingness to invest in industry. The case of Japan is an interesting exception to a general rule whose disagreeable effects are now giving much concern to Western policy-makers. Excluding the Communist solution the governments of backward countries are thus typically confronted with the problem of stimulating capitalist progress in the absence of a genuine capitalist class, a situation which leads to a good deal of rather half-hearted talk about "socialism" as a "middle way." In fact for all their socialist pretensions, which are frequently forced on them by the need to mobilise labor's political support against the representatives of the old regime, their real problem is to stimulate industrial growth—against the resistance frequently of merchant and middle-class elements more interested in speculation than in investment, and more inclined to import expensive American consumer goods than to expand domestic output. So far as self-interest goes, only the industrialists can be relied upon to use their profits for the purpose of constantly expanding production; but industrialism by itself is too bleak a gospel to make an appeal to the mass of people in "backward" or "underdeveloped" countries, whether governed in totalitarian fashion or (more or less) democratically.

Thus in the end the political issue impinges in the most direct manner upon the problem of capital formation, and it does so all the more urgently in proportion as the necessary capital has to be raised from peasant economies (governments able to tax large foreign holdings in mining or plantation farming are somewhat better off). Clearly there are political and psychological advantages attached to any program that effectively links capital accumulation to wider economic and social aims; and it may be suggested that under modern conditions nationalist regimes with a strong socialist flavoring are the ideal instrument of the "industrial revolution." But this is not quite the same as to say that socialism can become a "third force," or that its adoption will enable the governments of backward countries to evade the fundamental choice between Communist and democratic methods of political control.

CHAPTER VI

THE PATTERN OF CONFLICT

1: *East Against West*

WE HAVE NOW REACHED a point in this discussion where something like a coherent view of the Communist phenomenon becomes possible. The picture at first sight is puzzling. Here is a revolution originating in a relatively backward country that effectively challenges Western civilization in its strongholds; a totalitarian structure with quasi-Fascist features that still derives its ideological inspiration from the October Revolution; a society which is neither capitalistic nor, in the hitherto accepted sense, socialist; lastly, an expansion into backward, preindustrial regions, accompanied by a simultaneous threat to the political institutions of the industrialized West. The list of paradoxes could be extended almost ad infinitum; some of them are doubtless traceable to the intermediate position occupied by Russia, both geographically and culturally, between East and West: a central location that has made Communism what it is, since it has enabled the movement to assail Europe and Asia simultaneously. But for its expansion to take place, though at an uneven rate, in industrial and preindustrial societies alike, a common factor must be at work, over and above the influence radiating from the U. S. S. R. We know that Communist parties are now able to exploit the internal crises of an industrial democracy, though their successes in this field cannot as yet compare with those of European Fascism in the thirties; and it requires no proof that Communism is on the march in Asia. This realization that a movement originating from the 1917 upheaval in Russia has by now successfully adapted itself to East and West alike is at the bottom of the current panic about the survival of free institutions. For if Communism can supply a political framework for China and simultaneously present a genuine challenge to the democratic institutions of countries like France and Italy, there would seem to be no inherent limit to its expansion. A system that functions as a kind of ersatz capitalism in the most backward parts of Asia, and at the same time claims the inheritance of socialism in Europe, is as baffling as it is unprecedented; and one cannot altogether blame its theorists for proclaiming that history itself is on their side.

Yet reflection tells us that history—like liberty, fraternity, and equality—holds no such magic. History, as Marx was fond of pointing out, does nothing; and the fact that present-day Communists have, in this respect at least, strayed from the narrow path of orthodoxy is no reason why we should follow their bad example. Let us rather try to isolate the factors that have enabled Communism to transform itself into a world movement. The sheer impact of the Russian Revolution, although considerable, does not offer a satisfying explanation, for the peculiar combination of circumstances that made the 1917 combustion possible had no counterpart in any other country, European or Asian: the spontaneous "permanent revolution" of which Trotsky dreamed had to give way to Stalin's "permanent revolution from above" before Communism could become an effective challenge in East and West. This suggests a pointer to our problem, for we have seen that the essence of "revolution from above" is state control, and since Asian nationalists, no less than European revolutionaries, have shown themselves anxious—though for different reasons—to make such use of the concentrated power of the state machine, it is at any rate not surprising that they should have been attracted by the Soviet example. The crisis through which European democracy passed in the thirties was intimately bound up with the need to strengthen the state in an epoch of mass unemployment and unsolved social conflicts. But this same need was and is vastly more urgent in countries on the threshold of the industrial revolution: countries saddled with the *damnosa hereditas* of centuries of poverty and neglect. For all its bizarre terminology and the almost Byzantine atmosphere of its homeland, Communism is thoroughly modern in its acceptance of the world-wide drive toward economic planning. Barbarous in its methods and retrograde in its political and cultural physiognomy, it yet participates to some extent in a general movement that, under totally different conditions, raises the most subtle and intricate problems for a fully developed democratic society. Experience has shown that if the solution of these problems is inhibited, dissatisfaction with a "way of life" too glaringly divorced from reality can manifest itself in responses varying from indifference to outright rejection of the established order. No modern country, not even the United States, is immune to this challenge, but it is infinitely more unsettling in societies whose archaic structure is being shaken by the impact of industrial revolution. Hence the rapid advance of Communism in those backward countries which during and after the First World War were exposed to the full blast of European and American influence. For here the social framework crumbled at a time when the West stood plainly for *laissez-faire,* while Communism offered a new social integration. Here, too, the foreground was occupied by the typical colonial nationalist movement against imperialism, which also happened to be a movement against Western control. The situation was made to order for the new policies emanating from Moscow since the twenties; or, rather, the Asian stirrings complemented the upheaval in Russia, whose edge was likewise turned against the West: principally against Britain and the U. S. A.

Thus, there were all the elements of a Communist synthesis for Asia, at least a decade before Moscow was compelled to reckon with the far more baffling and complex problem of competing with the Fascist movements in Europe. As early as 1919, Trotsky had suggested to the Politburò that the road to Paris and London might run via Kabul and Bombay.[1] Ten years later the temporary defeat of Chinese Communism appeared to have blocked this approach; but the issue had merely been postponed. By 1949 the road was open once more—principally because the Kuomintang had lost control of a "bourgeois" revolution whose aims, as every Communist knew, could only be the classical nationalist ones of industrialization and intensive state control. Lenin's strategy of imposing Communist leadership upon an agrarian revolution had triumphed once more, this time in a social milieu far more backward than that of tsarist Russia; and because it had triumphed the West was henceforth excluded from a vast

[1] Cf. I. Deutscher, *The Prophet Armed,* Oxford University Press, 1954; p. 457.

region in which its interests had traditionally clashed with Russia's. At this point the integration of Soviet and Communist aims becomes, as it were, organic. That the whole of China would move into the Soviet sphere because Bolshevism had at one time worked out the strategy of controlling national-revolutionary movements was perhaps not fully expected even by the Soviet government. Yet when the landslide took place its results accorded perfectly with the forecasts made in an earlier and more optimistic phase of the Revolution.

It is of interest to compare Lenin and Stalin on this subject, because the events anticipated by the one have so largely had to be directed and controlled by the other. In his last piece of writing, the essay entitled *Economic Problems of Socialism in the U. S. S. R.*, Stalin devoted several pages to the seemingly irrelevant subject of the Second World War and its effect on the world market. "The disintegration of the single, all-embracing world market," according to him, "must be regarded as the most important economic sequel of the Second World War and of its economic consequences. It has had the effect of further deepening the general crisis of the world capitalist system." He then adds that the war "was itself a product of this crisis," and the general drift of his argument is to the effect that "capitalism"—*i.e.*, the world beyond the Soviet orbit—has entered a downward cycle, of which its territorial contraction is both cause and effect. The system, he thinks, is no longer developing, as it still was during and after the First World War, albeit by way of crises and conflicts; it has now entered a phase of stagnation and decay, most clearly reflected in its growing inability to find external outlets.

But it follows from this that the sphere of exploitation of the world's resources by the major capitalist countries (U. S. A.,

Britain, France) will not expand but contract; that their opportunities for sale in the world market will deteriorate, and that their industries will be operating more and more below capacity. That, in fact, is what is meant by the deepening of the general crisis of the world capitalist system in connection with the disintegration of the world market. This is felt by the capitalists themselves, for it would be difficult for them not to feel the loss of such markets as the U. S. S. R. and China. They are trying to offset these difficulties with the Marshall Plan, the war in Korea, frantic rearmament, and industrial militarization. But that is very much like a drowning man clutching at a straw (p. 36).

It seems probable that in publishing what was in effect his political testament, Stalin was deliberately linking up with Lenin's parallel (March 4, 1923) analysis of the prospects of the "two camps" after the first world upheaval.[2] Addressing the party for the last time through the medium of *Pravda*, Lenin in 1923 tried to lay down the general line of advance for the coming epoch, and in so doing gave the first clear formulation of the "two worlds" concept that was thereafter to become characteristic of Communist thinking:

At the same time, precisely as a result of the last imperialist war, a number of countries—the East, China, India, etc.—have been completely dislodged from their groove. Their development has definitely shifted to the general European capitalist lines. The general European ferment has begun to affect them, and it is now clear to the whole world that they have been drawn into a process of development that cannot but lead to a crisis in the whole world of capitalism.

Since Lenin in 1923 held that not only India but China had fallen under Anglo–U. S. control, this conclusion may seem startling, but he was of course convinced that the impact of industrialization under bourgeois *laissez-faire* direction would hasten the explosion. A few lines further on, he

[2] Cf. V. I. Lenin, *Selected Works*, London, 1947; Vol. II, pp. 844-55.

observes: "Precisely as a result of the first imperialist war, the East has been definitely drawn into the revolutionary movement, has been definitely drawn into the general maelstrom of the world revolutionary movement." The argument culminates in the well-known passage:

In the last analysis, the upshot of the struggle will be determined by the fact that Russia, India, China, etc., account for the overwhelming majority of the population of the globe. And it is precisely this majority that, during the past few years, has been drawn into the struggle for emancipation with extraordinary rapidity, so that in this respect there cannot be the slightest shadow of doubt what the final outcome of the world struggle will be.

The Soviet Union, however, cannot afford to remain inactive while confronting the hostility of the "west European counter-revolutionary states."

To ensure our existence until the next military conflict between the counter-revolutionary imperialist West and the revolutionary and nationalist East, between the most civilized countries of the world and the Orientally backward countries, which, however, account for the majority, this majority must become civilized.

That is to say, it must assimilate the technology of the West. Having done so, the "revolutionary and nationalist East" (the choice of phrase is instructive) will ally itself with the U. S. S. R. In 1923 Lenin did not dare forecast a Communist revolution in India or China, and his analysis is correspondingly more cautious in tone than Stalin's thirty years later. Yet he was convinced that the coming struggle between "imperialism" and "revolution" would resolve itself into a straight issue between the West and the East; this remarkable certainty throws a good deal of light on the intellectual antecedents of Bolshevism. It also explains why the Comintern saw no inconsistency in advising the Chinese Communists to join the Kuomintang, after the joint Sun-Joffe declaration of January, 1923, had affirmed the basic unity of purpose linking the Russian and Chinese revolutions. Whatever Trotsky might say (especially once Lenin was no longer there to pull him up), the alliance with Asian nationalism against "Western imperialism" was sound Leninist strategy.

It has never been easy for Western politicians and publicists to understand this kind of thinking, or to realize that it represents a genuine innovation. For the Bolsheviks, 1917 was a turning point in the history not only of Russia but of the world: it marked the defection of a major country from the world-wide capitalist nexus, and thereby opened up possibilities of development in Asia that the U. S. S. R., thanks to its geographical location, was well placed to exploit. In Communist thinking there is no distinction between internal and external politics, any more than between the political and economic spheres. The world revolution is an organic whole. At the political level it manifests itself in the East-West split, but this is due to the fact that the East is undergoing a social transformation for which the Russian Revolution sets the obvious example. Conversely, the loss of these gigantic markets must hasten the decline of the West, accentuate its internal crises, and enable the Communist movement to win power in Western industrial countries, at any rate to the extent that the Soviet Union is able to neutralize the political pressure exercised by the U. S. A. If the struggle should result in a third world war, the latter's probable outcome is suggested by the fact that the "camp of socialism" has the bulk of the globe's population behind it. After all, the "revolutionary and nationalist East," even where it is not Communist, cannot help sympathizing with the U. S. S. R. in its struggle to break the hold of the "imperialist West."

There is in all this an intricate mixture of fact and fancy, shrewd theorizing and illogical extrapolation, which is by no means easy to disentangle. Considerable harm has been done in recent years by naïve attempts to discredit "Communist imperialism," as though it were only necessary to stand a cliché on its head for the whole nationalist movement in Asia (and not only in Asia) to adopt a different orientation. The immense upheaval of the Chinese Revolution has in some quarters been treated as the consequence of a "conspiracy" by disgruntled Chinese intellectuals, or disaffected State Department officials, to bring Mao Tse-tung to power, and even at a somewhat higher mental level there is confusion about the manner in which Communism and nationalism tend to interlock. Because this subject has become so important, and because so many irrelevant or misleading theories about it are in circulation, it may be useful to start *ab ovo* by asking what it is that Communist doctrine itself postulates, and to what extent its tenets are in harmony with the facts.

2: *Nationalism and Revolution*

IT IS ONE OF THE MANY oddities of the contemporary situation that the whole subject is still for the most part discussed in terms of Lenin's now outmoded doctrine of nationalism, which the Stalinists no longer take seriously, although the Soviet government maintains it for internal use: principally as a weapon against the latent separatism of non-Russian nationalities. In its pure form, Leninism implies a distinction between the "natural" emotion of patriotism and the "bourgeois" concept of sovereign nationality. To be exact, Lenin, and subsequently Stalin (at any rate, in his essay on the national question [1913], which was probably in part written by Lenin himself), identify the emergence of the national consciousness with the destruction of precapitalist forms of society, the establishment of an economic nexus between people speaking the same language, the disappearance of regional autonomy—in short, the triumph of market forces over "simple commodity production," and the consequent rise of the bourgeoisie to social and political power. This notion was culled from Marx, and then given a characteristic twist, for Marx was, of course, aware that there are other sources of national consciousness—*e.g.*, participation in a common historical enterprise. It was one of his pet ideas that the French nation dated only from the French Revolution, and that Germany would have to undergo a similar democratic upheaval in order to acquire national unity and a national consciousness. In the original Marxian concept, democracy and the nation are thus two sides of the same reality. The nation constitutes itself in the act of the democratic revolution—*i.e.*, in the struggle to achieve political liberty and self-government. It follows that societies which have not gone through this phase cannot be classed as "nations," though they may have all the attributes of "national" sovereignty. Thus, Hohenzollern Germany was not fully a nation, although the national elements in its make-up were more important than in the case of the Hapsburg or Romanov empires, which had to cope with "national" minorities. To become a nation, Germany had to become a democracy, a process whose stages have accompanied us since 1918. The economic nexus linking people of the same language and culture is merely a precondition of national self-awareness, as is the existence of a

political frontier, which in any case (viz. Belgium, Switzerland, Canada) may include different ethnic and linguistic
groups. What really determines the fusion of such groups
into a nation is always a historical event, and in modern
times the principal determinant has been the democratic
revolution, in the course of which the masses of the people
acquire that political consciousness which was formerly the
privilege of a small ruling class. In this sense, democracy
and nationalism are one.

This whole concept, which clearly stems from the Jacobin
interpretation of the French Revolution, was so natural to
Marx that he hardly troubled to expound it systematically.
He took it for granted, and it was only at a later stage that
Marxists began to inquire how this doctrine stood in relation to the economic process that was the other side of the
bourgeois-democratic revolution. At this point, the "bour-
geois-revolution" concept acquires that ambiguity of meaning which has enabled modern Communist theorists to
disseminate so much semantic confusion. For Lenin the
nation is on the whole an authentic product of the capitalist
stage of development, a thesis faithfully parroted by Stalin
in the dreary polemical exercise already mentioned, on
which his fame as a theorist rests. There are occasions
(especially in his writings after 1917) when Lenin simply
equates the nation with the bourgeoisie, while the proletariat
incorporates socialist internationalism; just as there are
other times when he operates with the old democratic
national concept inherited from Marx and from the socialist
tradition generally.[8] It is useless trying to establish what
Lenin (and Stalin) "really" thought about nationalism, for
after 1917 they found themselves compelled to deal with

[8] Cf. his article "The National Pride of the Great Russians," *Selected
Works,* Vol. 1, pp. 626-30.

a situation which no one had foreseen, least of all themselves. But it is important to realize that neither of them had envisaged the case of a "proletarian" revolution as a result of which the Russian people would acquire a modern national consciousness. Yet this is precisely what happened. It was bound to happen, for once the masses had entered the political stage it became impossible to bind them to the state without at the same time giving them a sense of their own destiny. Soviet nationalism, like the republican-democratic nationalism of France after the Revolution, stems from this elemental need of hitherto passive and illiterate strata for common symbols and a common way of expressing themselves. As in the France of the 1790's, the first hurried attempts of the revolutionaries to provide such symbols were revised at a later stage, when the intellectuals who had led the movement were replaced by actual representatives of the new society. Thus, Trotsky's attempt to enshrine the "proletarian internationalism" of the utopian period of 1917-23 forever in the formal oath of the Red Army proved as short-lived as the republican internationalism of Saint-Just and Carnot. Yet the subsequent reaction did not go all the way: the red flag and the myth of the October Revolution as a proletarian upsurge had to be incorporated in the new integration, if the regime was to have any coherent ideology at all. The result, typically, was a compromise: internationalism disappeared, but Soviet nationalism took on some of the messianic and utopian characteristics of the formative period. Soviet culture ("national in form, socialist in content") became the symbolic expression of a new stage in the forward march of all mankind. That this "forward march" could on suitable occasions be equated with the triumphal advance of the Soviet army into regions still in need of liberation from capitalist and imperialist fetters made the new

doctrine eminently serviceable from the Kremlin's viewpoint, but did not alter its character. Like the Jacobins a
century and a half before, the Bolsheviks unwittingly created
a nation in the process of trying to abolish nationalism. They
now had to lead it, and it is scarcely surprising that the outcome brought an adaptation to traditional moods and concepts. Stalin's speeches during and since the "Great Patriotic
War" of 1941-45 are the best example of how this synthesis was effected—and the best possible comment on his
earlier attempts to prove that nationalism is a phenomenon
that arises and disappears with the capitalist epoch of
social history.

Had the process stopped at this point, the parallel with
Jacobinism would be complete. That it did not stop here was
due to the impact of the Russian Revolution on Asia and
its failure to have a corresponding effect in Europe. Thus,
the "proletarian" socialist component vanished very quickly,
and with it the doctrine of socialist internationalism and the
utopian attempt to raise the consciousness of the Russian
masses to the height attained by a handful of intellectuals
before 1917. On the other hand, the Soviet government and
the Comintern now found themselves confronted with huge
opportunities in Asia that required a different approach.
Broadly speaking, the situation called for a revival of the
earlier elements of Leninism, notably Lenin's old thesis that
in so far as it was a peasant movement the "bourgeois revolution" could be steered into antibourgeois channels. In the
mid-twenties the Bolshevik leadership was still hamstrung
by Trotsky's doctrinaire (and entirely un-Leninist) insistence on public proclamation of "proletarian dictatorship"
as the only possible instrument of revolution; but once this
obstacle had been got out of the way, it was not long before
Bolshevik strategy began to pay dividends in the backward

countries. It is true that the really impressive gains came
only after the U. S. S. R. had become a great power; but
the foundations were laid at an earlier stage, and where
Moscow still proved hesitant, the local Communist leadership might go further in developing the tendencies inherent
in Leninism beyond the point which the Comintern still regarded as orthodox. Thus, Mao Tse-tung inaugurated a
new epoch in Communist strategy by carrying matters to
the stage of leading a classical peasant insurrection against
the towns.[4] This was so well in accordance with Chinese
tradition that not only naïve Western observers, but even
lifelong Communists were for a time in doubt whether the
Chinese party could keep its original character. Bolshevism
had never been a labor movement in the generally accepted
sense of the term, but it had always had a hard core of labor
support; when Mao Tse-tung dispensed with this qualifica-
tion he was genuinely breaking new ground. The orthodox
view was that the peasant movement could be brought to
the point of making a Communist dictatorship possible, provided there was a nucleus of urban workers out of whom a
Communist party could be formed. In China that nucleus
was almost totally lacking, but its place was taken by the
intelligentsia, whose role was far greater even than in Russia:
a consequence of China's backwardness and semicolonial
status, and the resulting strength of the revolutionary drive
among classes other than the proletariat. Once the masses
were set in motion there was no force that could stop them,
and the task of setting them in motion could be shouldered
successfully by Communists who at first differed from other
revolutionary nationalists only on points that appeared to

[4] Trotsky's characteristic comment on this innovation was that revolutionary movements had hitherto taken Paris, rather than the Vendée,
as their model: a remark that showed how little he realized the potentialities of the new totalitarian age, particularly in Asia.

both sides to be secondary. Kuomintang and Communist
leaders stemmed from the same social milieu, shared the
common anti-Western and anti-imperialist bias, and during
the early stages of the movement, up to 1927, seemed to
differ only over the extent to which "the revolution" ought
to be pushed.

The situation today in other Asian countries is not fundamentally different, although the contrasting development
of China and India has introduced a new issue. Even those
nationalists who reject the Communist solution do so because they believe that "the revolution" can prosper without it. "The revolution" itself is never questioned, even
where it has already occurred and led to disappointments.
It is the common bond linking all factions of the movement,
the only unifying symbol possible at this stage. There is little
profit in inquiring whether such-and-such a political leader
is primarily a nationalist "or" a Communist. Nationalism
can be conservative, liberal, democratic, or totalitarian, de-
pending on the circumstances; it can be Communist or
Fascist. Tito is a nationalist, and so is Franco. Mao Tse-
tung is certainly a nationalist, and the Chinese Communist
movement as a whole is more profoundly national (in the
worst sense of the term) than the Kuomintang, with its
roots in the westernizing business community, ever was.[5]
Yet what really matters is not the ideology of this or that

[5] Cf. Professor George E. Taylor, in *Annals of the American Academy
of Political and Social Science*, September, 1951. Professor Taylor does
indeed doubt the genuineness of the Chinese Communist party's nationalism, but he lays due stress on its conformity to the very Chinese tradition
of rule by a privileged bureaucracy. "The Chinese Communist party . . .
is the ghost of the Middle Kingdom, sitting crowned on the grave
thereof." What is this but another way of saying that the regime is in
harmony with "national" tradition? It is true that, on our own assumption, China before the revolution was not a nation in the Western sense,
but that is another matter. Cf. also Professor Karl Wittfogel in *Review
of Politics*, Notre Dame, Indiana, October, 1954.

group, but the fact that nationalism is a necessary concomitant of "the revolution"—using that term in the broadest sense to signify the entry of the masses into some sort of political life, whether under Communist or democratic leadership. When it is borne in mind that this process is quite independent of the political direction given to the movement by the competing leadership cliques at the top, the fact that Communist parties have found it possible to integrate themselves into the national-revolutionary movement becomes less of a puzzle. The real driving force of the whole process, as Lenin pointed out long ago, is the peasantry; and the peasantry is the "national" class par excellence. This point is worth some elaboration.

3: *The Role of the Peasants*

IT HAS LONG BEEN a commonplace of Communist theorizing—although it still appears to be a closed book to most Western students of the subject—that Lenin's strategy, before and after 1917, was intimately linked with his changing views on the agrarian question. Unlike Trotsky and the Mensheviks, Lenin had around 1905 developed a strategy based on the assumption that a radical democratic (but nonsocialist) revolution in Russia was possible if the peasant movement obtained adequate leadership from "the workers," that is, from his own party. Thus, the "bourgeois revolution"—bourgeois in the sense that its aim was not socialism, but a *modern* form of capitalism within a republican-democratic setting—would temporarily take place under "proletarian" leadership. The resulting paradoxes did not worry him, and he consistently refused to trouble himself about Trotsky's "permanent-revolution" concept, which assumed that under Russian conditions the "bourgeois revolution" would lead straight to a socialist dictatorship. This attitude was closely bound up with his insistence on the central role of the peasantry in the coming upheaval. The agrarian movement, he thought, would facilitate the establishment of a democratic republic, and at the same time open the road for a much more rapid development of capitalism (he occasionally spoke of the need to substitute an "American" form of capitalist development for the "Asian" conditions characteristic of tsarist Russia). In sum, the democratic revolution had to be carried to its furthest possible limit, if only because there was no other way of really setting the peasant masses in motion:

> The peasantry is capable of becoming a wholehearted and most radical adherent of the democratic revolution. The peasantry will inevitably become such, if only the progress of revolutionary events, which is enlightening it, is not interrupted too soon by the treachery of the bourgeoisie and the defeat of the proletariat. Subject to this condition, the peasantry will inevitably become a bulwark of the revolution and the republic, for only a completely victorious revolution can give the peasantry everything in the sphere of agrarian reforms, everything that the peasants desire, of which they dream, and of which they truly stand in need (not for the abolition of capitalism, as the Social-Revolutionaries imagine, but) in order to emerge from the mire of semiserfdom, from the gloom of oppression and servitude, in order to improve their living conditions as much as it is possible to improve them under the system of commodity production.
>
> Moreover, the peasantry is drawn to the revolution not only by the prospect of radical agrarian reform but by its general and permanent interests. Even in the struggle with the proletariat, the peasantry stands in need of democracy, for only a democratic system is capable of giving exact expression to its interests and of ensuring its predominance as the mass, the majority. The more enlightened the peasantry becomes . . . the

more consistently and determinedly will it favor a thorough-going democratic revolution; for, unlike the bourgeoisie, it has nothing to fear from the supremacy of the people, but, on the contrary, can only gain from it. A democratic republic will become the ideal of the peasantry as soon as it frees itself from its naïve monarchism, because the deliberate monarchism of the bourgeois brokers (with an upper chamber, etc.) implies for the peasantry the same disfranchisement and the same down-troddenness and ignorance as it suffers from today, only slightly glossed over with the varnish of European constitutionalism.[6]

Thus, the program was, at the time of writing (1905), held within the limits of radical democracy, and the reason why so much stress was laid on "proletarian" (*i.e.*, Social-Democratic) leadership of the movement was fear of "bourgeois treachery"—*i.e.*, the nonexistence of a *republican* group among the bourgeois liberals. But this emphasis did not in the least signify that the coming revolution would be anything but "bourgeois" (in the Marxist sense):

The bourgeois nature of a democratic revolution expresses itself, among other things, in the fact that a number of classes, groups, and sections of society, whose stand is based entirely on the recognition of private property and commodity produc-tion, and which are incapable of going beyond these bounds, are led by force of circumstances to recognize the inefficacy of the autocracy and of the whole feudal order in general, and join in the demand for liberty. The bourgeois nature, however, of *this* liberty, which is demanded by "society" and advocated in a flood of words (and words only!) by the landowners and the capi-talists, is manifesting itself more and more clearly. At the same time the radical difference between the struggle of the workers for liberty and the struggle of the bourgeoisie, between prole-tarian and liberal democratism, becomes ever more obvious. The working class and its class-conscious representatives are marching in the van of the struggle and urging it forward, not

[6] Lenin, "Two Tactics of Social-Democracy in the Democratic Revolu-tion," *Selected Works*, Vol. I, pp. 414-15.

only without fearing to carry it to completion, but aspiring to go far beyond the uttermost limits of the democratic revolution.[7]

The point here, which is truly crucial for the understanding of the whole Bolshevist movement and its victory in 1917, is that liberalism and socialism, bourgeoisie and proletariat, are viewed as factors helping or hindering the "democratic revolution"—*i.e.*, an intermediate process of which the peasantry was expected to be the chief beneficiary. It is true that Lenin's tactics were elastic. In 1917 he virtually adopted Trotsky's position, but only after he had become convinced that "proletarian dictatorship" was necessary to make an end of the old order. Put somewhat schematically, the issue that confronted him from 1905 onward was whether the power of the landowners could be broken without breaking that of the bankers and industrialists as well. In 1917 it might seem for a moment that "democracy," in Lenin's sense of the term, had arrived; but the Provisional Government drew back. Its recoil from the essential task of making peace and giving the land to the peasants (which would have constituted the main items of the "bourgeois revolution") convinced Lenin that it was in fact impossible to strike at the landowners without breaking the power of the entire capitalist class. Thus, the "democratic" and the "socialist" revolution had to be telescoped, after all. This was the real sense of the Bolshevik party's "reorientation" after April, 1917, for until that moment Bolshevism had always refused to commit itself to anything beyond a democratic republic and a radical land reform. The underlying continuity was, however, preserved, for Lenin had always insisted that the party must go at least as far as was necessary to mobilize the peasantry. If, contrary to previous expectations, that involved shifting from a democratic to a socialist revolution,

[7] Lenin, *ibid.*, pp. 433-34.

he was ready to take the plunge. In social terms, if the bourgeoisie insisted on saving the landowners, they would both have to go simultaneously. The outcome might be chaotic, but nothing mattered, provided the "democratic revolution" was pushed as far as it could go. That the real driving force behind it was the peasantry Lenin never doubted for a moment.

This Leninist doctrine on the peasantry's role in the "democratic revolution" became the common property of all Communist parties after 1917, and in particular of the Communist parties in Asia. To imagine that Communism can ever truly become a democratic peasant movement is of course absurd, and to the extent that such notions may have played a part in confusing Western policy during the later stages of the Chinese civil war, their originators laid themselves open to justified charges of naïveté, if nothing worse. But it is no less mistaken to treat the Communist attitude toward the peasants as a mere stratagem. The fact is that the radical undercurrent of agrarian movements in backward countries has become a firmly integrated part of the entire Communist attempt to revolutionize their social structures. The motivations that animate the peasants are not simply faked or caricatured by the Communists in order to gain recruits in the countryside: they are the "mass basis" of the kind of Communism that has struck roots in countries like China, Indo-China, and Indonesia. Communism in Asia is, among other things, a revolutionary agrarian movement; just as it is, among other things, an anti-Western ("anti-imperialist") one. Owing to the backwardness of Asian society, compared with early-twentieth-century Russia, the genuinely democratic and the Communist-totalitarian strands of the movement against the old order are so closely interwoven that even the capitalist and entrepreneurial core

of the middle class—in other words, the industrial bourgeoisie—can to some extent be drawn into the revolutionary
ranks. This became manifest when the Chinese Communist
leadership began to distinguish between the "national bourgeoisie" and that section (the "compradors") which had
"entered the imperialist camp."[8] The consequent fostering of
a "national" form of capitalism under state control at first
struck some Western observers as a hopeful sign that the
regime was on the way to recognizing the merits of the
"mixed economy" and that it might in time lose its totalitarian character. The hope was groundless, for Communism,
being genuinely totalitarian, can manipulate *all* classes of
society without losing control of the state. Its dynamic is
strong enough to override class and sectional interests—
including, perhaps, even the peasant's interest in private
ownership of his plot of land—and while this state of
affairs lasts the regime can identify itself in turn with
every section of society, if it so chooses. Thus, Mao Tse-
tung's party in the thirties migrated from the towns to the
centers of agrarian unrest, and has now returned to the
great cities, where it was born. Thus, too, the regime won
over a section of the intelligentsia, which, after all, started
the whole national movement half a century ago. It is, of
course, strong among the industrial workers, but not because
it "represents" them; it represents nothing and nobody but
itself.

But if Chinese Communism was firmly rooted in the
Bolshevist tradition, it also inaugurated new developments
of its own. Chief among these was an awareness that the
political awakening of the countryside could be turned into
a powerful vehicle of the national-revolutionary movement.

[8] Cf. Mao Tse-tung, *Selected Works,* Lawrence and Wishart, London,
1954; Vol. 1, *passim.*

Here, the Russian example was less conclusive, for the October Revolution had been launched under internationalist slogans addressed to the Russian and west European working class. By contrast, Chinese Communism, as soon as it had emancipated itself from the leading strings of the Comintern—*i.e.*, after the 1927-28 catastrophe—worked out its own tactics, which were based on the fullest exploitation of the peasant movement in its two principal aspects: agrarian revolution and patriotic hostility to foreign oppression, then largely typified by Japan. The subsequent internal history of the world Communist movement has been profoundly affected by the discovery that Communism can come to power on the broad back of the peasant movement, even if there is no "revolutionary proletariat" to speak of; but no less significant was the parallel realization that the peasants respond to patriotic appeals, and that those who want to win their confidence must above all legitimize themselves as defenders of the homeland. Peasant movements are patriotic, and consequently a stimulant to the nationalism of the towns—*i.e.*, the urban middle class. To win power, Communism in Asia thus had to absorb not merely the urban nationalist movement, but the peasant movement as well. In effect they turned out to be two sides of the same reality.

It does not require much perspicacity to understand why this is so. The clue is provided by the word "homeland," for which other interchangeable expressions—*e.g.*, "fatherland," "motherland," "national soil," etc—may be substituted at will. Patriotism is fundamentally an expression of peasant mentality. This statement can only seem surprising to urban intellectuals who have lost the feeling of attachment to one's plot of land and substituted the much paler and more ideological concept of loyalty to the nation, the flag, or the state. The emotional patriotism of the peasant is profounder and more elemental than that. He really means it when he says that he is prepared to die for his bit of soil, and he readily extends this sentiment to the community, provided its symbols are such as to hold his loyalty. No other class has quite this naïve and untroubled relationship to the "country" (in both senses of the term), which is as good a reason as any why peasants or farmers make better soldiers than townspeople: always provided they are not given the impression (as the Russians were in 1914-17) that their interests are being recklessly sacrificed to incomprehensible aims. As long as he can identify his piece of land with the "country" in general, the peasant remains the backbone of every national movement and every national army, even if the ideologies of the city-bred leaders of the movement are strange to him. Of all the absurdities perpetrated by Communist theorists, which Communist organizers since 1917 have slowly and painfully had to correct, none surely has been more remarkable than the misunderstanding reflected in the phrase "bourgeois nationalism." Not that the bourgeoisie is incapable of nationalism; but its patriotic emotions, even at their strongest, are only pale echoes of the elemental passion welling up from the countryside, once its inhabitants have learned to identify their land with "the land." This process of identification, of course, is precisely what every national movement is about.

Because the rural population is emotionally dependent on symbols relating to the land, any movement that satisfies its social cravings can count on being able to channel its energies into a nationalist direction. This is the reality underlying the familiar statement that patriotism and democracy go together. Once again the French Revolution supplies a convenient example. As everyone knows, the movement reached the democratic stage because the Jacobin leadership was willing to go through with drastic measures benefiting the peasantry; having passed through this phase, it promptly acquired a "national" character, complete with war against France's neighbors. There was nothing in the original psychology of Jacobinism—a typical offshoot of the Enlightenment—to presage the democratic and patriotic rage of 1793-94. The upheaval simply reflected the sudden irruption of the urban and rural masses upon the political stage. The same thing happened in Russia after 1917, and more recently in China. The difference lies in the fact that while the Jacobins were overwhelmed by the sudden release of popular energies, their successors had worked out an appropriate instrument of control. Robespierre and Saint-Just had no totalitarian party machine at their disposal, and could be overthrown by a coalition of hostile forces in the Convention. If one ignores the dramatic circumstances of the time and the lavish use made of the guillotine, their fall was indeed merely the first of a long series of ministerial crises. The French parliamentary system was still in its infancy, and all concerned were excessively ready to employ violent methods; but in principle the mechanism whereby unpopular political leaders are eliminated had already been worked out. The threatening experiment in totalitarianism was cut short, and France obtained its first view of a parliamentary crisis and its uses. At this point the political power of the liberal bourgeoisie seemed to have been consolidated, but the army still had to be reckoned with, and so had the readiness of the peasants, in and out of uniform, to back a military dictator who safeguarded their newly gained possessions, and then led them all over Europe to defeat the enemies of "the revolution"—*their* revolution. The story is well known; its only relevance in our context is a reminder that agrarian revolutions typically release popular energies which an expansionist government can put to good use.

France, however, had no national problem within its borders, and so the example remained untypical. It took another century of political change, this time in central and eastern Europe, before the link between agrarian unrest and nationalism disclosed itself in all its fullness. For obvious reasons, Austria-Hungary supplied a particularly good field for experimentation. In Hungary, at any rate, the land question and the national question were one: the Hungarian Constitution before 1918 excluded the peasants, whether Magyar or Slav, from voting rights, and the Slovak, Rumanian, Croatian, and Ruthenian minorities were additionally subjected to "national"—i.e., cultural—oppression. The effect was to turn the emerging peasant parties into advocates of a national-democratic revolution. Since the towns were the seat of a ruling class that coincided with an alien "master race," the cultural dissociation became so great that the entire political and social structure fell apart. Pre-1918 Hungary was an extreme case, but similar conditions existed all over eastern Europe. They helped to promote both the war of 1914-18 and the subsequent wave of revolutions, and when the new nationalist regimes after 1919 proved unable to cope with the problem of rural poverty and overpopulation, a new cycle of political disturbances set in, this time characterized by competition between Fascist and Communist movements. The east European regimes established in the wake of the 1939-45 war have emerged from Communist parties that had gone through this cycle and evolved techniques of winning and holding power in predominantly peasant societies. They had not, however, at any time obtained the backing of more than a minority of the peasants, a circumstance which set them off sharply from the Communist-dominated national-revolutionary movements in Asia.

It is only in China and some of its borderlands that Communism has become fully integrated with a revolutionary national movement which is also a peasant movement. That is was able to do so was largely due to the previous impact of Western and Japanese domination, but the automatism of the economic process "at the village level" would in any case have caused the old social structure to burst apart. Communism merely profited from a situation brought about by the triumph of unregulated market forces. This factor is still insufficiently understood, but the broad outlines are not particularly mysterious. What happens in essentials is that, as the self-contained village community breaks down under the impact of modern technology, communications, taxation, conscription, and radio, the peasant forms a mental image of a country-wide peasant community which, for him, is the nation. If this process is hastened by agrarian upheaval, and the mental contours rendered sharper and clearer by foreign control—a more palpable object of dislike than the traditional rulers within one's own community —a situation may arise that an active minority can exploit to impose its own leadership. If this minority consists of Communists, the Communist party will dominate the movement, and Western observers will wonder how such a thing could happen, and how it squares with either "true" Communism or "true" nationalism (which by definition is "bourgeois"). This shows the inconvenience of being guided by Leninist textbooks. As against such naïve complaints it is sufficient to note that modern Stalinist doctrine describes national and social "liberation from imperialism" as a task to be carried out by the Communist party—itself no longer defined by its status within the international labor movement,

but by its fidelity to the Soviet Union (or the Chinese example) and the "teachings of Stalin" (or Mao). These teachings, it is true, are still for scholastic purposes related to a
wider corpus of doctrines suggesting that nationalism as such
is doomed to disappear with the bourgeois epoch; but that is
all. Orthodox Leninism (now proscribed in Russia as a
counter-revolutionary heresy and branded as the invention
of the archfiend Trotsky) is certainly no longer a guide in
the political field where Communist direction of national-
revolutionary movements is concerned. The fact is that,
although they are still hag-ridden by an inadequate and
outmoded doctrine, the Stalinists have gradually worked
themselves free of their doctrinal straitjacket and found a
way to synthesize peasant aspirations and national sentiments, as their opponents have not. Hence Vietminh; and
hence the Chinese Revolution.

It follows that attempts to play off nationalism against
"international Communism" must be viewed with skep-
ticism. As we have seen, nationalism in an agrarian milieu
is itself a revolutionary movement, being an aspect of the
countryside's political awakening. This truth has gradually
dawned on most Communists, while Western writers and
policy-makers—influenced perhaps by scraps of Leninist
doctrine acquired during their student days—have ridden
off in the wrong direction. "Bourgeois nationalism" is a
mirage; in so far as it exists it is unimportant. The notion
that nationalism "in itself," or *überhaupt,* can be mobilized
against Communism, *without being given a social content
and political direction,* is one of the numerous illusions to
which the political strategists of the cold war have fallen
victim. The submerged rural populations of backward
countries must inevitably make their political debut in national dress, but it does not follow that their national senti-

ment is devoid of social content. It has a very definite revolutionary edge, directed against the beneficiaries of the social order prevalent in a backward precapitalist milieu: landowners, usurers, merchants and officials, the latter existing primarily for the purpose of protecting the former. It is consequently useless to preach moderation and conservatism to the national movement of a backward country, or to beat the bushes for "safe" nationalist dictators who will respect established property rights. Regimes of this kind are no bulwark against Communism, for whatever else Communism does, it certainly causes the landowners to disappear; and that, to the peasants, is a blessing worth many tribulations.

These truths are in no way contradicted by the well-known phenomenon of rural conservatism. The very circumstance that the peasantry is the repository of society's oldest traditions makes it such an irresistible force once it is set in motion. Its archaic cast of mind becomes an asset to revolutionaries intent on giving a national character to the movement, although it also acts as a brake on the further development of the revolution. Since society has a past as well as a future, this interplay of conflicting tendencies at the height of a revolutionary crisis is hardly surprising. Ultimately it makes possible the reaction that is an essential part of every revolution, though it usually takes the leaders by surprise. The latter are normally by origin and upbringing somewhat remote from the peasant roots of national tradition. These roots reach back into archaic levels of folklore, behavior, and consciousness which are irksome and frequently repellent. Yet a completely urbanized society is conceivable only on the supposition that all links with the past are broken off—an evident absurdity, since a community of this kind would no longer constitute even the nucleus of a nation *in posse*. Resistance to tendencies promoting such a development forms the core of what is sane and healthy in conservatism, but it is fantastic to suppose that attachment to the past and to traditional folkways is *per se* a guarantee against revolutionary upheaval. In one way or another all political movements in a settled society draw upon the fund of traditions stored away in the collective consciousness, and the deeper they dig the closer they necessarily come to the rural sources of technology and culture. But this is merely another way of saying that the peasants have it in their power to give Communism a distinctly "national" character, and no one who has troubled to read the excruciatingly dull, but very instructive writings of Mao Tse-tung can doubt that in China this has in fact occurred.[9]

It is equally futile, and even more dangerous, to suppose that the democratic cause can benefit in the slightest degree from attempts to shore up the crumbling sociocultural framework of traditional Asian society. Thus, for example, the authoritarian family has for centuries been the keystone of all social arrangements in the East, and its dissolution is a precondition of gradual democratization in the political and

[9] Compared with Mao, even Stalin must rank as an original and penetrating thinker. It is the more important to stress this point because a conspiracy of silence has been allowed to develop on the subject of Chinese levels of thinking, whether the protagonists are in the democratic or in the totalitarian camp. Yet the simplest honesty compels the statement that contemporary Chinese writing, with a few obvious exceptions, is above all characterized by its naïveté. This of course facilitates Communist penetration a good deal more than Western counterpropaganda, since Soviet Marxism has already been filtered through the conceptual sieve of a comparatively primitive mentality. Intellectual achievements that seem unimpressive to us—*e.g.*, Lenin's quasiphilosophical writings—may have a powerful impact on minds not acquainted with the Western tradition of thought. Though Lenin was within a national tradition (that of the Russian "Enlightenment," typified by writers like Belinsky and Chernyshevsky) which had not evolved a genuinely critical manner of dealing with philosophical questions, even a tract like *Materialism and Empirio-criticism* displays a certain competence. One has only to compare it with Mao Tse-tung's naive little essay *On Practice* to realize that Russia stands in the same relation to contemporary China as the West does to Russia.

educational fields. In so far as Communism—in common
with liberalism and democratic socialism—furthers this disintegration, it is merely hastening a process which is long
overdue and which the younger generation in particular is
eager to complete. Yet, reputable organs of opinion in the
West have been found to deplore this state of affairs and to
suggest in all seriousness that the newly emancipated Eastern
nations should be helped to preserve their cultural traditions, which they are anxious to shed and which in most
cases are merely a decorative way of keeping women and
children under patriarchal control. Such sentiments are
naturally welcome to the powerful surviving conservative
and authoritarian elements, for the breakdown of the
patriarchal family releases energies that become available
for the new radical political movements. Nor is this
phenomenon confined to the East. It plays an important part
in the politics and the cultural life of southern Europe, from
Italy and Spain to Greece and Yugoslavia, much as in the
nineteenth century it did in France. If Communist parties
have unfortunately gained a disproportionate foothold in
some of these countries, a major root of their success
must be sought in their radical rejection of petrified cultural patterns, and in the corresponding timidity and half-
heartedness of competing democratic movements. To repeat
this disastrous experience on an even larger scale in the
East would be the best way to drive the more active and
intelligent members of the younger generation into the
totalitarian camp.[10]

[10] It is curious how little systematic attention has been given to this
subject. For an illuminating remark on modern Greece, see W. H. McNeill,
The Greek Dilemma, London, Gollancz, 1947; pp. 63-64: "EAM drew
much of its force from the fact that it appealed to the youth and
women of Greece. . . . Traditionally, in Greek society the father had
unchallenged control over the members of his family, and the place of
women was (and is) far lower than in the countries of western Europe

4: *The Communist Synthesis*

AT THIS POINT in our discussion we
may pause to ask what it is that has enabled Communism
to provide a synthesis of all the forces let loose by the collapse of traditional Eastern society. Some aspects of the
process have perhaps become a little clearer. We have seen
that in backward or agrarian countries—the terms are
interchangeable—nationalism is an aspect of the countryside's political awakening and that the recognition of this
fact is Communism's contribution to modern sociology. It
has also become evident that, like most discoveries, it was
made by accident: as Soviet and Comintern policy after
1917 collided with opponents in East and West, it was
gradually borne in upon the Kremlin that its best chance
lay with the exploitation of the anti-imperialist movement
in Asia. To Marxists it was obvious that this movement was
linked to the unrest caused by the dissolution of the self-
contained village economy and the impact of market forces
upon traditional society. Doctrinal evolution proceeded
slowly, but has now reached the point where Communism
has come to symbolize national and social awakening
throughout large regions of Asia. So far there is nothing very
surprising about the course of events, except perhaps that
the opponents of Communism should have behaved quite

. . . emancipation attracted many women, and they became among the
most fanatic EAM supporters. In general one may say that the development of EAM broke down the peasant family system of values and dis-
ciplines which had previously been dominant among the working classes
of the towns." The reverse side of this picture is the familiar clerical-
authoritarian complaint that the family, as well as the social order
generally, is menaced by "atheistic socialism and Communism." Such
sentiments are common to the clergy of most Roman Catholic countries
and they help to explain why some of these countries are plagued with
disproportionately large and virulent Communist movements.

so foolishly as they did. What still needs to be explained is
how the organizational model of Communism—the totalitarian state-party—was gradually fitted into the context of
national movements whose immediate aims were very far
from being revolutionary in the Communist sense. The
answer leads straight to the root of the whole Communist
problem. Presumably it is for this reason that entire libraries
have been written to obscure it.

The victory of Bolshevism in 1917 has made the world
familiar with the phenomenon of an elite of "professional
revolutionaries" becoming the core of a party that proved
capable of overthrowing a modern state. This could not
have been done by a democratic movement, however
broadly based. A movement of that character, whether
liberal, socialist, or "agrarian," would have been amenable
to class—*i.e.*, sectional—pressures which every dictatorial
regime must for a time override. It could be done only by
an organization that was already potentially totalitarian. Because the hard core of the Bolshevik party was "classless"
and composed of "professionals" it was able to take control
of the revolutionary mass movement in 1917, and for the
same reason it was able subsequently to establish the first
great totalitarian system in modern history. For the totalitarian political party comes close to being the ideal instrument of revolution. A party of this character is never simply
an expression of class interest. It arises from an interpenetra-
tion of sectional movements, at the point where their circumscribed activities are reflected, condensed, and syn-
thesized in the emergence of an entirely new and unprecedented factor standing outside all ordinary sectional conflicts: the nucleus of professional revolutionaries. The intelligentsia, as the only nonspecialist, or omnispecialized,
stratum in society, is the obvious reservoir and recruiting

ground of such groups, but once the "party of the new type" has come into being it ceases to represent the social milieu in which it arose. It represents no one but itself.

That, however, is precisely what enables it to win power and, having won power, to hold it. For this characteristic of indifference to class interests and sectional aspirations is something it shares with another entity—the state. The organization of professional revolutionaries, which on the morrow of its victory transforms itself into the nucleus of a new ruling class, is potentially totalitarian because it is independent of sectional interests. But this independence from, and indifference to, sectional pressures is ideally the chief trait of the state bureaucracy with which the revolution comes into conflict. If the state apparatus were not composed of functionaries whose outlook to some extent transcends sectional limitations, it could not operate at all. Civil servants are public functionaries—their consciousness, that is to say, takes shape at the point of intersection of group conflicts. Thus, the social function of the bureaucracy corresponds to that of the revolutionary elite, whatever their differences in political outlook. Both specialize, as it were, in general activities, and the peculiar *Weltanschauung* they have in common rests on the interrelation of sectional needs and viewpoints, and on the need to synthesize and manage them. Both groups are in consequence able to merge, once the revolution has taken place, in the totalitarian state-party, which thereafter—for all its internal "purges"—combines the stabilizing activity of the one with the revolutionary aims of the other.

This consummation is, however, possible only on condition that the "vanguard" is genuinely classless. A political organization of this type is potentially all-embracing—*i.e.*, totalitarian—only provided its origins are free from the taint of class interest. It can organize the whole of society because it is not organically linked to any part of it. That is its "professionalism," and the secret of its power and attraction. Were it genuinely part of any major social formation —as the Communist party claims to represent the working class—it could not become genuinely totalitarian; it could not, that is to say, become a state-party. For the state to become totalitarian, the party that captures it must have originated from a nucleus of "professional revolutionaries" *and continue to be subjected to its control.* That is why it has to be built from the top downward, and why the ordinary membership has to be excluded from all real decisions. A nucleus of this kind is highly fissionable material, and the eventual explosion can be devastating, as the October Revolution has shown. Building the nucleus and controlling the explosion is a professional job, but the professionals must be revolutionaries with a genuine belief in the importance of their cause. Experience in these matters can to some extent be institutionalized, but the revolutionary will that animates the whole fabric is as impenetrable and inscrutable as any other human motivation. In any event, every Communist party now has before it the image of a successful revolution imposed upon society by force and from above, *after* the capture of power. It is not too much to say that this concept, and the technique for realizing it, represent the central arcanum of Stalinism.

The nature of this challenge is still for the most part masked by the retention of traditional Leninist phraseology belonging to an earlier era. Essentially it rests upon the will to effect a revolutionary short cut from above, and the belief that Soviet experience has shown this to be possible. From the Communist viewpoint this grim vision has the character of an immense discovery: there is no need to accept things as they are! A means lies at hand to change the world as thoroughly as it was to have been changed, according to the older formula, by a victorious popular uprising. Total revolution is still possible, but it must be imposed from above! The managed revolution is the great discovery of Stalinism, its shibboleth, the sign by which the initiated recognize one another. It justifies all the horrors of the interim period, though it also exhausts a good part of the popular energies mobilized in the earlier, more spontaneous phase of the process. It may indeed exhaust them completely, leaving behind an inert mass held together by terror and propaganda alone. But although this is likely to be the eventual outcome, the regime can for some years conserve at any rate part of its original dynamic; and the suggestion may be hazarded that, in a country going through the earlier phases of an industrial revolution, this dynamic is powerfully reinforced by spontaneous processes arising from the operation of the social system itself.

Of the various reactions that this challenge has evoked, the most fruitful has been the search for democratic alternatives to Stalinism; the most sterile a tendency to shelter behind mere force, military or political. This is an age of substitutes, and the scene is crowded with synthetic regimes claiming to be able to satisfy the needs of a society in flux. Dictatorship is at a premium; and it is too often forgotten that most dictatorships are ineffective and short-lived. The Kemalist regime in prewar Turkey and the Titoist in present-day Yugoslavia are exceptions to the general rule, and their effectiveness was and is bound up with their quasitotalitarian character. The Kemalist revolution owed its original impetus to national revolution and to the break with Islam— hitherto a unique phenomenon—and it was carried through by a revolutionary junta that for decades tolerated no rival.

Marshal Tito's dictatorship would collapse if it were not propped up by the Yugoslav Communist party, and heretical Communist movements do not grow on trees. The Yugoslav miracle was an uncovenanted piece of luck, for which Western policy-makers have not ceased to apologize, as though it were something to be ashamed of. They are not likely to suffer a long succession of such embarrassments. It seems far more probable that the West will continue to be deluged with offers of support from conservative militarists, Perónist demagogues, and elderly bed-ridden intriguers in the distinguished succession of Drs. Mossadegh and Syngman Rhee. This is a misfortune, for there is reason to doubt whether a dictatorship not backed by a quasirevolutionary mass movement can nowadays function effectively over a lengthy period.

The cause must probably be sought in the growing complexity of modern society, which makes the task of co-ordination impossibly difficult for an old-fashioned regime of the military or bureaucratic kind. This problem is accentuated if the regime tries to bring about genuine changes—and if it does not, it is doomed anyhow. Revolutionary mass movements, with their organized youth sections, women's sections, and so forth, are indispensable to a central government trying to reach down into deeper strata of the population in order to mobilize popular support for a policy of modernization and reform. It follows that nontotalitarian dictatorships will tend to be socially conservative, while revolutionary regimes will develop totalitarian tendencies. Since social revolution and totalitarianism are alike distasteful to Western opinion, preference is likely to be given to "respectable" dictators who refrain from tampering with established property rights and who do not indulge in the modern practice of setting up as charismatic popular leaders. There is no doubt that governments of this kind are easier to get on with; unfortunately, they are also more likely to be swept away by the next wave of unrest.

It is arguable that under favorable conditions the worst consequences of "revolution from above" can be avoided and some measure of political liberty retained. But it may be as well to recognize that in some countries whose allegiance is important to the West, conditions in this respect are not favorable and will not become favorable for a long time. Apart from the need to mobilize mass support for the regime during a period of rapid social change and considerable economic pressure, there is the problem of building up an efficient state apparatus in countries notoriously backward in this respect. If this is not done under Western control it must be done by a home-grown regime so constituted as to place a premium on efficiency and reduce corruption to a minimum. The appeal of such a streamlined model to revolutionaries in countries ready for a social transformation is necessarily strong, even where Russian influence as such is remote and feeble. This explains why intellectuals and army officers in countries as widely separated from each other, and from Moscow, as Brazil and Pakistan should be liable to the infection. A revolutionary scheme that allots to the elite so important a role is certain to find a welcome where majority rule has not been securely established and for obvious reasons cannot for some time be made to square with social reality. With a slight twist, the party line can be turned into an esoteric doctrine stressing the omnipotence of the state if controlled by a revolutionary organization. The Stalinist amalgam of revolution and despotism thus attracts both the demagogue and the believer in "strong government." There is, of course, in all this an element of self-deception. The privileged Soviet elite, whose status appears so enviable to impoverished Middle Eastern or Latin-American intellectuals and civil servants, is hag-ridden with fears and repressions unknown elsewhere. But this dark side of the moon is invisible to people living in a prerevolutionary society, where an efficient totalitarianism can hardly be imagined. All they see is the promise of rapid transformation, coupled with power for themselves. That the state can be used to turn society upside down and inside out was an empirical discovery made in blundering fashion after 1917, and still half concealed from Lenin and the other leaders of the October Revolution. For the power-hungry intelligentsia of Asia and Latin America it is something like a revelation.

The totalitarian state may horrify liberals and socialist democrats, but it holds a very definite attraction for national revolutionaries in search of an instrument of control. For there is a radical difference between an ordinary old-fashioned authoritarian regime and a genuinely modern, streamlined, totalitarian one, in which the individual is kept under a close double check by his superiors in the party hierarchy as well as in the state. This issue is of crucial importance in societies where poverty, individualism, and an archaic family system have traditionally hindered the creation of an efficient state apparatus. A totalitarian party that does not shrink from challenging deeply rooted traditions (*e.g.*, the individual's primary allegiance to the family clan), and which maintains close control over the daily activities of its members, has the power to break the vicious circle of poverty, bribery, and inefficiency characteristic of a backward country. It may be very disagreeable, but it is a fact that such parties have a considerable advantage where circumstances favor a "revolution from above" and a dictatorial regime to suit it.

For under more liberal conditions the individual is less likely to establish that complete and all-embracing indentification of private and public aims which is the essence of totalitarianism. Every totalitarian party is both an army and a church; but the Communist party, with its cell structure, its rigid hierarchy, and its system of "democratic centralism," is particularly well suited to take over the entire private life of its members. It manages to do so even in countries with a long liberal-democratic tradition; no wonder it spreads like a cancer in societies lacking the kind of voluntary discipline and self-government we have come to associate with our own kind of world. It is all the more effective because, unlike "bourgeois" groups of the Indian Congress or Kuomintang type, it starts from scratch, unhampered by dependence on powerful pressure groups, and is consequently able to insulate its organization from the "masses" whom it claims to represent. Its remoteness from established social relations is thus a positive advantage to it; yet to win power the original nucleus of "professional revolutionaries" must sooner or later show its aptitude to govern, and government means state control. Communism stands a chance in Asia (and not only in Asia) because it is wholeheartedly committed to state management of the economy, and because even its opponents within the national-revolutionary movement are to some extent caught up in the same current.

That this current should have genuine force behind it is a consequence of the dilemma in which backward countries find themselves, once the preindustrial stagnation is broken and the race to catch up with the West has begun. Poverty and backwardness, whether reinforced by colonialism or not, result in a situation in which only the state, by centralizing all the available means of production, can speed up the process of modernization. Whenever the need

for capital investment becomes urgent, while private entrepreneurial activity is lacking, there will be a tendency to
rely on the government for a whole range of activities that
under different circumstances are left to private initiative.
At bottom it is a question of strengthening the authority of
the state by making the executive independent of sectional
pressure groups. This process is inevitable in a period of
rapid social change, if authority is not to disappear altogether. The modernization of a hitherto backward country
sets up stresses that reinforce the need for a strong central
government, and this is particularly true if industrialization
is accompanied by agrarian reform, as it must be if the
whole process is to be genuine and not a sham. But in the
last resort the reinforcement of governmental authority is
necessitated by the weakness of the middle class and the
low level of private savings. What the local bourgeoisie cannot or will not do must be done, *tant bien que mal,* by the
bureaucracy. Above all, the state must impose collective
savings far beyond the limit of what individuals would be
likely to save privately if left to their own devices. Where
average incomes are so low that voluntary savings are inadequate to finance the necessary investments, the saving has
to be done by the government. Land reform and the progressive recasting of income tax—the favorite panaceas of
modern liberalism—are irrelevant to this particular problem, for although in the long run they tend to raise productivity their immediate effect is to stimulate consumption,
just when the need for expansion of capital equipment calls
for an increase in investments. The redistribution of income,
therefore, must be accompanied by collective saving imposed
from above. If this is generally true of countries trying to
modernize their economy, it is doubly true of primitive
countries under urgent pressure to add to their stock of

private and public capital—plant and equipment, roads, railways, public utilities, etc. This process cannot, however, be isolated from the reform of the social structure, for it is only by withdrawing surplus labor from submarginal land and employing it in industry that a net addition can be effected to the community's total output, and such a policy calls for action of a kind that the entrepreneurial class is generally unable to take. Backward countries are typically plagued by the overcrowding of badly farmed, submarginal land by an expanding number of impoverished peasant farmers, working with antiquated tools on fragmented holdings, in debt to moneylenders and other pests, and unable either to increase the yield of their land or to find employment in urban industry. The economic case for the industrialization of such areas rests upon the existence of concealed rural unemployment and upon the wide discrepancy between agricultural and industrial productivity; and while there are legitimate differences of opinion as to the respective roles of public and private capital in such a situation, it is clearly absurd to propose that development must stand still until an entrepreneurial class has been formed which can direct the process. Where that class does not exist, or is plainly inadequate for the task, the state must step in, and in this age it generally will step in, even if it means outraging the feelings of orthodox bankers and economists.

It is this kind of situation which typically gives rise to the synthesis of revolutionary nationalism with some form of socialism or at least public intervention in the economic sphere. Whether the state merely underwrites private risks, whether it extends its investment activity to the private sector (as until recently it did in Turkey), or whether it undertakes the total reorganization of society—in every case there will be an initial concentration of authority on the political level, and consequently a struggle between various factions of the revolutionary movement to obtain control; the victorious faction will then proceed to organize society in its own image, but its rivals will be no less determined to utilize the state for this purpose. This assumption by the state of the entrepreneurial function, whether on totalitarian lines or not, is common to all genuinely modern attempts to hasten the industrialization of backward areas. The revolutionary regime derives its justification from it, and at the same time owes to it whatever inspiration it brings to the people under its control. It is the belief that only state action can shake society out of its rut that impels revolutionaries to seek power. It is consequently the weakness and not, as Lenin has it, the predominance of the national bourgeoisie that finds expression in the phenomenon of revolutionary nationalism. For if the entrepreneurs were able to direct the process of modernization on "classical" lines there would clearly be no need for national dictatorships, national organizations of capital and labor, state parties, state-controlled youth movements, and the other paraphernalia of modern dictatorial politics. Regimes of this kind need not be fully totalitarian, but they can hardly fail to be revolutionary and centralist. Whether they are Stalinist, Titoist, Socialist, Kemalist, Fascist, or Perónist depends on which faction of the revolutionary movement manages to seize power during the period that precedes the centralization of activity by, through, and under the state. But whatever the political regime, centralization is bound under these circumstances to become both the prime goal and the chief instrument of revolution.

The conviction that centralization of economic activity under state direction is "progressive"—*i.e.*, represents the *sine qua non* of rapid modernization—is the common bond linking all factions of the national-revolutionary movement. But for this common conviction there would be no common "anti-imperialist" platform, no united front, no Trojan horse, and no chance for the Communists to gain control of the movement. All disputes within a revolutionary movement of this kind are at bottom differences about the degree and form of centralization requisite for the task of building a modern nation. All political conflicts among the various factions go back to disagreements over the kind of state best suited to this purpose. Discussion always centers upon such questions as the scope left to private enterprise, the use made of the traditional governing classes (assuming they are not to be "liquidated"), the role of labor, etc. Generally speaking, the faction that can secure the adherence of organized labor and of the largest possible number of people in the managerial stratum will tend to come out on top. If it can persuade itself and others that its activities have something to do with "building socialism," so much the better for its morale. Thus, modernization will favor the extension of state control, even under conditions where power still lies with the entrepreneurs and allied groups. All the more will this be the case where a genuine revolution has taken place and the former ruling classes have been displaced. The mechanics of this process apply impartially to Latin-American dictatorship of the Perónist variety, Kemalism in the Middle East, and Titoism in Yugoslavia, and there is a sense in which the early stage of Mussolini's dictatorship in Italy belongs to the same pattern. That the Soviet Union should threaten to become the main beneficiary of what is really a world-wide phenomenon quite unrelated to Communist aims must be regarded as one of the by-products of the cold war. In the 1930's and early 1940's, Fascism held greater attraction for these movements than did Stalinism. Yet the prestige accruing to the Soviet Union from its military victory over Germany, and the progress of industrialization in Russia, do not wholly account for the change that has taken place. There is an element peculiar to Stalinism that favors a synthesis with national and colonial revolution. Unlike Fascism, with which otherwise it has so much in common, the Stalinist regime is able to exploit a revolutionary *mystique,* and its techniques are consciously directed toward a thorough transformation of society by revolution from above.

5: *The Western Dilemma*

WE HAVE SEEN that in the long perspective the cold war resolves itself into a struggle to determine the character of the society about to emerge from the impact of modern technology upon countries hitherto outside the historical mainstream. Until fairly recently, Russia was herself in this category, and her despotic methods of forced industrialization clearly make a strong appeal to the revolutionary intelligentsia of countries similarly situated. This is an aspect of the cultural lag dividing the West from the remainder of the world, a lag that the Soviet regime is both helping to fill and trying to exploit. Yet rural poverty, population pressure, the failure of the traditional governing class, and the presence of a nucleus of politically conscious workers in industry do not of themselves give rise to a revolutionary situation. The "subjective factor," whose absence in western Europe after 1918 the Comintern theorists found so hard to explain, is represented by the intelligentsia; to be precise, by that part of it which refuses to accept things as they are and turns to political action.

A good deal of the thesis set out in this chapter has in recent years become common ground among serious political analysts. There are, however, obstacles to a more general acceptance of the situation with which the West is confronted. The notion that the state can be employed as an instrument of revolution is both novel and frightening. There is obstinate resistance to the idea that nationalists may actually prefer Communism *because* it is totalitarian— *i.e.*, calculated to destroy all traditional obstacles to rapid modernization. Last but by no means least, there is considerable reluctance to admit that the intelligentsia of most Eastern and Islamic countries is far less enamored of libertarian principles than were its Russian predecessors during the nineteenth century.

Stalinism unfortunately appears to make a strong appeal to the educated minority of backward countries. This may be an aspect of the cultural lag already referred to, or it may be due to the even greater violence of the Western impact in recent decades and the need to react against the consequent cultural dislocation. Liberalism unsettles traditional society. Communism thereupon undertakes to settle its unrest, at a price that even intellectuals may not consider excessive. Revolutionary despotism is in the Eastern and Islamic tradition; democracy emphatically is not. If this assessment is correct, it seems to dispose of the belief, currently fashionable in Western quarters, that land reform and democracy are all that is needed to make the West popular in Asia and the Middle East. Apart from the fact that the kind of land reform apt to be sponsored by governments wedded to "free enterprise" is unlikely to do the peasant majority much good, there is reason to doubt whether the intelligentsia can make the necessary adaptation without going through a totalitarian phase. Dissolving cultures give rise to a powerful demand for a new integration that must be "total" if it is to fill the social and spiritual vacuum. Liberalism is an acceptable way of life for the plural society of the West, where religious wars came to an end centuries ago. It does not answer the needs of societies in transition from medievalism to modern conditions.

In the measure that these truths have in recent years penetrated the public mind, they have contributed to a more realistic assessment of the problem, but here and there they have also given rise to defeatism and even to a species of panic. Among the defeatists one must include those historians of culture who are obsessed with the "decline of the West" and in search of solutions transcending the political sphere. These solutions can only be long-term ones, and the attention given to them carries an implication that there is little hope of salvaging Western democratic society as such. It is doubtless to the credit of modern historians that it has become possible to take a dispassionate view of the culture to which we belong, but the present crisis is not going to be surmounted under the leadership of people who are fundamentally out of sympathy with the aims of an evolving democratic society. This society is becoming less and less like the Europe of the Middle Ages, and historians who regard the thirteenth century as the high-water mark of Western culture are bound to take an excessively gloomy view of our present prospects. It is in these quarters that Communism is taken seriously as a quasireligion, and much anxious thought is given to the possibility that Asia and Africa may yet escape the contamination by adopting Roman Catholicism (and Rome's doctrines on birth control?). The fact that Communism is spreading much faster in some Roman Catholic areas of Europe than Catholicism does in Asia appears to have escaped notice. On present evidence there seems no reason to believe that the international situation would be more manageable if China and Japan had been converted by Jesuit missionaries in the sixteenth and seventeenth centuries—a suggestion that startled some readers of Dr. Toynbee's recent writings.[11]

Such investigations as have been made into the subject suggest that the social conservatism of some predominantly Catholic areas in western Europe—notably western France, northern Spain, Austria, and Ireland—is a function of a certain kind of peasant ownership. The Catholic way of life, which combines a minimum of security with a profound pessimism as regards the possibility and desirability of change, has its attractions for conservatives; but it clearly requires specific social and economic preconditions for its functioning. In their absence, Catholicism is very far from being a bulwark of order—witness the stormy political history of Italy, the Iberian peninsula, and Latin America. Since the uncertain element in the cold war is not the industrial working class of highly developed countries, but the rural and semirural proletariat of societies in the earlier stages of industrialization, the importance allotted to the religious factor on *political* grounds is difficult to understand.

As he looks beyond the Mediterranean, toward the border regions between the Soviet empire and the West, the historian's gaze inevitably comes to rest upon the ancient and petrified authoritarianism of Islam. Inevitably, too, the dignified stagnation of Islamic society appeals to conservative instincts in the beholder. Cannot this archaic structure be reinforced with bits of concrete—treaties, air bases, arms,

---

[11] Cf. Arnold Toynbee, *The World and the West*, Oxford University Press, 1953; *passim*.

etc.—so as to become another defensive "bulwark"? This policy is now over a generation old. Its net achievement is a situation in which quite small "cadres" of Communists are potentially strong enough to upset all the established governments of the region—not, of course, under their own flag but by spearheading national-revolutionary movements. The exception is Turkey, where Islam was disestablished in the 1920's, with the result that the Republic is today the only genuinely westernized portion of the former Ottoman Empire (leaving Israel aside as not belonging to the Middle East proper). In the remainder of the area, Pan-Islamism is crumbling, while Pan-Arabism provides an excellent cover for rival Fascist and Stalinist cliques and an instrument for blackmailing the Western powers. The region has long been the favorite playground of politically minded Orientalists, historians anxious for a role in the cold war, and people who prefer horse-drawn vehicles to motor traffic. Various eminent members of this school were at one time or another associated with abortive projects for constructing a kind of Anglo-Arab caliphate from the debris of the Ottoman Empire, while others, slightly more up to date, busied themselves with schemes for fashioning a lasting alliance between British foreign policy and Pan-Arabism. The miscarriage of these curious experiments, and the postwar decline of British influence in the Middle East, have brought about a malaise that finds expression in gloomy Spenglerian prognostications and in persistent nagging at the Americans, the French, the Turks, and the Israelis: all of them unhampered by memories of personal and collective failure in building dream castles in the Arabian desert and consequently inclined to take a somewhat more robust view of Western prospects. It is primarily in these circles that discreet support is given to every utopian or reactionary scheme for driving the French from North Africa, pushing Turkey into a confederation with the creaking Islamic states of the Middle East, or removing that persistent thorn in the flesh, Israel. For why should these relative newcomers presume to interfere with the decline of the West? The erudite despair of the school is flavored with a liberal dose of malevolence toward successful competitors.

It is indeed undeniable that the impact of the West upon Islamic society creates a special problem. Islam is an authoritarian system that safeguards the culture of a society economically stagnant for so long that it cannot adapt peacefully or gradually to modern conditions. At the ideological level, where this failure to adapt enters the consciousness of the participants, it translates itself into a conflict between two sets of motives: an inflexible resolve to keep things as they are and a furious determination to break with the past at all cost. Both attitudes are clearly pathological; at least they would be so described in relation to an individual. In social terms they portend the kind of cycle of rebellion and stagnation that Spain has undergone since the early nineteenth century. Unlike Spain, though, the Middle East, apart from its Mediterranean fringe, could be incorporated into the Soviet empire at small cost to its inhabitants. The peasants obviously could not be worse off than they are, and the professional class might find satisfaction in running the revolution. The price demanded of it is not high: there is no intelligible sense in which countries like Iran or Iraq can be described as "nations"; what is more, there is no necessary link between nationalism and social conservatism, let alone between nationalism and affection for the "free world." There is no inherent reason why nationalism and Communism should not in the end form a stable amalgam in the Middle East, as they have done in China. In so far as

Islam is a "bulwark" against such a development, it is also an obstacle to modernization in general along non-Communist lines. It is precisely this fact which causes radical nationalists to form political alliances with Communists. A defensive association of the Western world with Islamic conservatism (perhaps via the Catholic Church: a notion favored in some influential quarters, in Rome and elsewhere) seems ideally designed to drive the entire nationalist movement in the Islamic Middle East into Moscow's arms. If the West is still capable of learning from its almost unbroken series of defeats in the cold war, it might do worse than study the example of Turkey since the Kemalist revolution modernized the country—*i.e.*, promoted that rupture with the decaying medieval tradition which Islamic conservatism seeks to impede elsewhere. The currently fashionable tendency to look for allies among the adherents of the various religious orthodoxies ("three hundred million Moslems") is a sign of mental aberration. There is no safety in numbers—or in anything else. If there is still a chance of winning the cold war it lies in gaining the support of those elements whom Western policy has, with some exceptions, cold-shouldered and driven into a sullen neutralism or into the enemy camp.

There is little to choose in this respect among self-styled conservatives, old-fashioned liberals with an unshakable belief in the beneficial effect of untrammeled competition, and newfangled democrats sentimentally attached to welfare economics that may be (and usually are) quite irrelevant to the basic issue of revolutionizing stagnant societies. Since 1945 all three schools have had ample opportunities to demonstrate the futility of their respective nostrums. Perhaps the highest compliment that can be paid to Western policy is that here and there—*e.g.*, in Yugoslavia and latterly in Bolivia—it has tried to assist, or at least undertaken

not to impede, a really promising attempt by local revolutionary forces to carry out the kind of radical reorganization that is essential to further progress along more or less
democratic lines.[12] Elsewhere, orthodox stupidity has triumphed, with results that are there for all to see. Nor can it
be seriously maintained that the Maginot Line of conventional thinking has been seriously dented by the half-
hearted assaults of British socialists or American liberals.
Both have since 1945 expended a good deal of rather vague
talk upon the subject of aid to backward countries, but
this program is invariably conceived as a technical rather
than a political operation. It is instructive that on this issue
British Labor has, if anything, proved less adventurous
than American liberalism. Having come into existence long
after the major issues of Britain's own industrial revolution
had been settled, in one way or another, on nonsocialist
lines, the Labor party is not well equipped to understand
the problems of a disintegrating agrarian society: the kind
of situation from which Leninism-Stalinism developed and
which it exists to deal with. This uncertainty appears whenever its leaders try to envisage ways and means of implant-
ing the welfare state in less favored territories, and *a fortiori*
whenever British authority comes into conflict with nationalist movements. It is customary to cite the Indian settlement
of 1947 as proof of British Labor's political maturity, but
its essence, after all, was the transfer of responsibility to
someone else—and even this solution had been inherited
by the Labor government, along with a good many other

[12] In the case of Bolivia, this intelligent policy of noninterference was
presumably facilitated by the fact that the revolutionary policies of the
Estenssoro government were backed by a labor movement under nationalist and/or Trotskyist control, so that it could at any rate not be
accused of promoting Soviet interests. As a harbinger of possible future
attempts to dissociate Western policy from crude antisocialism, the
experiment is relatively hopeful.

things, from the defunct Liberal party. On present evidence, British socialism (or what passes for such) is still in search of a *mystique* applicable to present and former colonial areas. Its dominant outlook remains obstinately insular, parochial, and utilitarian—more Methodist than Marxist, as its spokesmen are fond of pointing out. It is not a mentality well suited to the demands of the twentieth century.[18]

For an example of what is liable to happen when this amiable insular "consumer socialism" is confronted with an external challenge, one may turn to the Persian debacle of 1951. The problem posed by the sudden eruption of Persian nationalism was clearly one for which neither John Wesley nor the Webbs had prescribed a solution. It was not on that account entirely hopeless, but it did call for something more than a combination of routine diplomacy and democratic speechmaking. The Conservative reaction was on familiar lines: force was to be employed, and when that expedient failed or was not tried (largely because the dissolution of the Indian Empire had left a vacuum whose significance was not immediately appreciated) Conservative spokesmen fell back on their peculiar brand of historical fatalism, best exemplified perhaps by Sir Reader Bullard's diagnosis of the situation as a remote consequence of the battle of Poitiers, in A.D. 732.[14] Throughout this confused episode there was undoubtedly an element of genuine un-

[18] This applies also to that *enfant terrible* Mr. Aneurin Bevan. Although for long the hero of the left wing, he has always been characteristically vague on the subject of competing with Communism for control of nationalist movements in backward countries. It is true that he has laid it down that "the answer to social upheaval is social amelioration" (*In Place of Fear*, Heineman, London, 1952, p. 135.) But this is hardly definite enough. One has heard similar sapient observations from Mr. Walter Reuther and other moguls of American radical democracy. There is nothing very socialist about such pronouncements; they are in fact a hangover from the "bourgeois" radicalism of the nineteenth century.

[14] Cf. *The Listener*, November 20, 1952.

certainty over Britain's moral standing that affected both the government and its opponents. Was the British position as strong as the Foreign Office tried to make it appear? The Persians had a real grievance against the Anglo-Iranian Company, and against the British Treasury, which for years had appropriated the lion's share of the profits. They could also claim with some plausibility that the agreement of 1933, under which they bound themselves to refrain from measures of expropriation, had been signed under duress. But all this would not have unsettled the resolution, such as it was, of the British Cabinet and its supporters, had it not been for the use made by the Persians of the argument that they were merely "nationalizing" their own property. The dismay caused by this ingenious bit of sophistry was instructive because it showed what happens when the traditional integration breaks down in one of those countries which are now the principal buffer zone between the two worlds. Under "normal" conditions (which are fast ceasing to be normal, or even to exist at all) nationalist governments customarily combine their claim to sovereign independence and legislative omnicompetence with due regard for foreign investments and written agreements, even to the point of solemnly undertaking not to confiscate foreign property. In strict logic there is a paradox involved, since absolute sovereignty—the foundation myth of every national-democratic regime—must clearly be paramount and cannot be abrogated by treaty: a principle the Persian government conveniently remembered when it decided to "nationalize." For practical purposes, however, the arrangement usually works. Jacobin logic has its teeth drawn by the historical providence which ordains that nationalist regimes shall normally be anchored, on their social side, in propertied interests of the landowning or bourgeois kind. The silent pressure of this entirely unofficial state of affairs acts as an automatic safeguard against a literal application of the democratic principle that the sovereign legislature may do as it pleases. The sanctity of contracts and the doctrine of *volonté générale* can be brought into harmony, as the French Revolution has shown, on condition that both principles are professed by the same group of people. It is when this arrangement—known to liberals as "civilization" and to Marxists as "bourgeois democracy"—breaks down that serious trouble begins.

It is now a matter of record that such a breakdown occurred in Persia early in 1951 and that its consequences led to the collapse of the British position in that country. The fact that matters were subsequently patched up does not distract from the significance of the episode, for similar breakdowns are in principle to be expected wherever a nationalist regime tries to steal a march on Communism. Dr. Mossadegh's spectacular achievement, therefore, must stand as a warning, quite apart from its permanent effect on British (as distinct from American) interests. For although he failed in the end to steer a middle course between the old order and the revolutionaries, he demonstrated what can be done even by a weak and irresponsible regime that knows how to exploit the tension between nationalist passions and economic realities.

Here, if anywhere, is the challenge Western statesmanship has to face. It is the more urgent because in the long run it may determine the issue of "peaceful coexistence" between the two worlds. No one familiar with Communist thinking can really suppose that a succession of such debacles will have no effect on long-range political planning in Moscow and Peking. The temptation to "take over" strategically crucial areas by such means may in the end prove too great for world peace to be preserved. Nor should it be imagined that an effective answer can be found by a further development of the crude techniques of intervention displayed in the more recent case of Guatemala. Quite apart from the needless blundering and blustering which accompanied that affair, and which provided the other side with a rich supply of propaganda material for years to come, there is the simple fact that intervention on these lines can only aggravate the underlying tensions. Nationalism and revolution march together in backward countries, and those who go against the revolutionary current will eventually find themselves struggling with the nationalist tide. Indo-China, Persia, and Guatemala, in their various ways, have served as danger signs. There is still time to heed the signals, but in all probability not so much time as those in authority seem to think.

Meanwhile Communism runs away with the national-revolutionary movement and advertises its brand of despotic planning to power-hungry intellectuals who care little for democracy and much for some means to drag society out of its stagnation. The least that can be done in this situation is to recognize it for what it is. At bottom it is a question of controlling and directing the revolution that is now lifting the bulk of mankind to a new technological level. The West's opponent and rival in this process is the Soviet Union—both as a power and as a center of the world-wide Communist movement, whose leaders believe they have mastered the technique of the "revolution from above," by means of the totalitarian state-party and its instruments of terror and propaganda. These men have long shed their earlier utopian expectation of free popular support for the transformation they have in mind. Yet it would be wholly mistaken to suppose that they are insincere in claiming to represent the vanguard of the "proletarian revolution." This assertion forms part of the ideology of that totalitarian elite whose untrammeled future rule is prefigured by the Communist party's organizational structure. Like every myth, it has real power to move human beings to act. It therefore deserves to be taken seriously, and even to be treated with respect, in so far as it represents a conviction for which men are prepared to surrender their lives. But it ought not to be believed. The greatest mistake the West can make is to think of the Communist issue in terms of class, and to pit against a wholly mythical "proletarian" movement the resources of the traditional state and its governing groups, where the real issue lies between libertarian revolutionaries and others who can envisage the transformation of society only in terms of the Soviet experience since 1917. Revolution there must be, for no movement, however libertarian its ultimate aims, will renounce the hope of using the concentrated power of the state to end the dreadful poverty and squalor in which the bulk of mankind still lives at the present day. In the struggle to prevent the enemy from gaining control of the process, the West cannot succeed if it does not match his resolution.

CONCLUSION

SINCE THE END of the Second World War we have witnessed a regrouping of the nations allied in that struggle, the result of which has been to divide the world into mutually antagonistic groups or blocs. Although sometimes described as a conflict between East and West, it is in fact more complicated, since the Sino-Soviet bloc is confronted not merely by the nations organized under the North Atlantic Treaty, but also by Asian countries such as India and Japan. Irrespective of whether an Asian complement of the Atlantic Community will eventually emerge, the non-Communist world *de facto* includes all the countries not attached to the Sino-Soviet bloc. It follows that the problem of coexistence is basically political, not military. For if the Communist powers did not adhere to certain beliefs about the nature of their own society, and the trends at work in the outside world, the outlook for world peace would be very different.

Communist theory assumes that coexistence is possible and desirable, but only because it is in the long-term interest of the U. S. S. R. and its allies to gain time, while the Western world (which it wrongly identifies with the capitalist system) is on the downgrade; that the West's internal conflicts must periodically find an outlet in war, and that every such convulsion will leave the Communist "camp" stronger and better equipped for the last round. On these assumptions, a final grandiose clash is inevitable, but it is in the interest of the Communist powers to put it off as long as

228

possible. In the meantime, Communist movements will have a chance to revolutionize large portions of Asia, the Middle East, and perhaps Latin America—the so-called backward countries, where the industrial revolution is only now getting into stride. The Stalinist technique of "revolution from above" is considered adequate for the political control of such countries, because their nationalist movements are fundamentally interested in rapid economic development under dictatorial control. Communism can come to power by integrating itself with nationalist movements, and in the long run, as Lenin pointed out in 1923, the fact that Russia, China, and India together represent the majority of the world's population is a sure guarantee of victory.

As against this long-range strategy, democratic empiricism affirms the possibility of genuinely peaceful coexistence between the two blocs, pending the gradual reunification of the world society. Coexistence, however, does not exclude the possibility of local conflicts, which may turn into wars on the Korean or Indo-Chinese pattern. In the democratic view, there is no ineluctable fate driving the two "camps" to a final catastrophic test of strength, which under modern conditions could only mean the total destruction of all the major centers of civilization. If such a disaster were to occur, it would signify a breakdown of statesmanship. In fact, both sides, for reasons of self-preservation, must try to avoid it. From the West's viewpoint the problem then is how to stem the march of Communism without being drawn into all-out atomic war. It is conceivable that a short-term solution may be found in some tacit agreement to limit the use of armaments—either by not employing the most destructive weapons at all, or by making sure that total destruction is limited territorially to restricted areas of no great significance to either side. Only a Soviet advance into western Europe, or an "atomic Pearl Harbor," could justify general war with atomic weapons.

Assuming that the two camps can manage to live side by side for a decade or more, the cold war will take precedence over military problems. By the cold war we understand competitive attempts to alter the balance of power without overt resort to force. Since the uncertain factors in the global contest are the great undeveloped countries in the throes of an industrial revolution—principally India, the remainder of southeast Asia, the Middle East, and Latin America—the conflict reduces itself to a choice between Communism and democracy (not liberalism, since the modernization of backward areas may require quasisocialist planning techniques). If the Western democracies can demonstrate their ability to solve the social problems of the world under conditions of political freedom, the edge will be taken off the Communist drive for world domination. It is, however, a mistake to denounce "armaments" in the name of "social progress." Both are essential, for unless firmness and patience are combined, wavering elements may climb the Communist bandwagon. Coexistence and the cold war are in fact two sides of the same medal. To win the cold war is to make coexistence possible, and the cold war can be won if the West maintains a high rate of economic expansion, helps to modernize the backward countries, and keeps its powder dry. If this policy is successfully pursued over a considerable length of time, the Communist powers may eventually find it to their interest to abandon doctrinaire notions about the final inevitable collision. Until that happens, the rest of the world must learn to live with the cold war, even if it lasts a generation.

A strategy of this kind clearly demands time and patience; it also requires a realistic appreciation of what is likely to occur in the Communist part of the world. Here we are handicapped not merely by lack of factual knowledge, but by certain scholastic fashions that have begun to affect political thinking. It is not uncommon these days to come across learned essays apparently composed to demonstrate the Marxian orthodoxy of Lenin's or Stalin's or Mao Tse-tung's thinking and the importance Marxian theory in general is supposed to have for the understanding of Russian or Chinese affairs. In writings of this kind (often by reputable scholars) "surplus value," and even "dialectical materialism," are made to appear as causative factors shaping Communist policy, and we are given to understand that the behavior of the Moscow or Peking Politburo is in the last resort determined by the Engels-Plekhanov version of Marx's philosophy—a notion too flattering to intellectuals to be entirely convincing. It is, of course, equally unhelpful to be told that the rulers of the U. S. S. R. and China are actuated simply by the desire to maintain themselves in power. Yet even this arid generalization has in recent years been offered to the public as an "explanation" of Soviet affairs.

As against such academic exercises the political analyst does well to note certain material factors disclosed by the patient study of Soviet institutions. He will in particular give attention to the changing social composition of the Communist party in the U. S. S. R. and in the satellite countries—less is known about this phenomenon in China—and to the extra strain thrown upon the regime by the difficulty of persuading the workers that the party still represents their interests. He will ask himself whether it is possible for the system to remain in equilibrium once people have discovered that, so far from being "classless," the new society is operated in the interest of a self-contained managerial caste. He will, on the other hand, take note of the immense advantage available to the Communist movement in backward countries where the *mystique* of "planning" fits the longings of important strata other than the working class. He will also bear in mind that a revolution, to be successful, must have the support of a wide cross-section of society, and that such support will be forthcoming if the Communist party—or some other party—is seen to stand for radical measures calculated to overcome the inherited handicaps of a particular society. Lastly, he will remember that there are many varieties of socialist planning in the present world, and even some varieties of Communism; and in consequence he will not be perturbed if Titoist, Trotskyist, or other heretical Communist tendencies amalgamate with nationalist strains to produce yet another revolutionary regime. He will, on the contrary, welcome such variations, both for their intrinsic interest and because they help to diversify the international scene and *pro tanto* reduce the dangerous tendency for everyone to line up behind one or another of two exclusive and unalterable positions. In so doing he will indirectly pay tribute to the distinctive character of the "free world"—namely the fact that it really *is* free and therefore both decentralized and variegated, as against the totalitarian "camp," which defines itself by its rigidity and its inability to tolerate heresy. In short, he will exercise his critical function, as it cannot be exercised under totalitarianism. And by so doing he will contribute to the mental health of the society that shelters him.

Yet even if it could be assumed that expert advice were more or less unanimous, and that it were followed, we should still be confronting risks and threats on a scale for which there is no precedent. It has become a truism to say that the opportunities and the dangers created by modern

developments in technology are growing *pari passu,* and
that world government—or at least world peace—is now
the alternative to disaster. From the standpoint of scientists
and others committed to a rationalist view of world affairs,
it must seem an extraordinary piece of bad luck—almost
like the intervention of a malignant deity—that the public
disclosure of the powers inherent in modern science should
have been accompanied, on the political plane, by the division of the world into hostile blocs. In this somewhat narrow perspective, 1945 appears as a fateful date in the human
calendar: the year of the first atomic explosion, which was
also the year of the—unsuccessful—construction of a world
organization dedicated to the preservation of peace. Even if
one happens not to be committed to the particular species
of scientific rationalism reflected in the public pronouncements fashionable ten years ago, one may yet regard with
concern the course events have taken since then. It is unlikely, however, that real surprise will have been felt by anyone who saw the connection between the technological
upheaval whose fruits were witnessed in 1945 and the totalitarian organization of society over a great and growing area
of the planet. For the fact seems to be that—as Marx was
among the first to realize—every important step forward in
the mastery of nature is accompanied by a social upheaval.
The first wave of the industrial revolution made modern mass
democracy possible; the second wave has confronted us
squarely with the issue of centralized state control and with
the threat of totalitarianism, which has grown out of the
mishandling of this issue. It was therefore scarcely an accident that brought Hiroshima into such close and urgent
proximity with Lake Success, or that made the Soviet
Union a foundation member of a world organization
equipped with rudimentary powers of political control over

the whole globe. If one relinquishes the ideology that underlay the neoliberal utopianism of 1945, one begins to see
the common thread running through the Fascist and Communist experiments in totalitarian control, the planning
policies of democratic socialism, the attempt at world
organization inherent in the UN Charter, and, last but not
least, the new military strategy adopted by the major powers.
One realizes that one and the same process has made welfare planning possible and enabled dictatorial regimes to
achieve the total reorganization of society; one also sees
that the collapse of the pre-1914 division of labor was, in
the last resort, linked to the technological factors that supplied the economic base for socialist planning experiments
—and for their perversion under authoritarian control. In
short, one begins to discern a pattern at once more complex
and less baffling than the picture suggested by those fashionable alarmists who are now busy assuring us that the end of
the world is at hand, or, alternatively, that disaster can be
staved off by preventive war.

For if the totalitarian menace is at bottom a distortion of
the very urge for rationality and planning that inspired the
liberal idealists, the scientists, the economists, and the peacemakers of 1945, our condition is perhaps not entirely hopeless. Instead of regarding Communism as an incomprehensible monstrosity, we can begin to think of it as an impasse,
a perversion, or a stunted development of something that in
its origins was not so very different from the drive for a
rational world order that underlay democratic thinking in
the West. And conversely, it is not inconceivable that the
Communists—once their residual faith in universal revolution has evaporated—may come to recognize that the remainder of the world cannot be pressed into the strait jacket
imposed upon their own society. In brief, it may become

possible to discover common ground. It is, however, quite certain that such a discovery will avail us little if we fail to keep our powder dry. The best that can be hoped for, perhaps, is that this kind of uneasy equilibrium—punctured, no doubt, by local wars, in which each side proclaims its unshakable devotion to the cause of world peace and world order—will continue long enough for a sufficient number of people on both sides of the Iron Curtain to work out the elements of a genuine strategy of coexistence; a strategy, that is to say, which tacitly accepts the division of the world, realizes that its causes are linked to the universal groping toward a planned and controlled international order, and quietly works for a lowering of tension, until such time as the "two worlds" are ready to come together. While this interval lasts, and assuming that it is not suddenly cut short by the kind of catastrophe that will make an end of all our preoccupations, the political analyst can best assist the planner and the politician by reducing his concepts to the sort of methodical order that corresponds to the world we actually live in.

BIBLIOGRAPHY

ABRAMS, M., ed.: *Britain and Her Export Trade,* London, 1946
AMERY, L. S.: *The Washington Loan Agreements,* London, 1946
ARENDT, H.: *The Origins of Totalitarianism,* New York, 1951
ARON, R.: *Les Guerres en chaîne,* Paris, 1951
ARNDT, H. W.: *The Economic Lessons of the Nineteen-Thirties,* Oxford, 1944
BALOGH, T: *The Dollar Crisis,* Oxford, 1949
BERGSON, A., ed.: *Soviet Economic Growth,* Evanston, 1953
BORKENAU, F.: *The Communist International,* London, 1938
————: *European Communism,* London, 1953
CARR, E. H.: The Bolshevik Revolution 1917-1923, Vols. I-IV, London, 1950-54
————: *Studies in Revolution,* London, 1950
————: *Conditions of Peace,* London, 1943
CHURCHILL, W. S.: *The Second World War,* London, New York, 1948-54
CROSLAND, C. A. R.: *Britain's Economic Problem,* London, 1953
Department of State Publication; 3573, Far Eastern Series 30: *United States Relations with China,* Washington, 1949
DEUTSCHER, I.: *Stalin,* Oxford, 1949
————: *The Prophet Armed: Trotsky 1879-1921,* Oxford, 1954
————: *Soviet Trade Unions,* London, New York, 1950
DUVERGER, M.: *Political Parties,* London, New York, 1954
FEIS, H.: *The China Tangle,* Princeton, 1953
FINLETTER, Th. K.: *Power and Policy,* New York, 1954
FITZGERALD, C. P.: *Revolution in China,* London, 1952
FURNIVALL, J. S.: *Colonial Policy and Practice,* Cambridge, 1948
GERSCHENKRON, A.: *Bread and Democracy in Germany,* Berkeley, 1943

HALLGARTEN, G. W. F.: *Imperialismus vor 1914*, Munich, 1951

HARROD, R.: *John Maynard Keynes*, London, 1951

———: *The Dollar*, London, 1953

HAWTREY, R.: *Towards the Rescue of Sterling*, London, 1954

———: *Western European Union*, London-New York, 1949

HOLLAND, W. L., ed.: *Asian Nationalism and the West*, Institute of Pacific Relations, New York, 1953

HOSELITZ, B. F., ed.: *The Progress of Underdeveloped Areas*, Chicago, 1952

HUDSON, G. F.: *Questions of East and West*, London, 1952

JASNY, N.: *The Soviet Economy During the Plan Era*, Stanford, 1952

KAHIN, G. M.: *Nationalism and Revolution in Indonesia*, Cornell, 1952

KENNAN, GEORGE: *American Diplomacy*, Chicago, 1951

———: *Realities of American Foreign Policy*, Princeton, 1954

LANGER, W. L. and GLEASON, S. E.: *The Challenge to Isolation 1937-40*, New York-London, 1952

———: *The Undeclared War 1940-41*, New York-London, 1953

LENIN, V. I.: *Selected Works*, 2 vols., London, 1947

———: *Ausgewählte Werke*, 12 vols., Moscow-Zurich, 1932-39

LEWIS, W. A.: *Economic Survey 1919-1939*, London, 1949

———: *The Principles of Economic Planning*, London, 1949

LIPPMANN, W.: *Public Opinion and Foreign Policy in the United States*, London, 1952

MANDELBAUM, K.: *The Industrialization of Backward Areas*, Oxford, 1945

MAO TSE-TUNG: *Selected Works*, London, 1954

MARLOWE, J.: *Anglo-Egyptian Relations 1800-1953*, London, 1954

MARX-ENGELS: *Archiv*, ed. D. Ryazanov, Frankfurt, 1926

———: *Ausgewaehlte Briefe*, Berlin, 1953

———: *The Russian Menace to Europe*, ed. Blackstock & Hoselitz, London, 1953

McCALLUM, R. B.: *Public Opinion and the Last Peace*, Oxford, 1944

McNeill, W. H.: *The Greek Dilemma*, London, 1947

————: *America, Britain and Russia: Their Cooperation and Conflict*, Oxford, 1953

Meissner, B.: *Russland im Umbruch*, Frankfurt, 1951

Meyer, F. V.: *Britain, the Sterling Area and Europe*, Cambridge, 1952

Monnerot, J.: *Sociologie du Communisme*, Paris, 1949

Namier, L. B.: *Europe in Decay*, London, 1950

Nurkse, R.: *Problems of Capital Formation in Underdeveloped Countries*, New York, 1953

Perroux, F.: *L'Europe sans Rivages*, Paris, 1954

Philip, A.: *L'Europe Unie et sa Place dans l'Economie International*, Strasbourg, 1954

Purcell, V.: *The Chinese in South-East Asia*, Oxford, 1951

Robbins, L.: *The Great Depression*, London, 1935

Robertson, D. H.: *Britain in the World Economy*, London, 1954

Royal Institute of International Affairs: *Survey of International Affairs, 1939–1946:* The World in March, 1939, Oxford, 1952. *Hitler's Europe*, Oxford, 1954

Soviet Documents on Foreign Policy, ed. Jane Degras, Oxford, 1951-53

Japan's New Order in East Asia 1937-1945, ed. F. J. Jones, Oxford, 1954

Schumpeter, J. A.: *Capitalism, Socialism and Democracy*, New York-London, 1950

————: *History of Economic Analysis*, New York-London, 1954

Sering, P.: *Jenseits des Kapitalismus*, Nuremberg, 1947

Staley, E.: *The Future of Underdeveloped Countries*, New York, 1954

Schwarz, S.: *Labor in the Soviet Union*, New York, 1952

Stalin, J.: *Problems of Leninism*, Moscow, 1947

————: *Marxism and the National and Colonial Question*, London, 1936

————: *Economic Problems of Socialism in the U. S. S. R.*, Moscow, 1952

STAMP, L. D.: *Our Undeveloped World,* London, 1953

SETON-WATSON, H.: *From Lenin to Malenkov,* New York, 1954

TOWSTER, J.: *Political Power in the U. S. S. R.,* Oxford, 1948

TOYNEBEE, A.: *The World and the West, London,* 1953

TROTSKY, L.: *Die Permanente Revolution,* Berlin, 1930

United Nations Publications:

A Study of Trade Between Asia and Europe, Geneva, 1953

Economic Survey of Europe Since the War, Geneva, 1953

Economic Survey of Europe in 1953, Geneva, 1954

Economic Bulletin for Europe, Second Quarter, 1954, Geneva, 1954

Economic Survey of Europe in 1954, Geneva, 1955

WARD, B.: *The West at Bay,* London, 1948

WARRINER, D.: *Economics of Peasant Farming,* Oxford, 1939

WILSON, H.: *The War on World Poverty,* London, 1953

WOOTTON, B.: *Freedom under Planning,* London, 1945

ZINKIN, M.: *Asia and the West,* London, 1951

Pamphlets and Periodicals:

BEVAN, A.: *In Place of Fear,* London, 1952

BIRD, J.: *East-West Trade,* London, 1954

COLE, H. and SHANKS, M.: *Policy for the Sterling Area,* London, 1953

DEANE, M.: *Economic Ties in the Free World,* London, 1953

MEADE, J. E.: *The Atlantic Community and the Dollar Gap,* London, 1953

WARD, B.: *Britain's Interest in Atlantic Union,* London, 1953

Annals of the American Academy of Political and Social Science, Philadelphia, September, 1951

Atlantic Alliance, A Report by a Chatham House Study Group, London, 1952

Defense in the Cold War, A Report by a Chatham House Study Group, London, 1950

Economica, New Series, Vol. XXI, No. 83, August, 1954, London

Oxford Economic Papers, New Series, Vol. 6, Nos. 2 and 3, Oxford, June-September, 1954

The Manchester School of Economic and Social Studies, Vol. XXII, No. 2, Manchester, May, 1954

INDEX

Albania, 131
Acheson, Dean, 8
Acheson-Lilienthal Report, 7
Amery, L. S., 36
Anglo-Iranian Company, 224
Arnold, General, 20 (footnote)
Argentina, 94, 161, 163
Asian Despotism, 132. See: Stalinism
Atlantic Alliance, 100;
Community, 16, 28, 49, 60, 61, 63, 64, 69, 71, 85, 104, 228;
Council, 18, 67;
Pact, 3;
solidarity, 104;
Union, 63, 65, 69, 70;
world, 26
Atlantic Community; See: Atlantic Alliance
Atlantic Union; See: Atlantic Alliance
Atomic Weapons, control of proposed, 8, 9, 17; development of by Russia, 17
Austria, 30, 196, 218
Australia, 63, 71, 74 (footnote), 161
Autocracy, Soviet, 115, 116; opposition to by managerial caste, 125
Axis, challenge of, 91; imperialist ideology of, 42; threat of, 10, 12

Balkans, Anglo-French rivalry in, 28
Baltic, 133

Barcelona, 147
Barnard, Chester, 8 (footnote)
Belgium, 108, 161
Belinsky, 200 (footnote)
Benelux Group, 78
Berlin, airlift blockade, 23
Bevan, Aneurin, 223 (footnote)
Bilbao, 147
Bismarckian Era, 45
Black Sea, 133
Boer War, 38
Bolivia, 221, Estenssoro, 222 (footnote)
Bolsheviks, anti-capitalist policy of, 54; old guard purge by, 113; prejudices of toward West, 55; similarity of to Jacobins, 184
Bolshevism, intellectual antecedents of, 178; led by "professional revolutionaries," 203; not a labor movement, 185
Bombay, 175
Bonapartist Tendencies in Russian Revolution, 113
Boothby, Sir Robert, 101 (footnote)
Bourgeoisie, 33; in backward countries, 211; in China, 192; in Russian Revolution, 191; miscast in Lenin's theory, 213; nationalism in, 194; treachery of, 189
Brazil, 208
Bretton Woods Agreement, 12, 58

British Commonwealth, See: Commonwealth, British

Brüning, Heinrich, 106

Budapest, 43

Bulgaria, 134

Bullard, Sir Reader, 223

Bureaucracy, in Communist regime, 138; replaces bourgeoisie in backward countries, 211; social function of, 204

Bush, Vannevar, 8 (footnote)

Byrnes, James F., 8 (footnote)

Cambridge, school of thought at, 11

Canada, in dollar area, 78; opposed to Empire tariff, 36; reservoir of economic strength, 64; "underdeveloped" area, 163, 164; U. S. export market, 72; wheat output, 161

Castlereagh, 5

Catholic Church, 221; way of life, 218

Catholicism, Roman, birth control doctrine of, 217; influence of in Asia, 218; links of with Islam, 221; possibility of being used for "defensive association" in Asia and Africa, 221; support of, for authoritarianism, 202

Ceylon, 71; instances advantages of specialization, 96

Chamberlain, Joseph, 34; concern of with British Empire policy, 36; develops high tariff program, 35. See: Imperialism

Charismatic Leaders, 207, 208

Chernyshevsky, 200 (footnote)

China, as food producer, 161, 162, 163; Communist victory in, 93, 112; contrast of with India, 186; exemplifies revolutionary strategy, 191; industrialization of by Russia, 118; in Leninist-Stalinist doctrine, 175, 176, 177; representative of bureaucratic Asian systems, 132

Chinese Communist Party, defeat of in 20's, 57; policy of towards "national bourgeoisie," 198

Chinese Revolution, 24; effect of on world balance, 53; forecast of, 179; impact of on India and Japan, 63; significance of, 180

Churchill, Winston, acknowledges Pax Americana, 32; as coalition leader, 108; at Potsdam, 5; describes wartime conferences, 43; Fulton address of, 8; on Quebec agreement, 45 (footnote); remodels Conservative party, 35; role of, in Peace settlement, 10

Clark, Colin, 169 (footnote)

Clausewitz, 9

Cocoa, production of, 96

Coexistence, as major Western aim, 229, 230; compatible with limited war, 24; effect of on global power balance, 49; in Communist doctrine, 25, 228; in economic field, 118; peaceful, 19, 22

Cold War, 20; as global struggle, 59; "complements coexistence," 22; linked to economic contest, 230; struggle for backward areas, 24; totalitarian movements controlled by, 51

Colombo Powers, 62, 63; plan, 97

Colonial Policy, 91; during 1930-33 crisis; imperialism of, 97; laissez-faire, 159; linked to monopolistic capitalism, 97. See also: Lenin

Comintern, early defeats of in China, 57; loses control of Chinese Communist party, 193; unable to explain "subjective factor," 215

Commonwealth, British, 5; economic policies of, 75; evolution of from earlier Empire, 34; link of with liberalism, 38; nominal partner in 1945 settlement, 27; resistance of to Chamberlain program, 36; status of, compared with America, Russia, 39; within Atlantic Community, 104

Compradors, 192

Conant, James B., 8 (footnote)

Confederation, European, schemes for, 144

Conservatives, British, 35; support imperialism, 36. See also: Tories

Council of Europe, 144

Cracow, 135

Cripps, Sir Stafford, 110

Croatian Minorities, in Hungary, 196

Cyprus, 140

Czechoslovakia, 133-137, 141

Czestochowa, 136

Danielson, N. F., 153 (footnote) See also: Marx

Denmark, 161

Depression, 95; effect of on economic theory, 108; in Britain, 106; political impact of on labor opinion, 99. See also: Keynesianism, Unemployment

Disarmament, discussion on, 23

Dollar Area, 70; dollar balance improved, 80; drive, 72; European dollar problem, 74 sqq.; gap in, 71, 73; U.S. aid, 73. Cf. investment flow, 81; Paley Report, 81; Randall Report, 83

Dominions, British, as primary producers, 94

East Germany, 133, 137, 141

Eden, Anthony, 6

Egalitarianism, in British Labor movement, 131

Egypt, as modern food producer, 161; effect on of colonial regime, 162; exemplifies tradition of despotism, 129

Elite, Soviet, 127; of "professional revolutionaries," 203; totalitarian, 208

Empire, British, economic importance of to British exporters, 86; in Boer conflict, 38; in competition with Germany, 34 sqq.; 19th century conflict of with Russia, 24

Employment; See: Entrepreneurs; Fascism; Keynes, John Maynard; Unemployment

Engels, Friedrich, 231

Entrepreneurs, in backward countries, 167; influence of, affected by full employment, 109; function of, assumed by bureaucracy, 213

Espionage, atomic, 7

Estenssoro, See: Bolivia

Eurafrica, 65

Eurafrican Bloc, 65

Eurasian Bloc, 16; annexes East-
    ern Europe, 39; empire of,
    replaces traditional Russian
    state, 53; "heartland" of,
    43; juxtaposition of, to At-
    lantic Community, 26. See:
    Russian Revolution
European Payments Union, 70,
    74

Fabians, find some good fea-
    tures in imperialism, 103
Falange, 148
Fascism, as totalitarian variant,
    213-215; during world eco-
    nomic depression, 92; Eu-
    ropean, 57; imitates Com-
    munist methods, 139; in
    competition with Commu-
    nists, 175, 196; in Spain,
    147; reaction of toward
    mass unemployment, 98;
    successes of, in '30's, 173
Federalism, European, 141
Finland, 91
France, as co-guarantor of lib-
    eral world system, 32; as
    pillar of Versailles system,
    28 sqq.
Franck, James, 7
Franco, 146, 147, 186
Free Trade, abandonment of
    after 1931 debacle, 106;
    link of with democracy,
    105; policy of British Lib-
    erals, 37; supported by
    German Social-Democrats,
    107. See: Unemployment
French North Africa, Balkan-
    ization of, thought wise by
    some influential Americans,
    104; revolution in, 181,
    194; investment in, of pub-
    licly controlled capital, 97

Genocide, 31

Gladstone, William, 50
Gold Coast, 97 (footnote)
Gold Standard, 54
Greece, 139, 142, 143, 145,
    146, 201
Groves, Leslie R., 8
Guatemala, 226

Hapsburg Empire, 181. See:
    Austria
Harriman, William Averell, 151,
    155
Harrod, Roy, 11
Hegel, 9
Hilferding, Rudolf, 102, 108
    (footnote)
Hiroshima, effect of on U.S.
    allies, 67; obliteration of,
    7; symbol of technological
    revolution, 233
Hitler, Adolf, effect of on labor
    movement, 105-107; ex-
    cesses of, 4; era, 105; re-
    gime of, 88; rise to power
    of, 12
Hohenzollern Germany, 181
Holland, 161
Hoover, Herbert, 108. See: Un-
    employment
Hungary, constitution of, 196;
    defining characteristics of,
    133, 134; land question of,
    196; minorities problem of,
    196; invasion of by Soviet
    army, 43. See: Austria
Hydroelectric Power, 94
Hydrogen Bomb, cost of, 20;
    possession of, 44. See:
    Atomic Warfare

Iceland, 65, 68
Illiteracy, in southern Europe,
    142
Imperialism, adherence to by
    Chamberlain, 34, 35; Axis
    acceptance of, 42; British,

compared with German, 37; effect of, on backward countries, 159; factor in British politics, 35; ideology of, 42; in Boer War, 38; in Leninist doctrine, 97; in modern Communist parlance, 197; in Russia and Japan, 40, 41, sqq.; in Stalinist doctrine, 177; protectionist impasse, 38. See: Canada; Commonwealth, British; Conservatives.

India, as food producer, 161; confronts Sino-Soviet bloc, 228; Congress of, 210; excess manpower of, 163; industrial progress of, 91; in Leninist theory, 177; obtains sterling releases, 96; population, density of, 160

Indo-China, Communism in, 191; conflict of, 22; discloses UN paralysis, 62; land problem in, 163; nationalism of, 226; parallel of, to Korea, 24; pattern of, 229

Indonesia, Communism in, 191

Inflation, as aid to economic expansion, 169; fear of in pre-Hitler Germany, 108; under state control, 170; See: Hilferding

Intelligentsia, affinity of to totalitarian structures, 217, 218; as revolutionary group, 100; during British labor experiment, 131; in prewar Germany and Japan, 42; in U.S.R.R., 203, 215; key factor in Communist Revolution, 215; of Islamic countries, 216; partly won over to Chinese Communism, 192; political role of, in

Chinese revolution, 185; reservoir of professional revolutionaries, 203; role of under Communist regimes, 138

International Monetary Fund, 13

Investment, effect of on living standards, 144; European, overseas, 93 sqq.; in backward countries, 168; in post-war Poland, 137; political conditions of, 170; rate of, inadequate in southern Europe, 143; rate of, in Soviet, 120, sqq.; of U.S. capital in Europe, 84

Iran, See: Persia

Iraq, 220

Ireland, Catholicism in, 218; food producer, 161; part of densely populated west European group, 140

Irrigation, economic effects of, 162. See: Egypt

Islam, attractive to Conservatives, 221; authoritarian character of, 218; disestablished in Turkey, 206, 219; undemocratic tradition of, 216; Western impact on, 220. See: Toynbee

Israel, a Mediterranean country, 140; not properly a Middle-East country, 219; scheme for removing, 220

Italy, commodity exports of, to U.S.A., 78; Communist influence in, 201; inadequate funds of Cassa del Mezzogiorna, 145; overtaken by Poland as industrial producer, 141; regional differences of, 144; rural illiteracy and poverty in South, 159; under Mussolini, 139

Jacobins, doctrine of national sovereignty, 224; failure of experiment, 195; influence of on Marx, 182; interpretation of French history, 182; parallel with Bolshevism, 184

Japan, archaic pattern of, 42; as food producer, 161; Axis challenge, 91; capitulation of, 4; evolution of, into "Western" bridgehead, 66; exception to general Asian development, 170; land scarcity in, 163; parallel of, to Germany, 41; use of atom bomb against, 7

Java, 163

Jefferson, 50

Jesuit Missionaries, 218

Kabul, 175

Kautsky, 102

Kemalist Regime, dictatorship in, 213, 214; likely to be revolutionary and centralist, 213; revolution of, 206; rupture with Islam, 221

Keynes, John Maynard, apostatized from economic orthodoxy, 11; effect of his theory on British labor movement, 106; influence of, 15; Keynesian revolution, 108; Keynesian techniques, 100; theory of, considered in relation to backward countries, 169; theories of, foreshadowed in German full employment schemes, 107; Utopia of, 15

Keynesianism See: Keynes, John Maynard

Khrushchev, N., 119

Kipling, Rudyard, 37, 38

Kolkhoz, 126, 127, 132

Korea, 3; battlefields of, 23; effect on UN prestige of war in, 62; localized war in, 24; political stalemate unbroken by war in, 53

Kremlin, denounces Western imperialism, 55; evolves Asian strategy, 202; overrates revolutionary prospects, 54. See: Stalinism

Kronstadt Rising, 113

Kuomintang, cooperation with Comintern, 179; lacks totalitarian character, 210; loses control of Chinese revolution, 175; shares social traits with Communist party, 186

Labor Camps, 126, 130

Labor Government, British, committed to liberal postwar plans, 16; concentration of on welfare schemes, 110; confirms Potsdam decisions, 6; failure of to reorganize British industry, 131; Indian settlement of, 58

Labor Party, British, converted to planning for full employment, 106; effect of 1931 defeat on, 108; inadequate policy of for backward countries, 222; shift of, from free trade policy, 105; supports Liberals before 1914, 35, 36

Laissez-faire, accepted by Social Democrats, 107; during depression, 92; effect of on industrial investment, 159; in colonies, 98; modified in Spain under dictatorship, 147; planning required despite policy of Brüning government, 106; fanatics of, 18

Lancashire, 110

Latin America, 59, 71, 76, 170, 218, 230

League of Nations, 32

Lebanon, 140

Lenin, 54, 56; anticipates Stalin's policy, 176; introduces NEP, 113; lays down lines of advance, 177; on alliance with Asian nationalism, 179; on bourgeois leadership in national revolution, 213; on colonial imperialism, 98; on nationalism, 182; on peasantry's role in revolution, 187; on philosophy, 200; strategy of, 175; tactics in Russian revolution, 190. See: Trotsky

Liberalism, Utopia, 16; in Britain before 1914, 35-37; influence of on British labor broken by depression, 106; influence of in U.S.A., 18; Keynesian form, 15; link of with free trade, 104, 105

Lilienthal, David, 7, 8. See: Acheson

Lincoln, Abraham, 50

Luxembourg, Rosa, 102

Magyars, 196

Malaya, 71, 96

Malenkov, 119

Managerial Stratum, 100; group in state-party regime, 214; ideology of development of, 160; in U.S.S.R., 115; political role of in Soviet Union, 128; privileges of, 130

Mao Tse-tung, 180; as national leader, 186; as theorist, 200; opens new chapter in

Communist strategy, 185; writings quoted, 192

Marshall Plan, countries included in plan, 76; inadequacy of, 58; in Stalinist doctrine, 177; policy of, not followed up, 83; reflects supranational tendency, 144; successful as stop-gap, 13

Marx, Karl, correspondence of with Danielson and Zasulich, 153; critical of Russian development under Tsarism, 154; doctrine of national democracy, 181; free-trade bias of, 106; influence of on German Socialists, 106; Jacobin concepts inherited by, 182; laissez-faire inheritance rejected, 108; liberal implications of theory of, 106; on history, 173; on link between technological and social change, 233; on Russia, 153; on unplanned economic development, 152; rejects analogy between U.S.A. and Russia, 154; relevance of theory of to Communism, 231; shares classical view on labor supply, 169

McMahon, Brien, 20

Mediterranean, Anglo-French rivalry in, 28; fringe of, 220. See: Cyprus, Israel, Lebanon

Meloy, John, 8

Mensheviks, 187

Methodists, 223

Middle East, cold war in, 59; industrialization of, 170; Kemalism in, 214; living standards in, 118; military defense of, 161; political conflicts in, 220. See: Islam

Milner, 36. See: Conservatives, British

Mittleuropa, 31, 102. See: Pax Britannica

Mohammed Ali, 162. See: Egypt

Monnet, Jean, 13

Monoculture, 161. See: Specialization

Monopolism, See: Imperialism

Monsoons, 162

Moravia, 136

Moravska Ostrawa, 135

Moscow, Asian policy of, 175; center of world revolution, 59; imperialism of, 56; long-range planning of, 225

Moslems, 221. See: Islam

Mossadegh, 207, 225

Munich, 92

Mussolini, 139, 214

Mutual Security Administration, 72

Nagasaki, 7

Napoleon, 5, 31

Narodniks, 55

National Socialists, 99, 107

NATO. See: North Atlantic Treaty Organization

Nehru, Pandit, 164

Neoclassical Economics, 169

Neoliberalism, 11, 13, 18, 75, 160, 234

Neutralism, 21, 22, 29, 65, 68, 99

New Deal, 11, 15, 98, 106, 129

New Zealand, 71

Nigeria, 96

Nile, 162

North Africa, cold war in 59. See: Eurafrica, French North Africa

North America, dollar balance of, with Europe, 80. See: Dollar Area

North Atlantic Treaty Organization (NATO) balance of, with Sino-Soviet bloc, 10; establishment of, 8; German contingent of, 47; military expenditure of, compared with Soviet, 124. See: Atlantic Alliance

October Revolution, ideology of, 112; inspiration of, 172; internationalist slogans of, 193; legend of proletarian uprising, 183; launched by professional revolutionaries, 205; myth of, 51; new role of state disclosed, 209

OEEC, 84, 85

Oil, 94

Oppenheimer, J. Robert, 8

Ottoman Empire, 219

Ottawa Agreements, 36

Overpopulation, in backward countries, 159; in China, 162; in Spain, 146; rural, in Eastern Europe, 103

Oxford, economists of, 11

Paley Report, 72, 81

Pan-Arabism, 219

Pan-Islamism, 219

Pax Americana, 18, 32, 38, 61, 64, 67, 69

Pax Britannica, 31, 32, 33, 36, 38, 54, 102

Pearl Harbor, 23, 230

Peking, 225

Permanent Revolution, 173, 174

Peronism, 94; tendencies of, 207, 213, 214

Persia, 223-226

Philippines, 63, 96

Plekhanov, 231

Poland, independence of, 10; post-war industrialization of, 133-137, 141, 150; western frontiers of, 4
Point Four, 58, 97
Politburo, 175, 231
Portugal, 139, 142, 146, 149
Potsdam, 4, 7, 10, 134
Prague, 43
Pravda, 177. See: Lenin
Proletarian Revolution, dictatorship of, 190; in Lenin's 1905 concept, 189
Protection, 34, 105, 110

Quebec Conference, 45

Randall Report, 83
Republican Party, in U.S., 151
Reuther, William, 223
Roman Catholics. See: Catholicism, Roman
Romanov Empire, 181
Roosevelt, Franklin D., policy of toward U.S.S.R., 5; regime, 58; Roosevelt-Truman period, 151
Rubber, 96
Ruhr, 136
Rumania, 133, 134, 151
Rumanians, in Austria-Hungary, 196
Russia, aggregate industrial capacity compared to Germany's, 48; arms output before and during Second World War, 46, 47; comparison of with NATO, 124; industrial revolution in, 116, sqq.; military strength of, 44, sqq.; present military strength of, 122; rates of industrial growth in, 118 sqq.; revolution in, 112 sqq.; state of,

replaced by Soviet Empire, 53
Ryazanov, David, 153

San Francisco, 3, 4, 6
Saxony, 136
Scandinavia, 140
Schuman Plan, 13
Security Council, 14, 39, 69
Senate of United States, hears statement on atomic weapons, 20
Siberia, Tzarist colonization of, 55
Slavophiles, 55
Slovak, 196
Smith, Adam, 108, 169
Social Democrats, cling to laissez-faire, 106; converted to planning, 108; inherit Marxian doctrine, 106-108
Social Revolutionaries, 188. See: Lenin
Sociology, Communist contribution to, 202
South Africa, 71
Spain, 65, 70, 139, 140, 142, 143, 145-149, 161, 201, 218, 220
Specialization, economic, 93; favored by industrial progress, 94; in tropical colonies, 96; urged on primary producers, 168
Stalin, amalgam by of revolution and despotism, 208; appeals to intelligentsia in backward countries, 216; compared with Mao Tse-tung, 200; comparison of policy with that of Fascism, 214; death of, 114; doctrine outlined in *Economic Problems of Socialism*, 127; epoch of, 126; essay of, on nationalism, 181; pattern

of, in Asian revolution, 197; policy of despotism, 132; policy of maximum capital investment in heavy industry, 17, 125, sqq.; policy of "revolution from above," 174; poltical testament of, 177
State Capitalism, 97-99
State Department, 180
Sterling Area, 70, 72, 74, 96
Subsistence Farming, 149, 167
Sun-Joffe Agreement, 177
Sweden, 48, 78, 86, 87, 91, 108. See: Scandinavia
Switzerland, 86, 87, 182
Syngman Rhee, 207

Tariff, U.S., effect of, on European exports, 73, 102, 103
Teheran Conference, 6, 10, 43
Thermidor, 113. See: Stalin
Third Reich, 41
Thomas, Charles A., 8
Tin, 96
Tito, 186, 207
Titoism, 206, 213, 214, 232
Totalitarianism, age of, 185; elite of, 192, 201, 217, 227; party of, 204, 222; state of, 157, 205, 207, 209, 210, 232, 233
Toynbee, Arnold, 55, 218
Trotsky, on Comintern strategy, 175; on imperialism, 103; on permanent revolution, 173; on "Soviet Thermidor," 113; on strategy of Russian Revolution, 187; opposition of, to Chinese Communist tactics, 185; proscribed in Russia, 198; Red Army organizer, 183
Trotskyists, 222, 223
Tzarism, 40, 55, 153, 175, 188

Turkey, 139, 142, 143, 146, 149, 150, 206, 212, 219, 220, 222

Ukraine, 136
Underdeveloped Countries, 156; contrasted with backwardness, 159; food output of various regions compared, 161; land hunger and overpopulation of, 162; methodical difficulties, 158; modernization of, 157; not identical with primary producers, 165; problem of capital formation, 167-171
Unemployment, 90, 98; full employment, 105; German political collapse in thirties due to, 107; political impact of, in Britain, 108; political consequences of, 99. See: Keynes, John Maynard
United Nations, charter of, 3, 4, 11, 14, 17, 61, 66, 67, 69, 234

Versailles, 27, 28
Vietminh, 198
Vienna, 43
Voznesensky, 47

Washington, 67, 68, 105
White, Harry, 12 (footnote)
Wilson, Woodrow, 35
Winne, H. A., 8

Yalta Conference, 6, 10
Yangtze Delta, 160
Yugoslavia, 118, 128, 133, 139, 140, 142, 143, 145, 146, 148-150, 201, 206, 207, 214, 221

Zasulich, Vera, 153

For Product Safety Concerns and Information please contact our EU
representative GPSR@taylorandfrancis.com
Taylor & Francis Verlag GmbH, Kaufingerstraße 24, 80331 München, Germany

www.ingramcontent.com/pod-product-compliance
Lightning Source LLC
Chambersburg PA
CBHW070357270326
41926CB00014B/2594

9 780367 620752